THE BEST TEST PREPARATION FOR THE

ADVANCED PLACEMENT EXAMINATION *IN*

ENGLISH
Language & Composition

Linda Bannister, Ph.D.
Professor and Chair, Department of English
Loyola Marymount University
Los Angeles, California

Robert Liftig, Ed.D.
Adjunct Professor of Writing
Fairfield University
Fairfield, Connecticut

Ellen Davis Conner, M.A.
Instructor of English
Clear Lake High School
Friendswood, Texas

Luann Reed-Siegel, M.A.
Former Instructor of English
Linden High School
Linden, New Jersey

Research and Education Association
61 Ethel Road West
Piscataway, New Jersey 08854

The Best Test Preparation for the
ADVANCED PLACEMENT EXAMINATION
IN ENGLISH LANGUAGE & COMPOSITION

Printed in the United States of America

Library of Congress Catalog Card Number 93-84362

International Standard Book Number 0-87891-923-6

Research & Education Association
61 Ethel Road West
Piscataway, New Jersey 08854

REA supports the effort to conserve and
protect environmental resources by
printing on recycled papers.

CONTENTS

About Research and Education Association

Research and Education Association (REA) is an organization of educators, scientists, and engineers who specialize in various academic fields. Founded in 1959 with the purpose of disseminating the most recently developed scientific information to groups in industry, government, universities, and high schools, REA has since become a highly respected publisher of study aids, test preps, handbooks, and reference works.

Created to extensively prepare students and professionals with the information they need, REA's Test Preparation series includes study guides for the Advanced Placement Exams, the Scholastic Assessment Test (SAT), the Tests of General Educational Development (GED), the Test of English as a Foreign Language (TOEFL), as well as the Graduate Record Examinations (GRE), the Graduate Management Admission Test (GMAT), and the Medical College Admission Test (MCAT).

Whereas most test preparation books present few practice exams which bear little resemblance to the actual exams, REA's test preparation books present exams which accurately depict the official tests in degree of difficulty and in types of questions. REA's practice exams are always based on the most recently administered tests and include every type of question that can be expected on the actual exams.

REA's publications and educational materials are highly regarded and continually receive an unprecedented amount of praise from professionals, instructors, librarians, parents, and students. Our authors are as diverse as the subjects and fields represented in the books we publish. They are well-known in the respective fields and serve on the faculties of prestigious universities and high schools throughout the United States.

Acknowledgments

In addition to our authors, we would like to thank Dr. M. Fogiel, President, for his overall guidance which has brought this publication to its completion; Stacey A. Sporer, Managing Editor, for directing the editorial staff throughout each phase of the project; and Ita Belkowitz, Project Editor, for coordinating the development of the book.

AP

English Language & Composition

Study Schedule

Study Schedule

If you have less than four or five weeks before the exam, condense this schedule accordingly. If your time before the exam is very limited, start with chapter 4, "Preparing for and Taking the AP Exam", and then take the practice tests. They will help acquaint you with the format and time limitations of the exam.

Week 1	Read Chapter 2, "Learning about the 'Other' Literature," setting aside a few hours each day. Do not rush through. Read carefully and take notes on the chapter for later review. Make flash cards of the main ideas of the chapter and of the glossary words. This chapter will help you to develop critical reading skills.
Week 2	Read Chapter 3, "Writing About the 'Other' Literature". Again, take notes on the chapter and make flash cards of the main ideas. This chapter provides instruction on analyzing, critiquing and writing about the types of passages found on the exam.
Week 3	Read Chapter 4, "Preparing For and Taking the AP Exam". Take notes for later study. Take the first practice exam in real time, with the actual test conditions. Do not allow yourself to borrow extra time during or even between test sections, get up out of your seat, or take any phone calls. It would be best to match the time the actual test will begin by waking up as early as you would on the day of the test.
	Mark any confusing questions. You may answer a confusing question correctly at home, forget to look up the explanation, and then get a similar question wrong on the actual exam.
	Grade yourself and review the book's explanations of the answers. From this, diagnose your weaknesses and turn back to the chapters.
Week 4	Take the second practice exam, again mimicking the actual test conditions. Remember to mark any confusing questions. Grade yourself and review the answers.
Week 5	Take the third practice exam, using the same procedures as the first and second.

AP

English Language & Composition

Chapter 1

Chapter 1

Scoring High on the AP English Language & Composition Examination

About the Book

This guide provides complete preparation for the AP English Language and Composition Examination. In addition to test-taking techniques and the information required by the test (such as literary definitions and expected essay structures), you will find complete lessons that teach you the skills demanded by this test. The instructional passages of this book teach you criticial reading skills using material beyond the range of the AP examination. You will be taught by lesson and example how to write high-scoring essays that demonstrate all you have learned.

To compliment the chapters on cricital reading, Chapter 4 focuses on the test and functions to prepare you directly for it. Everything you need to know for the test is capsulated in this chapter. Also, you will find helpful facts about the AP exams, and a breakdown of the questions into easily recognizable types. As the time of the test approaches, you will be able to concentrate on this chapter for the most time-efficient preparation.

This book also provides three full-length practice tests. These practice exams include thorough explanations of the answers for added instruction and self-diagnosis of problem areas. Lastly, included for your reference is a glossary of literary terms with sixty-five fully defined entries.

About the Test

The Advanced Placement Examination in Language and Composition is taken by approximately 30,000 high school students each year. The test is geared towards the student who has studied the mechanics of writing and rhetoric at an advanced level, and wishes to pursue college credit.

It is possible to confuse the AP Examination in Language and Composition with the AP Examination in Literature and Composition. The **Literature** exam focuses on literature and literary criticism, while the **Language** exam deals with writing as a craft. This book is designed to help you to prepare for the AP Examination in Language and Composition *only*.

The AP Language Exam is divided into two sections:

Section 1 – Multiple-Choice (60 minutes)
- 5–6 reading passages, with an average of 10 questions each
- May include approximately 10 Sentence Rewrite questions

Section 2 – Free Response (up to 120 minutes)
- 3 Essay questions

The first section consists of five or six reading passages and sixty multiple-choice questions, which you will have an hour to complete. Each passage will be followed by an average of ten questions and thereafter the passage will not be referred to again. Do not feel pressured to remember each reading — just digest them one at a time and move on. After reading the passage, you will have approximately one minute to answer each question.

During some test administrations, the multiple-choice section includes ten or more questions that are not related to a reading passage. These questions ask you to rewrite complex sentences by changing key words. Each answer choice presents a version of the rewritten sentence, and you must choose the best answer. You will find a full explanation of how to answer these questions in the following chapters. Note that although these rewrite questions do not always appear on the AP exam, when they do occur, they are usually the first set of questions.

The second section of the AP Language Exam consists of three essay questions, and is divided such that you will have thirty-five minutes to write each essay. Do not expect to go back to an essay after the allotted time has elapsed. Note that each essay has very specific instructions, and most have a passage which you will read critically to answer the essay question. Your essays will be scored according to the essay structure, the clarity of your writing, and the extent to which you have answered the question.

Scoring of the AP Language and Composition Examination

The multiple-choice section of the exam is scored by crediting each correct answer with one point and deducting one-fourth of a point for each incorrect answer. Unanswered questions receive neither a credit nor a deduction. The free response essays are graded by over 1,500 instructors and professors who gather together each June for a week of non-stop AP essay grading. Each essay booklet is read and scored by four graders. Each grader provides a score for the individual essays. This score is a number on a scale from 0 to 9, 0 being the lowest and 9 the highest. These scores are covered up so that the next grader does not see them. When the essays have been graded four times, the scores are averaged, one score for each of the three essays, so that the free response section is comprised of three scores.

The three essays are weighted equally, and the total weight of the free response section is sixty percent of the total score. The multiple-choice section comprises forty percent of the total score. Each year the overall grades fluctuate because the grading scale depends upon the performance of students in past AP administrations. The following method of scoring and the corresponding chart will give you an **approximation** of your score. It does not indicate the exact score you would get on the actual AP English Examination, but rather the score you achieved on the sample tests in this book.

Multiple-Choice Scoring:

_____	− (¼ × _____) =	_____
Number correct	Number incorrect	Raw Score (Rounded to nearest whole number.)

Essay Scoring:

_____ +	_____ +	_____ =	_____
Question 1 (out of 9)	Question 2 (out of 9)	Question 3 (out of 9)	Essay Score (Rounded to nearest whole number.)

As you can see, there is a correction for guessing on the multiple-choice section, so you are discouraged from random guessing or filling in of answers. Depending on the number of multiple-choice questions, the Essay Score is multiplied by approximately 3.3 to 3.8. This is called the Weighted Essay Score. (If necessary, the Multiple-Choice Score is also weighted.)

Each section of the test is weighted according to time allotted to that section; that is, the Multiple-Choice Score counts approximately 60 points, and the Weighted Essay Score counts approximately 90 points, to make a total of approximately 150 points. The Multiple-Choice Score is added to the Weighted Essay Score to get a Composite Score, which is rounded to the nearest whole number. The Composite Score Ranges are then determined for the AP Grade. The following table is approximate since the Composite Score Range varies a few points from year to year.

Composite Score Range	AP Grade
101-150	5
90-100	4
70-89	3
50-69	2
0-49	1

You may want to give your essays three different grades, such as a 5, an 8, and a 6, and then calculate your score three ways: as if you did well, average, and poorly. This will give you a safe estimate of how you will do on the actual exam. Try to be objective about grading your own essays. If possible, have a friend, teacher, or parent grade them for you. Make sure your essays follow all of the AP requirements before you assess the score.

The Composite Score

To obtain your composite score, use the following method:

_____ = _____ (weighted multiple-choice score—**do not round**)
multiple-choice
raw score

3.333 x _____ = _____ (weighted free response score—**do not**
      free response   **round**)
      raw score

Distribution of Grades

Distribution of grades varies from year to year and from test to test. The following table is an approximate distribution of grades for an AP Language and Composition Examination and an approximation of the percentage of people earning the grade.

	Grade	Percent Earning Grade
Extremely well-qualified	5	10
Well-qualified	4	20
Qualified	3	35
Possibly qualified	2	30
No recommendation	1	5

How to Use This Book

It is important to note that critical reading is a skill, and that while memorization will serve for the mastery of literary terminology, practice is your only means to critical reading. Chapters 2 and 3 of this book have been designed to help you hone your critical reading and writing skills. Once you have practiced these skills, move onto Chapter 4 which coaches you for the format and time limits of the AP Language exam. If the test date is near, it may be a better idea for you to start with the coaching chapter and practice tests, since they provide direct instruction for the exam format.

In an ideal situation, employ the five week schedule at the beginning of the book, which was conceived with the busy student in mind. It should be compatible with even the most active students' schedules.

AP

English Language & Composition

Chapter 2

Chapter 2

Learning About the "Other" Literature

Literature Defined

In his recent book, *The Rhetoric of the "Other" Literature,* noted scholar W. Ross Winterowd argues that literature has been much too narrowly defined. Traditional genres (fiction, poetry, and drama) do not accommodate the huge volume of nonfictional texts that have been written over the past several centuries. According to Winterowd, any text of enduring value, regardless of its genre, is worthy of the name "literature."

Indeed, as a part of the AP Course in English Language and Composition, students may be exposed to a variety of these "other" literatures. Students may read the works of autobiographers, diarists, biographers, historians, critics, essayists, journalists, political commentators, scientific writers, and nature writers, among others. Whatever the discipline, excellent prose pieces share certain characteristics of style and arrangement. Similarly, there are strategies for critical reading that are useful for any prose passage.

A Brief Look at the Significance of the Essay

The "other" literature most often takes the form of an essay. Students in the AP Course in English Language and Composition will study essays written by writers from a variety of disciplines and periods. Over the last 400 years, many compelling essays have captured the audiences of their day with their powerful ideas and styles. The development of the essay as an art form is particularly interesting precisely because great essay writers have sprung from fields as diverse as politics and biology, education and art history. This fact speaks to the importance of conveying ideas in writing. The literary tradition of the essay has been shaped by thinkers who, regardless of their training, felt strongly about issues and ideas, and who had an impact on their audiences.

Despite its power to change people's thinking, the essay has not enjoyed the prestige of fiction, poetry, and drama. Montaigne, a sixteenth-century lawyer and writer, generally agreed upon by scholars as the father of the essay, helps us understand why. Montaigne articulated the problematic nature of the form when he defined the essay very loosely, saying anything could be included in it and that it could start and stop wherever it pleased. An essay could consequently include history and personal experience, fact and fiction, scientific discovery and philosophical musing. The "proper" length of an essay is nowhere specified, though it is generally read in one sitting. Essays are often written in the first person, and thus are easily seen as an expression of the author's persona or voice as well as the author's thoughts. An essay's style, therefore, is as significant as the information and opinion it contains. Essays are often superb examples of the marriage of form and content, the hallmark of great literature. It is indeed appropriate to consider essays the "other" literature.

Strategies For Critical Reading of Prose Passages

Critical reading is a demanding process. Linguists and language philosophers speak passionately of the importance of true literacy in human affairs. It is not enough to merely comprehend: true literacy lies in the ability to make critical judgments, to analyze, and to evaluate. It is with this end in mind—true literacy— that any reader should approach a text.

What Critical Readers Do

If you can summarize the main points of an essay, that's a start. If you can recall the plot twists in a short story, or articulate the line of reasoning in an argument, that's a start. But if you are able to offer an informed opinion about the purpose and merits of a text, then you are on the road to true literacy.

The AP Examination in English Language and Composition seeks to identify critical readers, readers who not only can describe *what* happened in a text they've read, but *why* it happened and *how* it happened.

More specifically, as a critical reader, you will:

- summarize and outline complex material,

- critically examine a text's reasoning,

- analyze the way a text achieves its effects, especially through stylistic choice,

- evaluate a text, deciding whether it is accurate, authoritative, and convincing,

- determine a text's significance,

- compare and contrast different texts,

- synthesize information from one or more related texts, and

- apply concepts in one text to other texts.

As a critical reader, you'll be an active participant, not a passive recipient. It may help to envision yourself in a dialogue with the author and other critical readers. As rhetorician and critic Mikhail Bahktin argues, language operates in a dialogic mode, where receivers are just as essential to effective transmission of messages as senders.

There are six strategies a critical reader can employ to participate fully in the "re-creative act" that is reading.

1. Get the facts straight.

2. Analyze the argument.

3. Identify basic features of style.

4. Explore your personal response.

5. Evaluate the text overall and determine its significance.

6. Compare and contrast related texts.

1. Get the Facts Straight

Read actively, pencil in hand, underlining important phrases or noting key points in the margin. Briefly record your reactions, questions, and conclusions. Though you may not have time to thoroughly annotate a prose passage during a test, if you rigorously practice annotating beforehand, you'll begin to do it less laboriously and with less written back-up.

Your first task as a critical reader is to learn everything you can about the text. You can begin by scrutinizing the implications of the title, trying to identify the author and general time period in which the text was written, and identifying the thesis. In short, a good reader looks for the main ideas, but also looks for other information (author, era, form) that may help him or her determine the slant of those ideas.

Once you've identified the essence of a passage, try to jot it down in your own words in a single sentence. This will help you focus on a text's meaning and purpose, a skill extremely useful when the detailed multiple-choice questions on the AP Examination present you with "blind alleys" or slightly off-base interpretations of a text.

There are really four activities you perform in order to "get the facts straight":

a. **Previewing** – looking over a text to learn all you can *before* you start reading (This is, of course, much more difficult with excerpts.)

b. **Annotating** – marking up the text to record reactions, questions, and conclusions (Hint: It's especially useful to underline what you think the thesis is.)

c. **Outlining** – identifying the sequence of main ideas, often by *numbering* key phrases

d. **Summarizing** – stating the purpose and main idea, the "essence" of a text

Once you've got the facts straight, you're ready to tackle the analytic and evaluative aspects of critical reading. Before addressing those, let's test your ability to get the facts.

Here's an essay titled "Education of Women" by William Hazlitt, an essayist and scholar who wrote during the early nineteenth century. Try your hand at previewing, annotating, outlining, and summarizing it. Then look at the following pages, where a proficient critical reader has done those operations for you. Compare your responses and see where you can improve. Remember, you don't have to take copious notes to get to the essence of a text.

Education of Women

We do not think a classical education proper for women. It may pervert their minds, but it cannot elevate them. It has been asked, Why a woman should not learn the dead languages as well as the modern ones? For this plain reason, that the one are still spoken, and may have immediate associations connected with them, and the other not. A woman may have a lover who is a Frenchman, or an Italian, or a Spaniard; and it is well to be provided against every contingency in that way. But what possible interest can she feel in those old-fashioned persons, the Greeks and Romans, or in what was done two thousand years ago? A modern widow would doubtless prefer Signor Tramezzani to Aeneas, and Mr. Conway would be a formidable rival to Paris.[1] No young lady in our days, in conceiving an idea of Apollo, can go a step beyond the image of her favorite poet: nor do we wonder that our old friend, the Prince Regent,[2] passes for a perfect Adonis in the circles of beauty and fashion. Women in general have no ideas, except personal ones. They are mere egoists. They have no passion for truth, nor any love of what is purely ideal. They hate to think, and they hate every one who seems to think of anything but themselves. Everything is to them a perfect nonentity which does not touch their senses, their vanity, or their interest. Their poetry, their criticism, their politics, their morality, and their divinity, are downright affectation. That line in Milton is very striking—

'He for God only, she for God in him.'

Such is the order of nature and providence; and we should be sorry to see any fantastic improvements on it. Women are what they were meant to

---

[1] Hazlitt was a theatre critic and had accused a popular Italian tenor, Tramezzani, of overacting in his love scenes. He also criticized actor William Conway in the role of Romeo.

[2] The Prince Regent was George, Prince of Wales, recently declared insane.

be; and we wish for no alteration in their bodies or their minds. They are the creatures of the circumstances in which they are placed, of sense, of sympathy and habit. They are exquisitely susceptible of the passive impressions of things: but to form an idea of pure understanding or imagination, to feel an interest in the true and the good beyond themselves, requires an effort of which they are incapable. They want principle, except that which consists in an adherence to established custom; and this is the reason of the severe laws which have been set up as a barrier against every infringement of decorum and propriety in women. It has been observed by an ingenious writer of the present day, that women want imagination. This requires explanation. They have less of that imagination which depends on intensity of passion, on the accumulation of ideas and feelings round one object, on bringing all nature and all art to bear on a particular purpose, on continuity and comprehension of mind; but for the same reason, they have more fancy, that is greater flexibility of mind, and can more readily vary and separate their ideas at pleasure. The reason of the greater presence of mind which has been remarked in women is, that they are less in the habit of speculating on what is best to be done, and the first suggestion is decisive. The writer of this article confesses that he never met with any woman who could reason, and with but one reasonable woman. There is no instance of a woman having been a great mathematician or metaphysician or poet or painter: but they can dance and sing and act and write novels and fall in love, which last quality alone makes more than angels of them. Women are no judges of the characters of men, except as men. They have no real respect for men, or they never respect them for those qualities, for which they are respected by men. They in fact regard all such qualities as interfering with their own pretensions, and creating a jurisdiction different from their own. Women naturally wish to have their favourites all to themselves, and flatter their weaknesses to make them more dependent on their own good opinion, which, they think, is all they want. We have, indeed, seen instances of men, equally respectable and amiable, equally admired by the women and esteemed by the men, but who have been ruined by an excess of virtues and accomplishments.

—William Hazlitt (1815)

1. Get the Facts Straight

A. Previewing "Education of Women"

A quick look over the text of "Education of Women" reveals a few items worth mentioning. This short essay is probably most closely related to an Op-Ed (Opinion-Editorial) piece written in a newspaper. Published in the *Examiner* in 1815, the essay begins with a proclamation, "We do not think a classical education proper for women." The term "we" suggests the assurance of numbers and power. It's safe to assume Hazlitt speaks for a significant group (perhaps educated men?). And lastly, the year 1815 is relevant to our reading because it suggests a time when women did not enjoy the rights and privileges that are commonplace in the late twentieth century, at least in most of the major industrialized cultures. If the year were not stated, as is the case in the AP exam, you could infer from the debate over educating women that the piece was written before the late twentieth century.

B. Annotating "Education of Women"

An annotation records reactions, questions, and conclusions. Underlining key phrases may help you find the theme. Here are excerpts from Hazlitt's essay with underlining and annotations alongside to facilitate easy reference.

Education of Women

We do not think a classical education proper for women. It may pervert their minds, but it cannot elevate them. It has been asked, Why a woman should not learn the dead languages as well as the modern ones? For this plain reason, that the one are still spoken, and may have immediate associations connected with them, and the other not. A woman may have a lover who is a Frenchman, or an Italian, or a Spaniard; and it is well to be provided against every contingency in that way. But what possible interest can she feel in those old-fashioned persons, the Greeks and Romans, or in what was done two thousand years ago? A modern widow would doubtless prefer Signor Tramezzani to Aeneas, and Mr. Conway would be a formidable rival to Paris.[1] No young lady in our days,

1. The Thesis! But, what was a "classical" education in 1815? Probably Latin and Greek, philosophy and the "classics" of literature.

2. Perversion, not elevation, is the result of education of women—learning "taints" women.

3. Women learn modern languages only to be able to speak to their lovers—women have a shallow purpose for education.

4. Allusion to "poor" actors of the day (see footnote) who are preferable to historical figures (Aeneas, Paris)—women

in conceiving an idea of Apollo, can go a step beyond the image of her favorite poet: nor do we wonder that our old friend, the Prince Regent[2], passes for a perfect Adonis in the circles of beauty and fashion. <u>Women in general have no ideas, except personal ones.</u> They are mere egoists. They have no passion for truth, nor any love of what is purely ideal. <u>They hate to think,</u> and <u>they hate every one who seems to think of anything but themselves.</u> Everything is to them a perfect nonentity which does not touch their senses, their vanity, or their interest. Their poetry, their criticism, their politics, their morality, and their divinity, are downright affectation. That line in Milton is very striking—

'He for God only, she for God in him.'

Such is the order of nature and providence; and we should be sorry to see any fantastic improvements on it. <u>Women are what they were meant to be;</u> and we wish for no alteration in their bodies or their minds. They are the <u>creatures of the circumstances in which they are placed,</u> of sense, <u>of sympathy and habit.</u> They are exquisitely susceptible of the passive impressions of things: but <u>to form an idea of pure understanding or imagination,</u> to feel an interest in the true and the good beyond themselves, <u>requires an effort of which they are incapable. They want principle,</u> except that which consists in an adherence to established custom; and this is the reason of the severe laws

have little interest in history or politics, only romantic self-gratification.

5. Women don't think, are selfish, frivolous.

6. Women's destiny—creatures of circumstance, habit. Women can't change.

7. They have impressions, not ideas. So women only feel, can't think? They aren't interested in any truths beyond what is true for them.

8. They "want" principle…They "want" imagination…Want means lack, not desire.

which have been set up as a barrier against every infringement of decorum and propriety in women. It has been observed by an ingenious writer of the present day, that <u>women want imagination.</u> This requires explanation. They have <u>less</u> of that imagination which depends on intensity of passion, on the <u>accumulation of ideas and feelings round one object,</u> on bringing all nature and all art to bear on a particular purpose, on continuity and comprehension of mind; but for the same reason, <u>they have more fancy,</u> that is <u>greater flexibility of mind,</u> and <u>can more readily vary and separate their ideas at pleasure.</u> The reason of that greater presence of mind which has been remarked in women is, that they are <u>less in the habit of speculating on what is best to be done, and the first suggestion is decisive. The writer of this article confesses that he never met with any woman who could reason, and with but one reasonable woman. There is no instance of a woman having been a great mathematician or metaphysician or poet or painter: but they can dance and sing and act and write novels and fall in love,</u> which last quality alone makes more than angels of them. <u>Women are no judges of the characters of men, except as men. They have no real respect for men, or they never respect them for those qualities, for which they are respected by men.</u> They in fact regard all such qualities as interfering with their

9. They don't synthesize ideas but rather "separate" them. Does this mean they can't compare issues, seeing things only in isolation?

10. Women go with the first idea, don't reason through alternatives. Where is his evidence?

11. Oh, here's the proof…he's met only one reasonable woman.

12. Women have accomplished little. Falling in love is their greatest skill. The double-standard in action; women are restricted to "non-cognitive" activity. The most they can aspire to: performing arts, romance.

own pretensions, and creating a jurisdiction different from their own.
Women naturally wish to have their
favourites all to themselves, and flatter
their weaknesses to make them more
dependent on their own good opinion, which, they think, is all they want.
We have, indeed, seen instances of
men, equally respectable and amiable,
equally admired by the women and es-   13. Women ruin men.
teemed by the men, but who have been
ruined by an excess of virtues and
accomplishments.

As these annotations illustrate, a reader approaching Hazlitt's text would have several questions and perhaps express surprise at Hazlitt's opinionated judgments. Your notes should, as the sample annotations do, reflect your reactions as the text progresses. Make sure you include any conclusions you have drawn as well as the questions that occur to you. The lines you underline or highlight, places where the text makes statement of "fact," will help you identify the main ideas later.

C. Outlining "Education of Women"

Go back to the statements you have underlined. Paraphrase and list them in numerical order, with supporting statements subsumed under key statements. Hazlitt's essay could be said to have the following key points, extrapolated from the underlining and written in outline form.

1. Classical education not proper for women

    a. modern language study better suits their romances

    b. no interest in history

2. Education is wasted on them because

    a. women have no ideas

    b. women have no passion for truth

    c. women hate to think

3. Women are what they are meant to be: frivolous, superficial

    a. creatures of circumstance, sympathy, and habit

    b. can't form ideas of understanding or imagination

    c. they lack principle

    d. they have fancy, flexibility of mind

   e. they can't synthesize ideas, but see ideas separately

   f. they take the first suggestion rather than speculate on what's best

   g. women can't reason

4. There are no examples of great women thinkers

5. Women are frivolous creatures

   a. women are only able to dance, sing, act, write novels, fall in love

   b. women cannot judge character

   c. women don't respect men for qualities considered good in women themselves (they're hypocrites)

D. Summarizing "Education of Women"

Read in this outline form, Hazlitt's essay is clearly an opinionated discussion of why women are not suited to education. Women are "born to" certain frivolous qualities of mind and behavior, and lack the mental capacity to reason, particularly in any principled fashion. The outline of key points and supporting statements lead the reader rather pointedly to this conclusion. Though at first Hazlitt's essay seems a disjointed litany of complaints, a sequence of reasons becomes more apparent after annotating and outlining the essay. It also becomes clearer how much Hazlitt relies on "accepted" opinion and his own experience rather than demonstrable proof.

We have just undertaken previewing, annotating, outlining, and summarizing the elements of "Get the Facts Straight." Very often at the conclusion of this stage of critical reading, the reader begins to get a handle on the text. The remaining five strategies after "Get the Facts Straight" seem to flow readily and speedily. To recap, these remaining five strategies are:

2. Analyze the argument.

3. Identify basic features of style.

4. Explore your personal response.

5. Evaluate the text overall and determine its significance.

6. Compare and contrast related texts.

Let's apply these remaining five strategies to Hazlitt's "Education of Women."

2. Analyze the Argument

An analysis examines a whole as the sum of its parts. Another brief look at the outline of "Education of Women" reveals the parts of Hazlitt's argument. In short, women should not be educated because they lack the qualities education enhances. They lack the capacity to entertain ideas because they have no passion for truth and hate to think. Women are naturally predisposed to acting precipitously rather than thoughtfully, with the use of reasoning. Evidence for these statements may be found in the lack of female contributions to human knowledge. Women can "perform" (and write novels, a less-than-respectable literary endeavor in 1815), and fall in love, but do little else. In short, things that require judgment are not suitable activities for women.

Hazlitt's essay has a rather simple argumentative structure. He asserts women are not educable and then provides "reasons" why. Hazlitt's "reasons" are primarily opinions, offered without any backing except the assertion that women have achieved little. The essay concludes with a final comment on the ability of women to ruin men, chiefly through flattery.

Analysis reveals that Hazlitt's essay has little to offer in support of the opinion it presents. Further, its statements seem more an emotional outpouring than a reasonable explanation. (The careful reader will also make note of how difficult it is to view Hazlitt's remarks in an unprejudiced fashion—the twentieth-century reader will, in all probability, find his assertions a bit ridiculous.)

3. Identify Basic Features of Style

Stylistically, Hazlitt's essay may be described as a series of blunt statements followed by reflection on how the statement is manifested in his culture. Hazlitt draws on anecdotal support—his observations of the women of his day, a line from Milton, and his own knowledge of the absence of women's accomplishments. Hazlitt's essay seems a collection of accepted or common knowledge: he writes as though his "reasons" are generally agreed upon, undisputed statements of fact. This structure suggests that because something is widely believed, readers should accept it. In all probability readers in 1815 did. Thus, the tone is both authoritative and perhaps a bit annoyed—annoyed with the problems women present.

Hazlitt's diction is largely straightforward, more plain than flowery. A few of the words and phrases he chooses have powerful or dramatic connotations, such as "pervert," "mere egoists," "perfect nonentity," "downright affectation," "hate to think," and "no passion for truth." But he relies largely on ordinary language and sentence structure. Only occasionally does he indulge in a syntactic permutation. For example, in the sentence "The writer of this article confesses that he never met with any woman who could reason, and with but one reasonable woman," Hazlitt shifts the modal verb "could reason" to the adjective "reasonable" with memorable effect. By and large, however, his sentences are simple declaratives, not difficult to read or interpret and not especially memorable stylistically.

This is an appropriate time to mention that most of the literary and rhetorical terms used in this discussion and the others that follow are included in the glossary at the end of these chapters on critical reading and writing.

4. Explore Your Personal Response

While nineteenth-century readers would probably have nodded in agreement as Hazlitt offered reasons why women shouldn't be educated, contemporary readers are probably surprised, dismayed, perhaps even angry. Review your responses in the annotations to the text. They will help recreate your personal reactions and the causes for those reactions. Do not always expect to agree with, or even appreciate a writer's point of view. You will find yourself disagreeing with texts rather regularly. The important thing is to be certain you can account for the sources and causes of your disagreement. Much of reader disagreement with Hazlitt's essay rests in what we would consider a more enlightened perspective on the abilities of women. An awareness of historical context does help explain "Education of Women," but probably doesn't increase twentieth-century sympathy for Hazlitt's position.

5. Evaluate the Text Overall and Determine its Significance

Hazlitt's essay "Education of Women" was a product of early nineteenth-century sensibilities. Its chief significance today is as a representative of its time, an indicator of a social and intellectual climate much different than our own. As a citizen of the Romantic period preceding the Victorian age, Hazlitt expresses an understanding of women that today we would deem, at the very least, incomplete.

6. Compare and Contrast Related Texts

A complete analysis of Hazlitt's essay would include a comparison of other essays of his, if available, on the subject of women and education. It would also be useful to examine other early nineteenth-century essays on this subject, and lastly, to contrast Hazlitt's essay with contemporary (i.e., late twentieth-century) essays that argue for and against the education of women. Through such comparison, a more complete understanding of Hazlitt's essay is possible. The AP Course in English Language and Composition uses comparative analysis regularly, while the AP Examination in English Language and Composition uses it in much more limited fashion. Occasionally you might be asked on the exam to contrast opposing (or similar) views on a single subject, but only within very narrow parameters. For instance, you might be questioned about two distinct styles used to approach the same subject and the resulting effects.

Although you may experience certain points of departure from the above discussion, most skilled readers will agree, in general, with its broad conclusions. This is because the text has been kept in mind and referred to throughout the discussion. If you read attentively, that is, if you attend to the text carefully, you are much more likely to reflect judiciously upon it. Thus, the components of our good reading definition—to read attentively, reflectively, and judiciously—are all present in the six broad strategies described and employed above.

The very *active* reading strategies employed on Hazlitt's essay "Education of Women" can be used with any text to help you "re-create" it with optimal effectiveness. That is to say, you as a reader should be able to very closely approximate the original authorial intentions, as well as understand the general audience response and your more particular individual response. The AP Course in Language and Composition is designed to help you practice these skills, while the AP Examination in English Language and Composition tests your mastery of them. In order to gain further valuable practice with these critical reading strategies, you may wish to read the following short essays. Remember to work with the six strategies in sequence. They are:

1. Get the facts straight.

    a. Preview

    b. Annotate

  c. Outline

  d. Summarize

2. Analyze the argument.

3. Identify basic features of style.

4. Explore your personal response.

5. Evaluate the text overall and determine its significance.

6. Compare and contrast related texts.

Read the following sample essays, each with brief comments by a professional reader employing the six strategies. These comments should enable you to check your own responses for accuracy and thoroughness. Once you become familiar with these strategies, they should become almost second nature to you and easy to employ. This familiarity is your best tool for success on the AP Examination in English Language and Composition.

Sample Essay #1

Female Suffrage

  I have read the long list of lady petitioners in favor of female suffrage, and as a husband and a father I want to protest against the whole business. It will never do to allow women to vote. It will never do to allow them to hold office. You know, and I know, that if they were granted these privileges there would be no more peace on earth. They would swamp the country with debt. They like to hold office too well. They like to be Mrs. President Smith of the Dorcas Society,[1] or Mrs. Secretary Jones of the Hindoo aid association, or Mrs. Treasurer of something or other. They are fond of the distinction of the thing, you know; they revel in the sweet jingle of the title. They are always setting up sanctified confederations of all kinds, and then running for president of them. They are even so fond of office that they are willing to serve without pay. But you allow them to vote and to go to the Legislature once, and then see how it will be. They will go to work and start a thousand more societies, and cram them full of salaried offices. You will see a state of things that will stir your feelings to the bottom of your pockets. The first fee bill would exasperate you some. Instead of the usual schedule for judges, State printer, Supreme court clerks, etc., the list would read something like this:

---

[1] The Dorcas Society was a benevolent religious organization for women.

OFFICES AND SALARIES

President Dorcas Society	$4,000
Subordinate Officers of same, each	2,000
President Ladies' Union Prayer Meeting	3,000
President Pawnee Educational Society	4, 000
President Of Ladies' Society for Dissemination of Belles Lettres among the Shoshones	5,000
State Crinoline Directress	10,000
State Superintendent of Waterfalls	10,000
State Hair Oil Inspectress	10,000
State Milliner	50,000

You know what a state of anarchy and social chaos that fee bill would create. Every woman in the commonwealth of Missouri would let go everything and run for State Milliner. And instead of ventilating each other's political antecedents, as men do, they would go straight after each other's private moral character. (I know them—they are all like my wife.) Before the canvass was three days old it would be an established proposition that every woman in the state was "no better than she ought to be." Only think how it would lacerate me to have an opposition candidate say that about my wife. That is the idea, you know—having other people say these hard things. Now, I know that my wife isn't any better than she ought to be, poor devil—in fact, in matters of orthodox doctrine, she is particularly shaky—but I still would not like these things aired in a political contest. I don't really suppose that woman will stand any more show hereafter than— however, she may improve—she may even become a beacon light for the saving of others—but if she does, she will burn rather dim, and she will flicker a good deal, too. But, as I was saying, a female political canvass would be an outrageous thing.

Think of the torch-light processions that would distress our eyes. Think of the curious legends on the transparencies: "Robbins forever! Vote for Sallie Robbins, the only virtuous candidate in the field!"

And this: "Chastity, modesty, patriotism! Let the great people stand by Maria Sanders, the champion of morality and progress, and the only candidate with a stainless reputation."

And this: "Vote for Judy McGinniss, the incorruptible! Nine children— one at the breast!"

In that day a man shall say to his servant, "What is the matter with the baby?" And the servant shall reply, "It has been sick for hours." "And where is its mother?" "She is out electioneering for Sallie Robbins." And such conversations as these shall transpire between ladies and servants applying for situations. "Can you cook?" "Yes." "Wash?" "Yes." "Do general housework?" "Yes." "All right; who is your choice for State Milliner?" "Judy McGinniss." "Well, you can tramp." And women shall talk politics instead of discussing the fashions; and they shall neglect the duties of the household to go out and take a drink with candidates; and men shall nurse the baby while their wives travel to the polls to vote. And also in that day the man who hath beautiful whiskers shall beat the homely man of wisdom for Governor, and the youth who waltzes with exquisite grace shall be Chief of Police, in preference to the man of practiced sagacity and determined energy.

Every man, I take it, has a selfish end in view when he pours out eloquence in behalf of the public good in the newspapers, and such is the case with me. I do not want the privileges of women extended, because my wife already holds office in nineteen different infernal female associations and I have to do all her clerking. If you give the women full sweep with the men in political affairs, she will proceed to run for every confounded office under the new dispensation. That will finish me. It is bound to finish me. She would not have time to do anything at all then, and the one solitary thing I have shirked up to the present time would fall on me and my family would go to destruction; for I am *not* qualified for a wet nurse.

—Mark Twain (1867)

Commentary on Mark Twain's "Female Suffrage"

Although this essay by famous American humorist Mark Twain also casts women in a less than favorable light, it is done in a light-hearted, hyperbolic fashion rather than with Hazlitt's straightforward seriousness. Contemporary readers are much less likely to take offense at Twain's intentional overstatement. His humorous, manufactured legislative offices, for example, "State Milliner" (hatmaker) and "Crinoline Directress" (petticoat manager), are intentionally facetious. This exaggerated style is a clue to Twain's intentions. Rather than mounting a serious argument about the unsuitability of women for legislative office, Twain is spoofing the results of women voting and holding office. The reader doesn't come away with the impression that Twain feels real rancor towards women, or completely lacks respect for their abilities, as Hazlitt seems to. A brief look at some textual evidence reveals why this is so.

Twain's list of "Offices and Salaries" created by women who vote and "go to the legislature" (take office) is delightfully silly. "Superintendent of Waterfalls" not biting satire, but openly, lightheartedly ludicrous. Later Twain compares men and women politicians, saying that "instead of ventilating each other's political antecedents, as men do, they [women] would go straight after each other's private moral character." And he parenthetically adds, "I know them—they are all like my wife." Here Twain is actually commenting on the superiority of the feminine perspective on suitability for office. Moral character is certainly a better measure of a person running for public office than their political connections. Twain's aside, which is generalizing from a particular, is an obvious humorous ploy, since Twain would not marry until three years after this essay was written.

Twain also compares the woman legislator to a "beacon light for the saving of others." He extends this metaphor when he predicts that "she will burn rather dim, and she will flicker a good deal." This metaphor may be interpreted as a suggestion that women are fallible and inconstant; still, they *are* a "beacon light" for others.

Twain ends the essay with a prediction that women will "talk politics instead of…fashion" and "neglect the duties of the household," and "men shall nurse the baby while their wives travel to the polls to vote." Furthermore, Twain's own circumstances will change. "That will finish me. It is bound to finish me." (Repetition for comedic effect is particularly well done here.) "She would not have time to do anything at all then, and the one solitary thing I have shirked up to the present time would fall on me and my family would go to destruction; for I am *not* qualified for a wet nurse." Twain's joking about male selfishness is nicely capped with a final punch line. Twain's essay is marked by a number of stylistic features that contribute to his hyperbolic humor. Though only a few examples have been mentioned, it is readily clear that Twain's essay is meant as a playful jibe, poking as much fun at men as it does women.

Sample Essay #2

The Handsome and Deformed Leg

There are two sorts of people in the world, who with equal degrees of health, and wealth, and the other comforts of life, become, the one happy, and the other miserable. This arises very much from the different views in which they consider things, persons, and events; and the effect of those different views upon their own minds.

In whatever situation men can be placed, they may find conveniences and inconveniences: in whatever company, they may find persons and conversation more or less pleasing; at whatever table, they may meet with meats and drinks of better and worse taste, dishes better and worse dressed; in whatever climate they will find good and bad weather; under whatever government, they may find good and bad laws, and good and bad administration of those laws; in whatever poem or work of genius they may see faults and beauties; in almost every face and every person, they may discover fine features and defects, good and bad qualities.

Under these circumstances, the two sorts of people above mentioned fix their attention,—those who are disposed to be happy, on the conveniences of things, the pleasant parts of conversation, the well-dressed dishes, the goodness of the wines, the fine weather, etc., and enjoy all with cheerfulness. Those who are to be unhappy, think and speak only of the contraries. Hence they are continually discontented themselves, and by their remarks sour the pleasures of society, offend personally many people, and make themselves everywhere disagreeable.

If this turn of mind was founded in nature, such unhappy persons would be the more to be pitied. But as the disposition to criticize and to be disgusted, is perhaps taken up originally by imitation, and is unawares grown into a habit, which though at present strong may nevertheless be cured when those who have it are convinced of its bad effects on their felicity. I hope this little admonition may be of service to them, and put them on changing a habit, which, though in the exercise it is chiefly an act of imagination, yet has serious consequences in life, as it brings on real griefs and misfortunes. For as many are offended by, and nobody well loves this sort of people, no one shows them more than the most common civility and respect, and scarcely that; and this frequently puts them out of humor, and draws them into disputes and contentions. If they aim at obtaining some advantage in rank or fortune, nobody wishes them success, or will stir a step, or speak a word, to favor their pretensions. If they incur public censure or disgrace, no one will defend or excuse, and many join to aggravate their misconduct and render them completely odious.

If these people will not change this bad habit, and condescend to be pleased with what is pleasing, without fretting themselves and others about the contraries, it is good for others to avoid an acquaintance with them, which is always disagreeable, and sometimes very inconvenient, especially when one finds one's self entangled in their quarrels.

An old philosophical friend of mine was grown from experience very cautious in this particular, and carefully avoided any intimacy with such people. He had, like other philosophers, a thermometer to show him the heat of the weather, and a barometer to mark when it was likely to prove good or bad; but, there being no instrument invented to discover, at first sight, this unpleasing disposition in a person, he for that purpose made use of his legs; one of which was remarkably handsome, the other by some accident, crooked and deformed. If a stranger, at the first interview, regarded his ugly leg more than his handsome one, he doubted him. If he spoke of it, and took no notice of the handsome leg, that was sufficient to determine my philosopher to have no further acquaintance with him. Everybody has not this two-legged instrument; but everyone, with a little attention, may observe signs of that carping, fault-finding disposition, and take the same resolution of avoiding acquaintance of those infected with it. I therefore advise those critical, querulous, discontented, unhappy people, that if they wish to be respected and beloved by others, and happy in themselves, they should *leave off looking at the ugly leg.*

—Ben Franklin (1780)

Commentary on Ben Franklin's "The Handsome and Deformed Leg"

Ben Franklin, noted inventor, philosopher, and eighteenth-century statesman, wrote prolifically on the morals of his time. In this essay he sets up a dichotomy and proceeds to investigate it. The dichotomy involves two sorts of people—those "who are disposed to be happy" and those "who are to be unhappy." Stylistically, Franklin is adept in this essay at stringing sets of opposites together in long list-like constructions. The second paragraph of the essay, for example, creates a rather comprehensive catalogue of the circumstances of life, in both its positive *and* negative aspects. Franklin uses this list to set up situations which people invariably react to. His essay is, in short, a commentary on the quality of those reactions.

Franklin calls his essay a "little admonition" and offers it as a service to others. Franklin is famous for his prescriptions for happy life, and this essay fits well within that category.

A few words about Franklin's title are well worth mentioning. Previewing the text inevitably focuses in on this rather perplexing title: the reader wonders whether Franklin intends it literally or figuratively. The answer comes in the concluding paragraph, which is an anecdote based on a philosopher friend's deformity. This fellow, lacking an instrument like a thermometer or barometer to discover unhappy, disagreeable people, made use of his legs—one handsome, one crooked and deformed. This philosopher felt that persons with a "carping, fault-finding disposition" would regard "his ugly leg more than his handsome one" and would even "speak of" the ugly leg. The philosopher would then "have no further acquaintance with him." Franklin concludes the anecdote and his essay with his advice: "I therefore advise those critical, querulous, discontented, unhappy people, that if they wish to be respected and beloved by others, and happy in themselves, they should *leave off looking at the ugly leg.*" The title and the anecdote are now linked, and Franklin's advisory essay is firmly rooted, via analogy, in the reader's mind.

Sample Essay #3

The following text is an excerpt of a long essay by Charles Lamb.

A Bachelor's Complaint of the Behaviour of Married People

As a single man, I have spent a good deal of my time in noting down the infirmities of Married People, to console myself for those superior pleasures, which they tell me I have lost by remaining as I am.

I cannot say that the quarrels of men and their wives ever made any great impression upon me, or had much tendency to strengthen me in those antisocial resolutions which I took up long ago upon more substantial considerations. What oftenest offends me at the houses of married persons where I visit, is an error of quite a different description;—it is that they are too loving.

Not too loving neither; that does not explain my meaning. Besides, why should that offend me? The very act of separating themselves from the rest of the world, to have the fuller enjoyment of each other's society, implies that they prefer one another to all the world.

But what I complain of is, that they carry this preference so undisguisedly, they perk it up in the faces of us single people so shamelessly, you cannot be in their company a moment without being made to feel, by some indirect hint or open avowal, that *you* are not the object of this preference. Now there are some things which give no offence, while implied or taken for granted merely; but expressed, there is much offence in them. If a man were to accost the first homely-featured or plain-dressed young woman of his acquaintance, and tell her bluntly, that she was not handsome or rich enough for him, and he could not marry her, he would deserve to be kicked for his ill-manners; yet no less is implied in the fact, that having access and opportunity of putting the question to her, he has never yet thought fit to do it.

The young woman understands this as clearly as if it were put into words; but no reasonable young woman would think of making this the ground of a quarrel. Just as little right have a married couple to tell me by speeches, and looks that are scarce less plain than speeches, that I am not the happy man,—the lady's choice. It is enough that I know I am not: I do not want this perpetual reminding.

The display of superior knowledge or riches may be made sufficiently mortifying, but these admit of a palliative. The knowledge which is brought out to insult me, may accidentally improve me; and in the rich man's houses and pictures,—his parks and gardens, I have a temporary usufruct at least. But the display of married happiness has none of these palliatives: it is throughout pure, unrecompensed, unqualified insult.

Marriage by its best title is a monopoly, and not of the least invidious sort. It is the cunning of most possessors of any exclusive privilege to keep their advantage as much out of sight as possible, that their less favoured neighbours, seeing little of the benefit, may the less be disposed to question the right. But these married monopolists thrust the most obnoxious part of their patent into our faces.

Nothing is to me more distasteful than that entire complacency and satisfaction which beam in the countenances of a new-married couple,—in that of the lady particularly: it tells you, that her lot is disposed of in this world: that *you* can have no hopes of her. It is true, I have none: nor wishes either, perhaps: but this is one of those truths which ought, as I said before, to be taken for granted, not expressed.

The excessive airs which those people give themselves, rounded on the ignorance of us unmarried people, would be more offensive if they were less irrational. We will allow them to understand the mysteries belonging to their own craft better than we, who have not had the happiness to be made free of the company: but their arrogance is not content within these limits. If a single person presumes to offer his opinion in their presence, though upon the most indifferent subject, he is immediately silenced as an incompetent person. Nay, a young married lady of my acquaintance, who, the best of the jest was, had not changed her condition above a fortnight before, in a question on which I had the misfortune to differ from her, respecting the properest mode of breeding oysters for the London market, had the assurance to ask with a sneer, how such an old Bachelor as I could pretend to know anything about such matters!

But what I have spoken of hitherto is nothing to the airs which these creatures give themselves when they come, as they generally do, to have children. When I consider how little of a rarity children are,—that every street and blind alley swarms with them,—that the poorest people commonly have them in most abundance,—that there are few marriages that are not blest with at least one of these bargains,—how often they turn out ill, and defeat the fond hopes of their parents, taking to vicious courses, which end in poverty, disgrace, the gallows, etc.—I cannot for my life tell what cause for pride there can possibly be in having them. If they were young phoenixes, indeed, that were born but one in a year, there might be a pretext. But when they are so common—

I do not advert to the insolent merit which they assume with their husbands on these occasions. Let *them* look to that. But why *we*, who are not their natural-born subjects, should be expected to bring our spices, myrrh, and incense,—our tribute and homage of admiration,—I do not see.

"Like as the arrows in the hand of the giant, even so are the young children"; so says the excellent office in our Prayer-book appointed for the churching of women. "Happy is the man that hath his quiver full of them." So say I, but then don't let him discharge his quiver upon us that are weaponless;—let them be arrows, but not to gall and stick us. I have generally observed that these arrows are double-headed: they have two forks, to be sure to hit with one or the other. As for instance, where you come into a house which is full of children, if you happen to take no notice of them (you are thinking of something else, perhaps, and turn a deaf ear to their innocent caresses), you are set down as untractable, morose, a hater of children. On the other hand, if you find them more than usually engaging,—if you are taken with their pretty manners, and set about in earnest to romp and play with them,—some pretext or other is sure to be found for sending them out of the room; they are too noisy or boisterous, or Mr. _____ does not like children. With one or other of these forks the arrow is sure to hit you.

I could forgive their jealousy, and dispense with toying with their brats, if it gives them any pain; but I think it unreasonable to be called upon to *love* them, where I see no occasion,—to love a whole family, perhaps eight, nine, or ten, indiscriminately,—to love all the pretty dears, because children are so engaging!

—Charles Lamb (1825)

Commentary on the Excerpt from Charles Lamb's "A Bachelor's Complaint of the Behaviour of Married People"

Lamb's essay opens with a summary of his essential thesis, and the remaining text is an amplification of that thesis. Lamb objects to married people for several reasons. He says first that they are too loving but clarifies this by saying loving in and of itself is not the real issue, rather married people's carrying their "preference [for one another] so undisguisedly" that they make single people feel that they "are not the object of this preference." In short, Lamb's problem is not the married state itself, but the air of superiority married people attach to it and the propensity of married people to display their "state" for the improvement of single folk. He goes on to say that the "display of married happiness has none of these palliatives: it is throughout pure, unrecompensed, unqualified insult." Here he does more than lament marriage's "superior" stance: he almost seems envious of it.

Lamb is fond of elevated diction. Words like palliative ("reduction of pain or intensity"), usufruct ("enjoyment"), and patent (meaning "contract") appear throughout Lamb's text. Similarly, his syntax is often rather complicated, sometimes masking his satiric barbs under an elitist syntactic respectability. Take this sentence as an example: "The excessive airs which those people give themselves, rounded on the ignorance of us unmarried people, would be more offensive if they were less irrational." This "more-less" construction accuses the married folk of several sins: excessive airs, ignorance, and irrationality. In fact, it is only this irrationality that saves them from being even more offensive. This jab satirizing the married state is framed in a sentence requiring rather careful processing to achieve understanding. Lamb seems to relish poking fun in this complex way.

Lamb includes a humorous anecdote about a "young married lady of his acquaintance." In fact, this young married woman was married less than two weeks (a fortnight), when she "sneered" about Lamb, "old Bachelor" that he was, "pretending" to know about breeding oysters for market. The reader is expected to smile here at the young woman's lack of experience at being married, but also at the foolish notion that marriage somehow dispenses an immediate knowledge of commerce that bachelors aren't privy to. Lamb laughs gently, not acerbically. His tone is bemused, not intolerant.

The selection ends with a commentary on the further airs married people put on when they have children. Lamb speaks so disparagingly of children that his remarks have become funny. Lamb laments, "If they were young phoenixes...but when they are so common—." The mythical phoenix, which rises up from its own ashes every five hundred years, is contrasted with those "so little a rarity," children. Lamb finds a rather involved way of stating that children are abundant. He then alludes to Christ's nativity when he speaks of parents expecting homage, indeed "spices, myrrh and incense," from appropriately doting single people. Here Lamb suggests that parents consider their children nothing less than divine. He ends with the elaborate metaphoric joke comparing children to arrows, double-headed arrows, "to be sure to hit with one or the other (head)." The explanation of the metaphor follows. When you enter a house full of children and fail to notice them properly you are "untractable, morose, a hater of children," the first half of the double-headed arrow. But if you play with them in earnest (the second half of the arrow), they are sent out of the room. Guests cannot be too popular with the children; parental jealousy sets in. This is clearly a no-win situation for the unsuspecting single person. The double-headed arrow strikes, one way or the other.

Lamb's style, deliberately old-fashioned, is the voice of a bemused observer. He is less didactic than he is a satirist of the foibles he observes. In this essay, married people are the targets.

Conclusion

These commentaries are far from complete, but they begin to apply the most significant of the six critical reading strategies. Students preparing for the AP Examination in English Language and Composition should test their responses against these brief commentaries, and then move on to other essays, always attentive to the marriage of form and content that is the hallmark of excellent prose.

AP

English Language & Composition

Chapter 3

Chapter 3

Writing About the "Other" Literature: A Critical Dialogue

Critical Writing

As we discussed in the chapter on critical reading, literature is a term descriptive of much more than the traditional genres of fiction, poetry, and drama. While some traditional literary genres are included, the AP Course in English Language and Composition and the AP Examination in English Language and Composition both feature a variety of "other" literatures, chiefly nonfiction, especially the essay. In addition to demonstrable skill in critical reading of essays, biographies, journalistic prose, political, historical, and scientific treatises, students are expected to write about these texts effectively. The primary form written responses will take is the critical essay.

Writing as Dialogue

The critical essay may be thought of as a written dialogue with another text. The writer responds to the effects created by a text he or she has read, not with a mere overflow of feeling, but with a keenly critical eye, looking to the *how* of the text under scrutiny as well as the *what*. Most readers of *Beloved*, the Pulitzer Prize-winning novel by Toni Morrison, will vividly recall moments when the text overwhelmed them emotionally. When Sethe, a black mother, tries to kill her own children rather than give them up to slavers, reactions of fear, pity, love, and even loathing are reported. Though these reactions to the text are sincere, they are "monologues," involved in the text of *Beloved* only indirectly. The critical writer becomes involved directly and enters into dialogue with the text by attempting to discern how it created the responses it did. The critical writer may also take issue with a text, entering into a dialogue with it in order to evaluate and analyze it. Unless a writer enters into dialogue with the texts he or she reads and responds to, the written response will be either a superficial expression of emotion or a banal summary of what took place. Dialogue is crucial to critical writing. In the previous chapter on critical reading, much useful information is afforded the critical writer as well. It is good practice to apply the six strategies for critical reading to any text that you eventually have to write about. These six strategies are the beginning of the dialogue you'll enter into with any text. Putting your dialogue into words is the next challenge and the topic of this chapter.

Writing for the AP Examination

The English Language and Composition exam assumes that students are fluent in standard English syntax and grammar. They are also expected to be able to organize their thoughts in coherent, well-expressed expository prose. Most will be amply familiar with the standard five-paragraph theme with its introduction, three body paragraphs, and conclusion. Beyond an ability to use this basic form, however, students need to be aware of the different stylistic effects created by different syntactic and lexical choices. That is to say, when students choose a particular word or construct a very short or very complex sentence, they need to be in control of their choices, realizing how these choices affect their readers. They need to be aware of the effects of the text on the audience. This awareness is useful in both the analysis *and* creation of expository prose.

Fiction and poetry are natural locations for observing syntactic choice and diction, but exploring the rhetoric of the "other" literature (nonfiction) reinforces the strategies the AP Exam expects students to employ in their own prose. A key skill in writing about the "other" literature is the ability to analyze stylistic strategies. In addition to analyzing prose style, students will be asked to write argumentative essays (with appropriate support/evidence) in response to various readings. These readings are often excerpts rather than whole essays and thus offer additional challenges.

Strategies for Analysis and Argument

Since rhetorical analysis and argumentation are the two important expository forms, this chapter will suggest strategies for improving their work in these two forms. In short, students will learn how to create dialogues with the texts they are asked to read and write about. These dialogues may be analytic and/or argumentative, but in both cases they employ critical acumen and style. Thus, the following chapter has two sections:

1. Analytic Writing: A Critical Dialogue

2. Argumentative Writing: A Critical Dialogue

1. Analytic Writing: A Critical Dialogue

Most competent writers know that an essay has three basic parts: a beginning, a middle, and an end. But that basic organizational scheme may be stretched and altered in myriad ways. Think of an essay draft as an unconditioned athlete. With practice, even ordinary people of average ability can stretch and tone their muscles until they are capable of impressive feats of athletic endurance, flexibility, and strength. Similarly, with practice an essay can become much more than an ordinary five-paragraph theme. That essay, through proper attention to style, can become a toned and effective piece of rhetoric. ("Rhetoric" is meant here in its best sense—effective, compelling communication—rather than in its perjorative sense—sham or false persuasion.)

Starting with Style

In order to flex your essay-writing muscles, you must consider matters of style. Good analytic writing focuses on a text's substance and style, and is itself written in an appropriate style.

Writing critically *about* style and writing critically *with* style are our first concerns. Bearing in mind our framework of the dialogue, let's enter into a dialogue with a particular text and its style. In the following essay by Washington Irving, "The Voyage," several interesting stylistic strategies may be noted. In order to analyze Irving's work, you must be attentive to how these stylistic strategies support his thesis. In fact, voice, style, tone, and other rhetorical considerations are usually well-chosen reflections of an author's purpose and subject. Entering into a dialogue with a text can reveal how form and content reinforce one another—thus adding to the impact of the text.

Irving's essay is printed on the next page and the analytic response, in the form of a dialogue, follows. In order to prepare for your own analysis (and to better understand the professional analysis given), you should read Irving's essay using the same critical reading strategies recommended in the previous chapter. By

1. getting the facts straight,

2. analyzing the argument,

3. identifying basic features of style,

4. exploring your personal response,

5. evaluating the text overall and determining its significance, and

6. comparing and contrasting related texts,

you will muster a wealth of data about the text that will enable you to compose an astute analysis.

The Voyage

Ships, ships, I will descrie you
Amidst the main,
I will come and try you,
What are you protecting,
And projecting,
What's your end and aim.
One goes abroad for merchandise and trading,
Another stays to keep his country from invading,
A third is coming home with rich and wealthy lading.
Halloo! my fancie, whither wilt thou go?

Old Poem

To an American visiting Europe, the long voyage he has to make is an excellent preparative. The temporary absence of worldly scenes and employments produces a state of mind particularly fitted to receive new and vivid impressions. The vast space of waters that separates the hemispheres is like a blank page in existence. There is no gradual transition by which, as in Europe, the features and population of one country blend almost imperceptibly with those of another. From the moment you lose sight of the land you have left, all is vacancy until you step on the opposite shore, and are launched at once into the bustle and novelties of another world.

In traveling by land there is a continuity of scene, and a connected succession of persons and incidents, that carry on the story of life, and lessen the effect of absence and separation. We drag, it is true, "a lengthening chain" at each remove of our pilgrimage; but the chain is unbroken: we can trace it back link by link; and we feel that the last still grapples us to home. But a wide sea voyage severs us at once. It makes us conscious of being cast loose from the secure anchorage of settled life, and sent adrift upon a doubtful world. It interposes a gulf, not merely imaginary, but real, between us and our homes—a gulf subject to tempest, and fear, and uncertainty, rendering distance palpable, and return precarious.

Such, at least, was the case with myself. As I saw the last blue line of my native land fade away like a cloud in the horizon, it seemed as if I had closed one volume of the world and its concerns, and had time for meditation, before I opened another. That land, too, now vanishing from my view, which contained all most dear to me in life; what vicissitudes might occur in it—what changes might take place in me, before I should visit it again! Who can tell, when he sets forth to wander, whither he may be driven by the uncertain currents of existence; or when he may return; or whether it may ever be his lot to revisit the scenes of his childhood?

I said that at sea all is vacancy; I should correct the expression. To one given to day-dreaming, and fond of losing himself in reveries, a sea voyage is full of subjects for meditation; but then they are the wonders of the deep, and of the air, and rather tend to abstract the mind from worldly themes. I delighted to loll over the quarter-railing, or climb to the maintop, of a calm day, and muse for hours together on the tranquil bosom of a summer's sea; to gaze upon the piles of golden clouds just peering above the horizon, to fancy them some fairy realms, and people them with a creation of my own;—to watch the gentle undulating billows, rolling their silver volumes, as if to die away on those happy shores.

There was a delicious sensation of mingled security and awe with which I looked down, from my giddy height, on the monsters of the deep at their uncouth gambols. Shoals of porpoises tumbling about in the bow of the ship; the grampus slowly heaving his huge form above the surface; or the ravenous shark, darting, like a spectre, through the blue waters. My imagination would conjure up all that I had heard or read of the watery world beneath me; of the finny herds that roam its fathomless valleys; of the shapeless monsters that lurk among the very foundations of the earth; and of those wild phantasms that swell the tales of fishermen and sailors.

Sometimes a distant sail, gliding along the edge of the ocean, would be another theme of idle speculation. How interesting this fragment of a world, hastening to rejoin the great mass of existence! What a glorious monument of human invention; which has in a manner triumphed over wind and wave; has brought the ends of the world into communion; has established an interchange of blessings, pouring into the sterile regions of the north all the luxuries of the south; has diffused the light of knowledge and the charities of cultivated life; and has thus bound together those scattered portions of the human race, between which nature seemed to have thrown an insurmountable barrier.

We one day descried some shapeless object drifting at a distance. At sea, everything that breaks the monotony of the surrounding expanse attracts attention. It proved to be the mast of a ship that must have been completely wrecked; for there were the remains of handkerchiefs, by which some of the crew had fastened themselves to this spar, to prevent their being washed off by the waves. There was no trace by which the name of the ship could be ascertained. The wreck had evidently drifted about for many months; clusters of shell-fish had fastened about it, and long seaweeds flaunted at its sides. But where, thought I, is the crew? Their struggle has long been over—they have gone down amidst the roar of the tempest—their bones lie whitening among the caverns of the deep. Silence, oblivion, like the waves, have closed over them, and no one can tell the story of their end. What sighs have been wafted after that ship! What prayers offered up at the deserted fireside of home! How often has the mistress, the wife, the mother, pored over the daily news, to catch some casual intelligence of this rover of the deep! How has expectation darkened into anxiety—anxiety into dread—and dread into despair! Alas! not one momento may ever return for love to cherish. All that may ever be known, is, that she sailed from her port, "and was never heard of more!"

The sight of this wreck, as usual, gave rise to many dismal anecdotes. This was particularly the case in the evening, when the weather, which had hitherto been fair, began to look wild and threatening, and gave indications of one of those sudden storms which will sometimes break in upon the serenity of a summer voyage. As we sat round the dull light of a lamp in the cabin, that made the gloom more ghastly, everyone had his tale of shipwreck and disaster. I was particularly struck with a short one related by the captain.

"As I was once sailing," said he, "in a fine stout ship across the banks of Newfoundland, one of those heavy fogs which prevail in those parts rendered it impossible for us to see far ahead even in the daytime; but at night the weather was so thick that we could not distinguish any object at twice the length of the ship. I kept lights at the mast-head, and a constant watch forward to look out for fishing smacks, which are accustomed to lie at anchor on the banks. The wind was blowing a smacking breeze, and we were going at a great rate through the water. Suddenly the watch gave the alarm of 'a sail ahead!'—it was scarcely uttered before we were upon her. She was a small schooner, at anchor, with her broadside towards us. The crew were all asleep, and had neglected to hoist a light. We struck her just amid-ships. The force, the size, and weight of our vessel bore her down below the waves; we passed over her and were hurried on our course. As the crashing wreck was sinking beneath us, I had a glimpse of two or three half-naked wretches rushing from her cabin; they just started from their beds to be swallowed shrieking by the waves. I heard their drowning cry mingling with the wind. The blast that bore it to our ears swept us out of all farther hearing. I shall never forget that cry! It was some time before we could put the ship about, she was under such headway. We returned, as nearby as we could guess, to the place where the smack had anchored. We cruised about for several hours in the dense fog. We fired signal guns, and listened if we might hear the halloo of any survivors: but all was silent—we never saw or heard anything of them more."

I confess these stories, for a time, put an end to all my fine fancies. The storm increased with the night. The sea was lashed into tremendous confusion. There was a fearful, sullen sound of rushing waves, and broken surges. Deep called unto deep. At times the black volume of clouds over head seemed rent asunder by flashes of lightning which quivered along the foaming billows, and made the succeeding darkness doubly terrible. The thunders bellowed over the wild waste of waters, and were echoed and prolonged by the mountain waves. As I saw the ship staggering and plunging among these roaring caverns, it seemed miraculous that she regained her balance, or preserved her buoyancy. Her yards would dip into the water: her bow was almost buried beneath the waves. Sometimes an impending surge appeared ready to overwhelm her, and nothing but a dexterous movement of the helm preserved her from the shock.

When I retired to my cabin, the awful scene still followed me. The whistling of the wind through the rigging sounded like funeral wailings. The creaking of the masts, the straining and groaning of the bulk-heads, as the ship labored in the weltering sea, were frightful. As I heard the waves rushing along the sides of the ship, and roaring in my very ear, it seemed as if Death were raging round this floating prison, seeking for his prey: the mere starting of a nail, the yawning of a seam, might give him entrance.

A fine day, however, with a tranquil sea and favoring breeze, soon put all these dismal reflections to flight. It is impossible to resist the gladdening influence of fine weather and fair wind at sea. When the ship is decked out in all her canvas, every sail swelled, and careering gayly over the curling waves, how lofty, how gallant she appears—how she seems to lord it over the deep!

I might fill a volume with the reveries of a sea voyage, for with me it is almost a continual reverie—but it is time to get to shore.

It was a fine sunny morning when the thrilling cry of "land!" was given from the mast-head. None but those who have experienced it can form an idea of the delicious throng of sensations which rush into an American's bosom, when he first comes in sight of Europe. There is a volume of associations with the very name. It is the land of promise, teeming with everything of which his childhood has heard, or on which his studious years have pondered.

From that time until the moment of arrival, it was all feverish excitement. The ships of war, that prowled like guardian giants along the coast; the headlands of Ireland, stretching out into the channel; the Welsh mountains, towering into the clouds; all were objects of intense interest. As we sailed up the Mersey, I reconnoitered the shores with a telescope. My eye dwelt with delight on neat cottages, with their trim shrubberies and green grass plots. I saw the mouldering ruin of an abbey overrun with ivy, and the taper spire of a village church rising from the brown of a neighboring hill—all were characteristic of England.

The tide and wind were so favorable that the ship was enabled to come at once to the pier. It was thronged with people; some, idle lookers-on, others, eager expectants of friends or relatives. I could distinguish the merchant to whom the ship was consigned. I knew him by his calculating brow and restless air. His hands were thrust into his pockets; he was whistling thoughtfully, and walking to and fro, a small space having been accorded him by the crowd, in deference to his temporary importance. There were repeated cheerings and salutations interchanged between the shore and the ship, as friends happened to recognize each other. I particularly noticed one woman of humble dress, but interesting demeanor. She was leaning forward from among the crowd; her eye hurried over the ship as it neared the shore, to catch some wished-for countenance. She seemed disappointed and agitated; when I heard a faint voice call her name. It was from a poor sailor who had been ill all the voyage, and had excited the sympathy of everyone on board. When the weather was fine, his messmates had spread a mattress for him on deck in the shade, but of late his illness had so increased, that he had taken to his hammock, and only breathed a wish that he might see his wife before he died. He had been helped on deck as we came up the river, and now was leaning against the shrouds, with a countenance so wasted, so pale, so ghastly, that it was no wonder even the eye of affection did not recognize him. But at the sound of his voice, her eye darted on his features;

it read, at once, a whole volume of sorrow; she clasped her hands, uttered a faint shriek, and stood wringing them in silent agony.

All now was hurry and bustle. The meetings of acquaintances—the greetings of friends—the consultations of men of business. I alone was solitary and idle. I had no friend to meet, no cheering to receive. I stepped upon the land of my forefathers—but I felt that I was a stranger in the land.

—Washington Irving (1819)

Analytic Writing: A Critical Dialogue with Washington Irving's "The Voyage"

In 1815, Washington Irving crossed the Atlantic on business to England, Germany, and Spain and stayed abroad for 17 years. His best known book, *The Sketchbook*, was produced during this period and is the source of "The Voyage." In fact, "The Voyage" marks not only Irving's passage from America to England and the European continent, but also the passage from the culture and young traditions of the New World to the much longer established traditions of the Old World. William Makepeace Thackeray said that Irving was "the first ambassador whom the New World of letters sent to the Old." This background information, usually published in a headnote to a text, or readily available in a literary biography, is a useful place to begin a look at "The Voyage." (This process may be considered part of the "previewing" recommended in the previous chapter on critical reading.) In fact, this information helps the reader "center" the text, or place it in the tradition of arts and letters. It also helps the reader conjecture about Irving's intentions in writing this text and perhaps even speculate about some of his attitudes toward the subject. It seems likely, for example, that Irving, as an American, might feel some anxiety traveling abroad. Also, the hazards of a long sea voyage were considerable in the early nineteenth century. As we analyze Irving's style as further revealing his subject matter, we should be on the lookout for any of Irving's attitudes that are revealed, directly or indirectly. The careful reader/analyst is well aware that the influence of an author's attitude toward a subject can have on tone and style.

Irving begins his essay "The Voyage" by quoting an Old Poem—no author is mentioned. The poem muses about sailing ships and the various purposes for which they set to sea. This romantic, prefatory poem helps set the tone of Irving's essay. The critical reader/writer in dialogue with the text would begin by asking, "Why did Irving choose this old ditty?" The answer seems readily apparent: the subject of the essay is a sea voyage, and Irving is simply setting the scene. However, the poem's focus on the purposes of sea voyages may be a link worth remembering and considering as the essay unfolds. Now that we have launched into our dialogue, let's change to a format that will help us visualize the reader's interaction with the text. From now on, the analytic questions and comments will come from a "Reader" and the "Text" of "The Voyage" will answer.

Reader: The text of "The Voyage" is an account of Irving's Atlantic crossing. There are several moments when Irving gives information about his feelings on the journey.

Text: Yes, in the third paragraph Irving speaks rather wistfully of America, "now vanishing from [his] view, which contained all most dear to [him] in life": he worries about what "vicissitudes" might occur in his absence and what changes might occur in himself. He wonders when he may return and even *if* he will return to "revisit the scenes of his childhood."

Reader: But Irving's trepidation isn't so powerful that it prevents him from sailing. The tone here, Irving's "voice," is best described as a mixture of wistful fondness for the familiar and a fearful curiosity about the future. This ambivalence is mirrored in the physical fact of Irving's sailing—he is between the old and the new. What is the structure of the ensuing essay; are Irving's fears realized?

Text: Irving begins by describing his daydreams at sea, romanticizing the "piles of golden clouds just peering above the horizon, to fancy them some fairy realms, and people them with a creation of my own;—to watch the gentle undulating billows, rolling their silver volumes, as if to die away on those happy shores."

Reader: These musings on the clouds and waves are a departure from Irving's earlier abstract philosophizing. Here, he is caught up in the wonders of the sea and waxes almost poetic. In fact, the following two paragraphs are heavily imaginal and descriptive: the fourth paragraph is a series of metaphors about sea creatures (monsters gambol like lambs, porpoises are tumblers, sharks are spectres). The language here ("fathomless valleys," "shapeless monsters," "wild phantasms") is reminiscent of that used in the supernaturally charged "Legend of Sleepy Hollow," Irving's most famous work. Paragraph five is another philosophical ascent, speculating on a sail on a distant horizon. Here Irving harks back to the "Old Poem" of his opening. The sail is called a "fragment of the world, hastening to rejoin the great mass of existence." The sail, which stands for all types of sea-going vessels, brings the continents into contact with one another. Many purposes exist for travel by sea, but Irving sees them all as a way of binding "together those scattered portions of the human race." Perhaps he sees himself as a participant in the great cycle of connective journeys.

Text: Paragraph six describes passing the wreck of an unknown ship. Poignant details, like "the remains of handkerchiefs, by which some of the crew had fastened themselves to the spar, to prevent their being washed off by the waves," are abundant in this section.

Reader: Yes, Irving asks where the crew is and speaks sadly of their "bones whitening" in the deep. When he speaks of the "sighs wafting after that ship," and the "prayers offered up at the deserted fireside of home," it's not difficult to imagine the anxiety of Irving's own friends and relatives as he set out on his long, dangerous voyage. The description of the wreck indirectly suggests Irving's fearfulness. More of the same is found in the Captain's anecdote, which follows.

Text: The Captain's story of the large ship hitting and sinking the small schooner seems all the more pathetic because of the unprepared, sleeping crew, who "start from their beds to be swallowed shrieking by the waves."

Reader: These stories of shipwreck increase Irving's fear and end his fanciful musing on the sea. When a storm blows in, Irving describes its awful progress a bit melodramatically. "As I heard the waves rushing along the sides of the ship, and roaring in my very ear, it seemed as if Death were raging round this floating prison, seeking for his prey: the mere starting of a nail, the yawning of a seam, might give him entrance." Irving's mortality is an overwhelming preoccupation. In these lines, Death might enter through any crack: Irving certainly has let him in through his imagination. Stylistically, these dark thoughts seem to demand a respite in the text, and soon.

Text: Irving now turns to the "gladdening influence of fine weather and fair wind at sea." And shortly thereafter, land is sighted. Irving then returns to his theme of New World citizen sailing back to the Old World. He speaks of the "delicious throng of sensations which rush into an American's bosom, when he first comes in sight of Europe…It is the land of promise, teeming with everything…"

Reader: Irving is now filled with buoyant expectation and his syntax and diction are likewise speedy and ebullient. "Teeming," "stretching," "towering," and "rising" are some of the words that he uses to convey the enormous possibilities that await him. Why does he then shift gears and end with the sad reunion between the poor, ill sailor and his wife waiting at the dock?

Text: An answer might be found in the final line, "But at the sound of his voice, her eye darted on his features; it read, at once, a whole volume of sorrow."

Reader: So even in the happy moment of arrival, a scene of anxious sorrow intervenes. In fact, Irving shares this sorrowful mood. "I alone was solitary and idle. I had no friend to meet, no cheering to receive. I stepped upon the land of my forefathers—but I felt that I was a stranger in the land." So, at least the sick sailor is met at the dock by a loved one; Irving's voyage, however, ends with all the anxious fear strangers feel.

The above hypothetical dialogue between a reader and the text of Washington Irving's "The Voyage" pinpoints a number of revealing stylistic strategies. The stylistic choices Irving makes reflect his attitudes toward his subject and lead the reader to the essence of his text. Through this analysis, which focuses on style, it is readily clear that Irving was anxious about this voyage, a feeling that manifested itself in several ways and never left him, even when he was safely on shore. The anxiety felt on a sea voyage, though tempered by joyful expectation, may be seen as a reflection of his anxiety at visiting the Old World. Indeed, all Americans abroad in the early nineteenth century probably experienced it and would appreciate Irving's extended metaphor of a perilous sea voyage.

Students preparing for the AP Examination in English Language and Composition will find constructing dialogues with sample essays excellent practice for composing stylistic and thematic analyses. The dialogues themselves may be used as frameworks for the analytic essays the students then write. A good rule of thumb in analytic writing is to refer to the text regularly, using it to support your conclusions and engender your questions.

Exercise: Using the dialogue on Irving's "The Voyage," write a brief analysis (500 words) that incorporates the key elements of textual evidence and reveals Irving's reasons for writing. Remember, purpose is a significant determiner of style.

2. Argumentative Writing: A Critical Dialogue

Argument is a particularly human skill. Almost from the cradle, human beings manifest disagreement, sometimes very vocally! But argument, and argumentative writing, is not simply skillful disagreement. Essays that argue a particular point usually also involve the analytic skills emphasized in the previous section. The AP Examination in English Language and Composition will ask students to respond to a text by taking an opposing stand. To respond effectively and advance a successful argument, students will need to analyze the opposing argument as part of their response.

This section will offer practice in responding to argumentative texts, including performing the analysis that is so crucial to mounting a successful counter argument. The AP Exam frequently presents students with an argumentative text or an excerpt of an argument, and asks them to take the opposing view, sometimes regardless of their personal feelings on the subject. Or, students will be asked to compare and contrast two arguments to determine the more effective of the two.

In order to address all these possibilities in this review chapter, you will be presented with two arguments on a similar topic, a comparative analysis of their relative strengths and weaknesses, and instruction in composing your own argumentative response. Thus, the several skills of argumentative writing are all included.

As in the previous section, you will view the writing process as a critical dialogue. This methodology helps articulate the essential issues you will analyze and oppose. Students will also be given a brief review of sound argumentative essay structure and a few of the writing devices that regularly appear in effective argumentative essays. In addition, you will find many useful rhetorical and literary devices in the glossary at the end of this chapter.

The two arguments that you will analyze and compare follow. Presented chronologically, the first essay excerpt, taken from "Idleness an Anxious and Miserable State," was written in 1751 by Samuel Johnson, the famous eighteenth-century literary critic and essayist. The second essay excerpt, taken from Robert Louis Stevenson's "An Apology for Idlers," was published in 1876 and has since become a classic. Robert Louis Stevenson is a noted American author, perhaps most famous for *Treasure Island.*

Idleness an Anxious and Miserable State

Who knows if heav'n, with ever-bounteous pow'r,
Shall add tomorrow to the present hour?

I sat yesterday morning employed in deliberating on which, among the various subjects that occurred to my imagination, I should bestow the paper of today. After a short effort of meditation by which nothing was determined, I grew every moment more irresolute, my ideas wandered from the first intention, and I rather wished to think, than thought upon any settled subject; till at last I was awakened from this dream of study by a summons from the press; the time was now come for which I had been thus negligently purposing to provide, and, however dubious or sluggish, I was now necessitated to write...

There was however, some pleasure in reflecting that I, who had only trifled till diligence was necessary, might still congratulate myself upon my superiority to multitudes, who have trifled till diligence is vain; who can by no degree of activity or resolution recover the opportunities which have slipped away; and who are condemned by their own carelessness to hopeless calamity and barren sorrow.

The folly of allowing ourselves to delay what we know cannot be finally escaped, is one of the general weaknesses, which, in spite of the instruction of moralists, and the remonstrances of reason, prevail to a greater or less degree in every mind...

It is indeed natural to have particular regard to the time present, and to be most solicitous for that which is by its nearness enabled to make the strongest impressions. When therefore any sharp pain is to be suffered, or any formidable danger to be incurred, we can scarcely exempt ourselves wholly from the seducements of imagination; we readily believe that another day will bring some support or advantage which we now want and are easily persuaded, that the moment of necessity which we desire never to arrive, is at a great distance from us.

Thus life is languished away in the gloom of anxiety, and consumed in collecting resolutions which the next morning dissipates; in forming purposes which we scarcely hope to keep, and reconciling ourselves to our own cowardice by excuses, which, while we admit them, we know to be absurd. Our firmness is by the continual contemplation of misery, hourly impaired; every submission to our fear enlarges its dominion; we not only waste that time in which the evil we dread might have been suffered and surmounted, but even where procrastination produces no absolute increase of our difficulties, make then less superable to ourselves by habitual terrours...

To act is far easier than to suffer; yet we every day see the progress of life retarded by the *vis inertiae*, the mere repugnance to motion, and find multitudes repining at the want of that which nothing but idleness hinders them from enjoying...

There is nothing more common among this torpid generation than murmurs and complaints; murmurs at uneasiness which only vacancy and suspicion expose them to feel and complaints of distresses which it is in their own power to remove. Laziness is commonly associated with timidity...

Among all who sacrifice future advantage to present inclination, scarcely any gain so little as those that suffer themselves to freeze in idleness. Others are corrupted by some enjoyment of more or less power to gratify the passions; but to neglect our duties, merely to avoid the labour of performing them, a labour which is always punctually rewarded, is surely to sink under weak temptations...

The certainty of life cannot be long, and the probability that it will be much shorter than nature allows, ought to awaken every man to the active prosecution of whatever he is desirous to perform. It is true, that no diligence can ascertain success; death may intercept the swiftest career; but he who is cut off in the execution of an honest undertaking, has at least the honour of falling in his rank, and has fought the battle though he missed the victory.

—Samuel Johnson (1751)

An Apology for Idlers

Just now, when everyone is bound, under pain of a decree in absence convicting them of *lèse*-respectability[1], to enter on some lucrative profession, and labour therein with something not far short of enthusiasm, a cry

---

[1] A play on *lèse-majesté*, a crime or offence committed against a king.

from the opposite party who are content when they have enough, and like to look on and enjoy in the meanwhile, savours a little of bravado and gasconade. And yet this should not be. Idleness so called, which does not consist in doing nothing, but in doing a great deal not recognised in the dogmatic formularies of the ruling class, has as good a right to state its position as industry itself...

Where was the glory of having taken Rome for these tumultuous barbarians, who poured into the Senate house, and found the Fathers sitting silent and unmoved by their success? It is a sore thing to have laboured along and scaled the arduous hilltops, and when all is done, find humanity indifferent to your achievement. Hence physicists condemn the unphysical; financiers have only a superficial toleration for those who know little of stocks; literary persons despise the unlettered; and people of all pursuits combine to disparage those who have none.

But though this is one difficulty of the subject, it is not the greatest. You could not be put in prison for speaking against industry, but you can be sent to Coventry for speaking like a fool. The greatest difficulty with most subjects is to do them well; therefore, please to remember this is an apology. It is certain that much may be judiciously argued in favour of diligence; only there is something to be said against it, and that is what, on the present occasion, I have to say...

It is surely beyond a doubt that people should be a good deal idle in youth. For though here and there a Lord Macaulay may escape from school honours with all his wits about him, most boys pay so dear for their medals that they never afterwards have a short in their locker, and begin the world bankrupt. And the same holds true during all the time a lad is educating himself, or suffering others to educate him. It must have been a very foolish old gentleman who addressed Johnson at Oxford in these words: "Young man, ply your book diligently now, and acquire a stock of knowledge; for when years come upon you, you will find that poring upon books will be but an irksome task." The old gentleman seems to have been unaware that many other things besides reading grow irksome, and not a few become impossible, by the time a man has to use spectacles and cannot walk without a stick. Books are good enough in their own way, but they are a mighty bloodless substitute for life. It seems a pity to sit, like the Lady of Shalott, peering into a mirror, with your back turned on all the bustle and glamour of reality. And if a man reads very hard, as the old anecdote reminds us, he will have little time for thought.

If you look back on your own education, I am sure it will not be the full, vivid, instructive hours of truantry that you regret; you would rather cancel some lack-lustre periods between sleep and waking in the class. For my own part, I have attended a good many lectures in my time. I still remember that the spinning of a top is a case of Kinetic Stability. I still remember that Emphysteusis is not a disease, nor Stillicide a crime. But though I would not willingly part with such scraps of science, I do not set the same store by them as by certain other odds and ends that I came by in the open street while I was playing truant. This is not the moment to dilate on that mighty place of education, which was the favourite school of Dickens and of Balzac, and turns out yearly many inglorious masters in the Science of the Aspects of Life. Suffice it to say this: if a lad does not learn in the streets, it is because he has no faculty of learning. Nor is the truant always in the streets, for if he prefers, he may be out by the gardened suburbs into the country. He may pitch on some tuft of lilacs over a burn, and smoke innumerable pipes to the tune of the water on the stones. A bird will sing in the thicket. And there he may fall into a vein of kindly thought, and see things in a new perspective. Why, if this be not education, what is?

Extreme *busyness*, whether at school or college, kirk or market, is a symptom of deficient vitality; and a faculty for idleness implies a catholic appetite and a strong sense of personal identity. There is a sort of dead-alive, hackneyed people about, who are scarcely conscious of living except in the exercise of some conventional occupation. Bring these fellows into the country, or set them aboard ship, and you will see how they pine for their desk or their study. They have no curiosity; they cannot give themselves over to random provocations; they do not take pleasure in the exercise of their faculty for its own sake; and unless Necessity lays about them with a stick, they will even stand still. It is no good speaking to such folk: they *cannot* be idle, their nature is not generous enough; and they pass those hours in a sort of coma, which are not dedicated to furious moiling in the gold-mill...

If a person cannot be happy without remaining idle, idle he should remain...

And what, in God's name, is all this pother about? For what cause do they embitter their own and other people's lives? That a man should publish three or thirty articles a year, that he should finish or not finish his great allegorical picture, are questions of little interest to the world...

The ends for which they give away their priceless youth, for all they know, may be chimerical or hurtful; the glory and riches they expect may never come, or may find them indifferent; and they and the world they inhabit are so inconsiderable that the mind freezes at the thought.

—Robert Louis Stevenson (1876)

Reader: So the essential difference between Johnson's thesis and Stevenson's thesis is in their *definition* of idleness. Johnson sees it as a "weak temptation" that results in a "neglect of duty" and a misuse of precious time. Because life "cannot be long" every man should be awake "to the active prosecution of whatever he is desirous to perform." Stevenson, on the other hand, argues that idleness, particularly in one's youth, should be cherished and cultivated, for it is in idleness, in contemplation and observation, that true education occurs.

Text: Yes. Stevenson offers a lengthy example on the value of "street education" as opposed to poring over books, saying that "books are good enough in their own way, but they are a mighty bloodless substitute for life."

Reader: Stevenson even says idleness can help one avoid bitterness and concludes that an absence of idleness in life expends "priceless youth." After all, he argues, "[whether] a man should publish three or thirty articles a year," is a question of "little interest to the world." Furthermore, "the glory and riches they expect may never come."

A Critical Dialogue on "Idleness an Anxious and Miserable State" by Samuel Johnson and "An Apology for Idlers" by Robert Louis Stevenson

Reader: These two essay excerpts really present varying perspectives on idleness. Is it too easy to say Johnson is against it and Stevenson is for it?

Text:[1] Not really. That is, in a superficial sense, the basic point of departure. Finding the thesis in each essay will clarify their opposition.

Reader: Essentially, Johnson believes that idleness is evil because it means missed opportunity.

Text: Yes, he says idlers can never "recover the opportunities which have slipped away" and that they are "condemned by their own carelessness to hopeless calamity and barren sorrow."

---

[1] "Text" in this dialogue refers to *both* the Johnson and Stevenson excerpts.

Reader: That's a pretty strong condemnation of idleness; it's probably related to Johnson's indolent youth and his accompanying guilt. It's well known that Johnson's father died in his sickbed while the "lazy" Samuel refused to take over his father's booksellers business, and that Samuel repeatedly finished contracted essays while the printer waited at the door.

Text: Yes, your research is accurate. Samuel Johnson's essays are meant to teach his middle-class readers, and relentless self-examination is part of his style. See, for example, the opening to this essay where he refers to his difficulty in composing it and speaks of "trifling" till diligence was necessary. This self-reflection was used to derive moral lessons for his readers.

Reader: Stevenson's message is much less "moralizing" in tone and substance. He thinks idleness is okay if it makes you happy.

Text: He actually goes farther than that, saying that "extreme *busyness*...is a symptom of deficient vitality; and a faculty for idleness implies a catholic appetite and a strong sense of personal identity."

Text: Comparing Johnson's and Stevenson's argument at the level of definition of terms is indeed fruitful. How would you summarize the difference?

Reader: Well, it boils down to the purpose of life. Johnson seems to value producing and doing most highly. Stevenson wants to stop and smell the roses. I see value in *both* approaches to idleness. If I were to construct a counterargument, I might suggest that there is a time for idleness and a time for productivity. Stevenson seems to recognize that better than Johnson, perhaps because Johnson had such a hard time with indolence in his own life. He can't give himself a break!

            But western civilization has a powerful work ethic and idleness for its own sake would be hard to justify. If I were going to support my moderate position, I'd probably look for authoritative backing, the testimony of great thinkers on the value of idleness, perhaps an example or two of a "eureka" experience that accompanied an afternoon of daydreaming. I would also, however, provide examples of people who were too often idle and managed to do nothing with their lives.

Text: Though Johnson might agree with that tactic, Stevenson might retort, but if they were happy, what does it matter?

Reader: Ah ha! Now I've got *my* conclusion. I think true happiness is impossible when inactivity is complete or total. I guess I'll need evidence from psychologists or sociologists on the value of work—all work, physical and mental. I have my own definition of idleness now.

The hypothetical dialogue between a reader and the texts written by Johnson and Stevenson should help you "walk through" the process of analyzing and responding to arguments. In your own argumentative essay you should be aware of (and able to make use of) the many rhetorical and literary strategies that will bolster your case. Remember to peruse the Glossary, where these strategies are defined.

A Brief Review of Argumentative Structure

Composing an argument is a little like preparing a debate. You should approach the subject by first carefully defining it *and* by defining it from the opposition's perspective. Sometimes it's at this level, definition, that the real controversy is revealed. Certainly that was true of the two essays on Idleness.

The next step is to offer reasoning and evidence which supports your definition (or understanding) of the issue. Good evidence can take a variety of forms, and fallacious reasoning is equally abundant. (Check the glossary for examples of each, i.e., "analogy," "authority," and "example," which are good evidence, and "begging the question," "either-or reasoning," and "non-sequitur," which are common fallacies in argument.) In this stage of the argument, your job is to make clear *how* and *why* you arrived at your position. The reader should be able to follow your logic readily and should trust your evidence.

The next step involves covering your opponent's objections. In any argument, two or more positions may legitimately exist. Rather than discount your opposition out of hand (since this merely alienates; it doesn't win arguments), you should make a reasonable effort to deal with the major points of conflict and demonstrate where the opposition errs.

Lastly, your argument should offer a solution to the issue's problem(s). No reader likes to read an argument that complains without offering alternatives.

To make the above recommendations clearer, an outline of argumentative strategy is provided below.

Argument Outline

1. State premise or thesis; define issue(s)

   a. provide details about the nature of the issue

   b. articulate how your definition differs from the opposition; analyze their argument carefully

   c. define by denotation, connotation, division, example, and/or cause and effect

2. Offer reasoning and evidence

   a. provide readers with the logic that led you to your conclusion

   b. offer supporting evidence (comparison, analogy, authority, quotation, statistics, personal experience, etc.)

   c. check your reasoning and evidence for fallacies

3. Cover the opposition's objections to your position

4. Offer a solution or alternative

By following this outline you can create a reasonable, well-founded argument. Remember, careful analysis of your opponent's argument is the starting point for success—in any argumentative essay and on the AP Examination in English Language and Composition.

AP
English Language & Composition

Chapter 4

Chapter 4

Preparing for and Taking the AP Exam

The Advanced Placement English tests put out by the College Board are rigorous and challenging. A good score on an AP test is useful in college placement; most universities give placement and/or credit for college courses if students perform well on the tests. In some universities, you can earn as many as 12 hours of English credit with an assigned grade of "A" if you score a "5" on both the AP English Language and Composition Examination as well as the AP Literature and Composition Examination. You are urged to write your university and inquire about specific details and policies.

Format of the AP English Language and Composition Examination

The AP English Language and Literature Examination is divided into two parts, multiple-choice and essay. The multiple-choice section has approximately 60 questions divided among five or six reading passages (the exact number varies from year to year). There will be from five to fifteen questions per reading passage. You are allowed 60 minutes for the objective portion. Most years all students finish the multiple-choice section. Occasionally, the College Board will produce a test that almost no students finish within the allotted time; however, this is rare. Generally speaking, the test is geared so that most good students can finish within the time limits. The second part of the AP English Language and Composition Examination consists of three essay questions, and you will be allowed 120 minutes to complete this portion of the examination. You will be given interim time limits for each individual essay question.

Critical Reading of Passages

There are usually five or six reading passages in the multiple-choice portion of the AP English Language and Composition Exam. The poetry or prose passage will be taken from a variety of time periods and sources; therefore, contemporary pieces will be mixed with excerpts from earlier centuries. Also, the point of view (i.e., the literary device that describes the narrator of a fiction or other work) will vary. At least one selection will be written from the first person point of view, others being from third person point of view—objective, omniscient, or limited omniscient. Some passages will be casual, and some will be formal.

As you read each passage in the multiple-choice portion of the practice tests in this book, ask yourself the questions below. Not all of these questions will apply to every selection, of course. You should practice with these questions regularly in your reading. You would do well, for example, to have a copy of these questions as you read novels recommended by the College Board for the AP test.

Genre

1. Is the passage persuasive? Although essays range widely in subject matter, they will vary in tone and style from serious to satirical, from humorous to tragic, and from light inquiry to active—even aggressive—assertion. Typically, these nonfiction essays seek to fulfill the four purposes of academic nonfiction prose: describe, explain, inform, or persuade. More often than not, authors will use all their skills and all their minor purposes (i.e., describing, explaining, or informing) to support their ultimate purpose: to persuade you to some point of view.

   Aristotle is still not a bad guide to the means of persuasion. In his *Rhetoric*, he outlines three fundamental types of persuasion stemming from these three sources: *Ethos, Pathos,* and *Logos.* An author, for example, may rely upon his or her own reputation, character, spirit, or—in modern terms—"image" (or "ethos") to move the audience or readers to accept a thesis. Again, the author may rely primarily on the audience's feelings and appeal to them (i.e., "pathos") to sway readers to the thesis, or the author may attempt to reason with the audience, and use powerful logic (i.e., "logos") to get the reader to see the truth of the thesis in question. Of course, the best authors will employ all three to persuade the audience, but one element of persuasive argument will dominate the author's discussion. When you read the test essays, see if you can't tell what is most important to the writer as the basis for his or her persuasive effort.

2. Is the passage an excerpt from a work of fiction, a novel or short story? These passages tend to be a description of character or location, seldom a philosophical commentary. Sometimes a character's dialogue with another may be given to you to analyze.

Organization

1. If the passage is descriptive, is it organized spatially or by order of importance? What is the overall effect?

2. If the passage is narrative, is the chronological order of events interrupted by flashback, foreshadowing, episodic events? Is the plot framed or circular?

3. If the passage is expository, are any of the following devices or methods used: definition, cause and effect, deductive order, inductive order, comparison/contrast, division and classification, examples, extended example, analogy?

4. If persuasion is used, what methods does the author use to bolster the argument? Does the author deal with opposing evidence? Where is the thesis—at the beginning or at the end? Does the author fall into any logical fallacies?

Setting

1. Where does the story take place?

2. Is the description real or imaginative or a combination of both?

3. What are the details of weather, countryside, building(s), language, actions, dress?

4. What imagery is used (appeals to the senses, or from history, literature or mythology)?

5. How does the setting create mood?

6. How does the setting affect the character(s)?

7. Is personification used to describe buildings or society, weather, or nature? Are there any other figures of speech used in the description of setting?

8. How does the setting create or tie in with conflict or symbolism?

9. Is setting important to the theme?

10. How does the setting create mood or conflict?

Plot and Conflict

1. What is the conflict (self versus others, self versus self, human versus nature, humans versus God or fate)?

2. What is the situation at the beginning? How does this relate to the conflict? theme? character development?

3. Upon what past action, if any, is the plot dependant?

4. Is the plot **episodic** (one scene following another with the only linking device that of a change in time or place) or **paradigmatic** (i.e., a sort of logical puzzle, such as a mystery, or an inescapable design whose outcome is inevitable, such as those associated with myth)?

5. What is the first complicating incident? What is the climax? Are problems resolved in the falling action?

6. Is there a resolution or denouement?

7. Are there any subplots? If so, how do they tie in with the main plot?

8. How is suspense maintained, particularly once the climax has passed? Does the author continue the revelation of clues? Is the identity of a key character withheld? Does the dialogue or action become more intense?

9. Is the main thrust of the literature comic or serious?

10. If the literature is primarily serious, do any scenes offer comic relief?

11. If the literature is primarily humorous, are there any serious scenes? What is the point of the author's satire?

12. Is there flashback or foreshadowing?

13. Are there any parallel plots?

Character

1. Who is the main character?

2. What is the character like (list three adjectives to describe the character)?

3. Do you like the character? Does the character seem to be ethical or unethical?

4. Who or what are the **protagonist** (character trying to accomplish something) and **antagonist** (character or force opposing the protagonist)?

5. What are the motives of the character(s)?

6. Does the character have a good self-knowledge? If not, is he or she unreliable, self-deluding, or complacent?

7. Is the character in the process of changing, or is the character static?

8. Does the character reflect on a past dilemma? Is that dilemma resolved? How?

9. Do minor characters play an important role? Do they **complement** (appear similar), or do they serve as a **foil** (opposite personality or traits)? Do any provide comic relief or commentary?

10. How does the central character view the setting, conflict, other characters?

11. What are the **ethics** (moral position or beliefs) of the central character? Is the character being pressured to compromise?

12. Is the story one of changes: initiation, symbolic birth or rebirth, fertility, or death?

13. Are any of the characters symbols or stereotypes?

For example, do some characters seem to stand for an idea or other abstraction, such as Love, Innocence, Truth, or Greed? Do some characters appear to be undifferentiated "models," of their role, such as the spinster, the mad scientist, the country doctor, the wayward youth, the ingenue?

Point of View

"Point of View" in this sense is the literary device the author uses to narrate the fiction. This device is not to be confused with the author's attitude, or point of view (discussed below), toward the subject or theme. Typically, the point of view from which the fiction is told is that of some narrator or other, who then also may become an important character in the narration of the story, helping the plot to move forward, or in fact, functioning as a central figure in the development and outcome of the story. You should examine carefully the nature and character of the fictional narrator of the story, who is not the same person as the historically and biologically real author of the fiction, e.g., David Copperfield is the fictional narrator of the novel of that name, and Charles Dickens is the author. They are not the same!

1. What sort of narrator does the author employ: omniscient, limited omniscient, first person, third person?

2. If there is a first person narrator, does he or she provide an accurate self-analysis?

3. In an omniscient or limited omniscient point of view, in whose mind does the author dwell the most?

4. If the point of view is objective, what effect is created? Is it cold, unemotional, logical, or scientific?

5. With which character does the point of view encourage you to sympathize or relate?

Theme

1. What is the passage's theme?

2. Is the theme **explicit** (stated) or **implicit** (implied)?

3. Is there a universal truth, or simply a comment upon a particular situation or location?

4. How are the other elements of fiction—setting, character, plot, irony, symbolism, tone, mood—related to the theme?

Tone and Mood

1. What is the mood created by the **selection** (effect upon the reader)?

2. What is the **tone** (author's attitude toward the subject)?

This question may ask you to consider and decide how the *author* seems to feel toward the subject of a fiction. Be careful to make distinctions between how the *narrator's* attitude toward the subject and how the *author's* attitude may differ or coincide. Is the *narrator*, for example, sympathetic towards a character that the *author* treats as a symbol of Greed? Imagine the way that suggests how the author feels about the narrator! Be sure to review all the elements (character, plot, diction, imagery, and setting) and how they interact before you decide on how the *author* feels toward the theme or subject of the fiction.

Words Useful in Describing Tone

admiring	dramatic	mournful
angry	ecstatic	neutral
apprehensive	effusive	nostalgic
bantering	elegiac	objective
benevolent	facetious	patronizing
biting	factual	pedantic
bitter	fanciful	petty
candid	flippant	pretentious
clinical	hopeful	respectful
colloquial	impartial	restrained
compassionate	incisive	sardonic
complimentary	indignant	satiric
concerned	inflammatory	scholarly
condescending	informative	scornful
confident	insipid	sentimental
contemptuous	insolent	solemn
contentious	ironic	somber
cynical	irreverent	sympathetic
detached	learned	taunting
determined	lugubrious	threatening
didactic	mock-heroic	turgid
diffident	mocking	urbane
disdainful	mock-serious	urgent
disgusted	moralistic	worshipful

Language and Style

The narrator's language and style are those of a character in a fiction you read. For example, if a narrator always uses choices such as "interface," "input," "feedback," "output," and "bytes" to describe the interaction with other characters, the effect may be to suggest that the narrator is rather "mechanical" and insensitive to human relationships since this diction comes from the language used to describe the artificial intelligence of computers and not flesh and blood.

Similarly, the author may use a consistent set of metaphors and symbols during the descriptive passages in a pattern to generate feeling in the reader. For example, metaphors of the sea ("voyaging across the seas of conflict," "arriving on the shores of decision") may be used to suggest some universal relationship of the theme to life or say, overwhelming odds.

Be careful, when relevant, to distinguish among the narrator's, other characters' and the author's tone. They may be varied.

1. What is the word choice? Is it colloquial, idiomatic, scientific, Latinate, formal, concrete, abstract, scholarly, or allusive?

2. To what senses does the author appeal?

3. What literary devices of sense does the author use (personification, metaphor, simile, allusion)?

4. What literary devices of sound does the author use (alliteration, assonance, consonance, repetition)?

5. Does the language have rhythm?

6. Are the sentences long or short? Where does the author use short sentences or fragments for special emphasis? Where are there long sentences or run-ons for special effect?

7. Are the sentences simple, compound, complex, or compound-complex? Where does the author use sentence variety to emphasize an idea?

   See the glossary for detailed examples of the terms cited in questions 8 and 9.

8. What specialized sentence structure does the author use? The following are emphatic types of sentence structures: balanced, freight-train, inverted, parallel, periodic. Also, the author can employ anaphora, antithesis, asyndeton, chiasmus, negative-positive restatement, polysyndeton, tricolon.

9. Do any sentences begin or end with a significant word or phrase? Do any sentences have the main idea "hidden" in the middle, in an interrupter, so as to create surprise or suspense?

10. Does the author use colors to enhance moods, characterize someone in the story, or to develop the setting description (e.g., are there many references to red or shades of red to heighten the mood of danger or of bloody action)? Consider Poe's classic "Masque of The Red Death."

11. What are the best-worded phrases or best-chosen words?

An Explanation of Style

Style is the habitual, repeated patterns that differentiate one writer from another (or, one singer or painter from the other, for that matter). Salvadore Dali painted in the surrealist style, with his most famous painting being that of the clocks and watches dripping and oozing off the sides of tables. Claude Monet painted in the impressionist style, with bits of color that blend together to form a coherent whole only if the viewer stands back from the picture; Monet was interested in the use of color to form an impression, rather than the absolute realistic portrayal of a scene. In literature, Hemingway is well known for his terse, sparse, objective style indicative of the isolation of people in the twentieth century; Hawthorne for his flamboyant, exaggerated word pictures that create a mood of horror or fearful introspection.

So, the first part of style is the repeated patterns. The other component of style is deviations from the customary patterns. Hemingway, for example, deviates from his usual short sentences and few descriptive words when he describes nature. In those passages, you will find long, flowing sentences and lyrical descriptions of nature, such as a river, to show the peace that man obtains when he escapes the jarring, destructive effects of civilization and is comforted by the healing beauty of nature.

Expectation (the pattern) and **surprise** (the deviation from the pattern) are the component parts of style. A discussion of style is also a discussion of the **well-chosen word or phrase**. A discussion of the well-chosen word or phrase depends on your ability to be discriminating about language and to recognize good writing.

The AP English Language and Composition Examination tests your knowledge of style in two ways: through multiple-choice questions that closely analyze reading passages, and through an essay question (or two) that asks you to demonstrate your ability to analyze style in a passage.

The MOST IMPORTANT thing about discussing style is to show its relationship to the theme or main idea of a nonfiction or fiction passage, or to some element of a fiction. A discussion which does no more than list fancy terms and give examples of each will not get a good grade on the AP test. The graders wish to see how you interpret the link between theme and language, or between characterization and language, or between description of setting and language. The graders wish to see that you can recognize and discuss (in essay format) or identify (in multiple-choice questions) how style highlights the central idea, characterization, setting, symbolism, and how, in a well-written piece of literature, all elements interrelate. In an essay analyzing style, it is not enough to discuss theme, or to discuss style—you must relate each to the other in a fluid, organized manner.

For example, if the **theme** is about fertility and success, does the author have the story setting in the spring and use **images** of blossoming, growth, or fruition? Are the **characters** getting married? Is the **tone** optimistic, hopeful, humorous? Does the **word choice** have connotations of positive, safe, or loving feelings? Is the **plot** one that climaxes in marriage, good fortune, or renewal? Your job is to understand, and in your essay response, to show **how** the author blends these elements to produce an experience of the **theme** viscerally, emotionally, **and** intellectually.

To discuss style in detail, you should be familiar with the terms listed under "Language and Style."

Colloquial word choice is not standard grammatical usage and employs idiomatic or slang expressions; this word usage develops a casual tone. Scientific, Latinate (words with Latin roots or origins), or scholarly language would be formal and employ standard rules of usage. Concrete words form vivid images in the reader's mind, while abstract language is more appropriate for a discussion of philosophy. Allusive style uses many references to history, literature, or other shared cultural knowledge to provoke or enlighten the reader. Appeals to the senses make the writing more concrete and vivid. Since prose does not have a natural rhythm, an obvious metrical pattern in a passage signals an important idea.

Authors also employ other poetical devices in their writing to emphasize important ideas. Any time the author cares enough to use similes or metaphors, or any of the other common poetic devices, it is because the author wants to draw attention to that particular characteristic and perhaps suggest a more complex relationship to the implied or stated theme. Therefore, you should pay attention, too.

See the "Glossary of Literary and Rhetorical Terms" on page 81 for a list and explanation of common literary tropes.

If the author suddenly or obviously varies sentence structure or length of a sentence, this signals important ideas. Short sentences (seven words or fewer) or fragments usually signal important ideas. You should look out for them. If, in the midst of a variety of sentence structures and lengths, the author inserts two or three short, simple sentences, this is something you should notice as being significant. Most certainly, a detail or action will appear in these sentences that the author considers crucial.

Faulkner is an author who uses the interrupter to foreshadow details that later become significant. Humorous writing employs the interrupter for contrast or to give the author's real point.

An author can pick from a variety of specialized sentence patterns or structures to create emphatic sentences. Most sentences in the English language are **loose** sentences; that is, the main idea appears at the beginning of the sentence (subject first, then predicate, then additional modifiers) and much of the predicate part of the sentence can be cut off without serious damage to the main idea. Any time an author wishes to call attention to an important idea, he or she can use a different sentence structure. These different structures are called **emphatic** because they emphasize the ideas contained therein.

In analyzing an author's style, then, seek out patterns, habitual wording or phraseology, and then attempt to spot variations from the norm. Suppose an author employs many rather lengthy, balanced sentences with the frequent use of parallelism and anaphora, and the word choice is formal and Latinate. You can then make intelligent observations about the formal, balanced style. If this same author then includes one or two short sentences, a metaphor, and an inverted word order, you can point out these constructions and discuss the importance of the ideas contained in and signaled by these constructions. In addition, you should be on the lookout for the well-chosen word, for the compelling turn of a phrase. Don't forget: all discussion of style should show the relation to the tone or theme of the selection.

Logic and the AP Exam

Occasionally, an AP Literature and Language multiple-choice question will ask about logic or logical fallacies.

Formal logical arguments can be inductive or deductive. Inductive argumentation lists cases, examples, facts, and then ends with a logical conclusion (particular to general). Deductive argumentation begins with a statement of opinion and proceeds to prove it with cases, examples, facts (general to the particular). The basic form of the deductive argument is a three-part format known as a **syllogism**. The syllogism, you may recall, has a major premise, a minor premise, and a conclusion. If your audience accepts your premises, then your conclusion is usually accepted.

For example:

Premise One: Most Americans love violence.

Premise Two: Football is violent.

Conclusion: Therefore, most Americans love football.

Sound reasoning can be undermined by logical fallacies. The following is a list of common logical fallacies you are expected to know for the AP English Language and Composition Examination.

Attacking the Person

(Argumentum ad hominem) attacks the personality of the individual instead of dealing with the arguments and issues.

Example: John Smith can't tell us anything about the faithfulness of dogs because he has no faith at all in anything.

Begging the Question

Assumes something to be true that needs proof. The arguer uses as proof the very argument that needs proving.

Example: The reason George is so smart is because he is very intelligent.

(In other words, A is true because A is true. Just a minute, here! I've got to show why George is intelligent—the condition that stands in need of proof can't be the source of the proof! "Intelligent" is just a synonym for "smart," not evidence for it.)

Creating a False Dilemma

Uses a premise that presents a choice which does not include all the possibilities.

Example: People hate politics because politicians often lie.

(The premise that "people hate politics" is not necessarily true; somebody is sitting in those chairs in Washington.)

Since rabbits are responsible for destroying most suburban lawns, homeowners should shoot rabbits on sight.

Describing with Emotionally Charged Terminology

Uses vocabulary carrying strong connotative meaning, either positive or negative.

Example: Senator Jones is a commie, pinko, bleeding heart liberal who hates his mother, babies, apple pie, *and* the American way.

(This form of the tactic—name-calling—is perhaps most common. Poor Senator Jones is getting a terrible review; apparently, he hates all the things we love, and is the things we hate, so our emotions are likely to be *transferred* from them to him by association, whether they are true about him or not.)

Either/Or Fallacy

Does not allow for any shades of meaning, compromise, or intermediate cases.

Example: Either we abolish cars, or the environment is doomed.

(Probably other factors contribute to this possibility besides cars.)

Generalizing from Insufficient Evidence

(Hasty generalization) uses too few of the examples needed to reach a valid conclusion.

Example: Only motivated athletes become champions.

(Maybe not. What are the other factors in becoming champions? Good health? Superior genes?)

Circular Reasoning

(Post hoc ergo propter hoc) attempts to prove something by showing that because a second event followed a first event, the second event is a result of the first event.

Example: He went to the store to buy shoes, and therefore, the house burned down.

(I doubt it. Probably somebody lit a match. Buying shoes doesn't make a house burn down.)

Answering Multiple-Choice Questions

Reading attentively takes practice. Use the following tips while you practice.

1. Scan the reading passage to determine the type of prose, and perhaps the overall tone.

2. Ask yourself, "What is the SUBJECT of this passage?"

3. Read the stems of each question. (Don't read the answer choices, yet!)

4. Underline or circle the key word, usually the main verb which directs the skill being tested and the noun which provides a subject for the question's analysis.

5. Allot 30 minutes to read and 30 minutes to answer questions.

6. Don't spend too much time on one question—they all count the same. Make educated guesses to improve your odds of getting the question right.

7. If you are in doubt about which answer is correct, eliminate as many wrong choices as you can and concentrate on the two or three probable choices.

8. Your first guess is usually the right choice, so don't "second-guess" yourself.

Study these choices carefully before you take a multiple-choice practice test. Soon, you will begin to see the patterns in the questions and be able to predict the answer before you see the answer choices.

Rewriting

This question type does not always occur on each year's tests, but it is important for you to be familiar with it just in case. This rewriting section is part of Section I of the test when it occurs, and is usually the very first 12 to 15 questions of the test. The following pages will more than adequately prepare you for this rather unique set of questions.

A rewriting question consists of a grammatically correct, well-written sentence and directions to make a specific structural change while maintaining the meaning of the sentence. The directed change will refer to one or a few words that will spawn other changes in another part of the sentence in a cause-and-effect relationship. Your answer choices will include various versions of the "effect" part of the new sentence.

Sentence: Arriving before he was expected, he turned the tables on the party givers.

Directions: Change <u>Arriving</u> to <u>He arrived</u>.

    (A)   and so he turned
    (B)   and turned
    (C)   and then turning
    (D)   and had turned
    (E)   and there he had turned

The rewritten sentence should be: "He arrived before he was expected and turned the tables on the party givers," making (B) "and turned" correct. Answers (A), (C), and (E) have extraneous words and therefore are not concise enough to qualify as good writing. Answer (D) changes the sequence of the events because "had turned" grammatically must occur before "He arrived."

Your primary goals in answering these questions revolve around the formulation of the new sentence. The new sentence should carry, as much as possible, the same meaning as the test's original sentence. It should be the most fluid and natural in its construction and phrasing. The new sentence must adhere to the requirements of standard written English. And finally, your new sentence should be well-written—concise, logical, and idiomatic.

The questions of this section fall into definable types, which mostly draw on sentence structure as a basis for change. In the example given on the previous page, the original sentence has a dependent clause, "Arriving ... expected," and an independent clause, "he turned ... givers." The directions instruct a conversion of the dependent clause into an independent clause. A quick glance at the answer options—the repeated "and ... (verb)"—tells us that the orginal independent clause will remain independent, even if it shares the subject with the other predicate. "And" is a conjunction, joining equal things.

Like most of these question types, the exam has a mirror image of such questions. Holding to the principle that to truly know something you must be able to do it backwards and forwards, another type of question requires you to rewrite two independent clauses as a dependent clause and an independent clause. The conjunction will be eliminated, and you must recognize which answer will properly convert one of the clauses into a dependent clause.

In certain instances, dependent-independent conversions as a type will help you find the answer. When an independent clause is converted to a dependent clause, another clause from the sentence must become an independent clause. Look at the following example.

Sentence: Such topics as the role of fraud and its detection were not addressed in the debate on welfare reform, which idealistically concentrated on incorporating recipients back into the work force.

Directions: Begin with <u>Rather than address</u>.

(A)   detection, the debate that
(B)   detection in the debate, it
(C)   detection, the debate
(D)   detection, instead the debate
(E)   detection, concentrating

The original clause "Such ... reform" is independent, but changing the beginning to <u>Rather than address</u> will make it dependent. The original clause "which idealistically ... work force" was dependent, and must now become the independent clause in the new sentence. Answers (A), (D), and (E) require the "work force" clause to be dependent with their use of "that," "instead," and the "ing" ending of "concentrate." The correct answer is (C) "detection, the debate", because, unlike answer (A), it is open to allowing the "work force" clause to be independent. Answer (B) also meets this qualification, but it awkwardly makes the subject of the sentence "it" with the antecedent in the prepositional phrase of the dependent clause. Of answers (B) and (C), answer (C) is better written.

The fourth and final type that depends on the status of clauses is the conversion of a description to an independent clause.

Sentence: His seemingly offhand remark struck many in the group with pangs of self-doubt.

Directions: Change <u>struck</u> to <u>but it struck</u>.

(A)   remark seemed

(B)   remark, and it seemed
(C)   remark which seemed
(D)   remark, seemingly
(E)   remark, despite seeming

The change to <u>but it struck</u> requires that the original subject of the sentence now become an entire independent clause. To accomplish this, "the fascinating woman" becomes "the woman is fascinating." In our question, "seemingly offhand remark" becomes "remark seemed offhand." Only answer (A) places "remark" as a subject in any clause.

The next two types of questions are derived most directly from good reading and writing. The sentence "Mutual hostility was the result of his uncaring actions" uses a linking verb, which is a nonactive sentence structure that equates the subject and its object, making it reversible to "The result of his uncaring actions was mutual hostility." The noun "result" has another usage as a verb, and some test questions will require you to change the first sentence above to "His uncaring actions resulted in mutual hostility." Because so many words have both noun and verb forms, these sentences vary greatly and can be very complex. However, they tend to hinge on a linking verb that will be replaced by a former noun.

The last potentially complex question form requires a transition from a passive sentence, in which the subject recieves the action, to an active sentence, in which the subject performs the action. An active sentence is often considered to be more aggressive than a passive sentence, so their alternating uses are important to authors stylistically.

Sentence: The little boy was overcome with fear only a few minutes into his fruitless search for his mother.

Directions: Begin with <u>Fear</u>.

(A)   searched for
(B)   fruitlessly searching
(C)   was overcoming
(D)   overcame
(E)   had overcome

In the original sentence, the boy did not have any action, but was acted upon. He was overcome. The word "fear" had the action, but the sentence was written passively. To begin the new sentence with <u>Fear</u> will require you to make the sentence active for the sake of avoiding an awkward construction. Immediately you can eliminate answers (A) "searched for" and (B) "fruitlessly searching" because "search" need not change in our new sentence. The correct answer is (D) "overcame". It is active, concise, and in the right tense. Answers (C) and (E) should be eliminated because the first is too wordy in light of option (D) and the second is the distant past tense and therefore differs in meaning from the original sentence. Be aware that some test questions may instead require a conversion from active to passive.

Some simpler types of questions test very basic rules. The Should-If question contrasts these constructions, requiring you to know their appropriate connections to "would" and "will." "Should you forget, I would be furious," becomes "If you forget, I will be furious." The quote to non-quote question requires a conversion from "He said, 'My dog has fleas'" to "He said that his dog has fleas," which hits on the punctuation of quotes and the points of view of pronouns. The Most-Few question is another case of points of view, or optimism vs. pessimism. It requires a conversion from "Most know little" to "Few know much." The answer options on Most-Few questions strenuously test your ability to maintain the meaning of the original sentence.

Identifying these basic question types will help you to orientate yourself when you come to each new question. You will know from the type of question what form the rewritten sentence should take, and thereby eliminate two or three of the incorrect answer choices. From this point, you will have the time to test the remaining answers in your mind. Discerning the correct answer will depend on your ability to recognize good writing. You will find the sentences that are clear, concise, logical, and meaningfully equivalent, a skill you will be able to rehearse in the practice examinations.

Questions about the Speaker

For these questions, you are asked to make observations about the speaker or author. You are asked to judge how the speaker views himself or herself, what effect certain objects or events have on the speaker, what is important to the speaker, and how the speaker obtains/has obtained information about the world.

Questions usually appear in the following format:

In lines _____ the speaker depicts himself/herself as _____.

In lines _____ the speaker depicts himself/herself as all of the following EXCEPT _____.

For the speaker, _____ (subject) has the effect of _____.

For the speaker, _____ (subject) is _____ (evaluation of meaning or importance).

Which of the following is probably the main source of the speaker's knowledge of _____?

In "_____" (quotation containing action or description) the author is _____ (conclusion about that action or description).

Questions about Attitude

For these questions, you are asked to determine or make judgments about the attitude of the speaker or author toward the subject being described or discussed. You may be asked to do the following:

- identify a shift
- analyze the effect of the author's attitude
- decide what the author believes
- determine the atmosphere/mood
- determine the tone/atmosphere

Questions usually appear in the following format:

The shift in point of view has the effect of _____.

The author's attitude toward _____ can be described as _____.

The speaker assumes that the audience's attitude will _____.

The author believes/apparently believes _____.

The point of view indicated in _____ is that of _____.

The atmosphere is one of _____.

In "_____" which of the following most suggests a humorous attitude on the part of the author?

The passage is an appeal for _____.

Questions about Word Choice and Selection of Details

For these questions, you are asked to analyze the fine points of language and specific word choice. You are asked to determine the meaning of a word/phrase/sentence, identify elements of fiction, analyze important details or quotations, determine meaning of a word or phrase from the context, identify parts of a sentence, such as subject of a verb or antecedent of a pronoun, or analyze the style of a passage.

Sometimes, you will be asked to tell the meaning of a word in the context of the paragraph. You may not have seen the word before, but from your understanding of the writer's intent, you should be able to figure out what it is s/he's after.

For example, read the following paragraph:

Paris is a beautiful city, perhaps the most beautiful on Earth. Long, broad avenues are lined with seventeenth and eighteenth century apartments, office buildings, and cafés. Flowers give the city a rich and varied look. The bridges and the river lend an air of lightness and grace to the whole urban landscape.

In this paragraph, "rich" most nearly means

(A) wealthy.
(B) polluted.
(C) colorful.
(D) dull.

If you chose (C) "colorful" you would be right. Although "rich" literally means "wealthy," (that is its **denotation**, its literal meaning) here the writer means more than the word's literal meaning, and seems to be highlighting the variety and color that the flowers add to the avenues, that is, richness in a figurative sense.

The writer is using a non-literal meaning, or **connotation** that we associate with the word "rich" to show what s/he means. When we think of something "rich," we usually also think of abundance and variety and color, not just plain numbers.

Questions about word choice and selection of details usually appear in the following format:

Which of the following best describes what _____ symbolizes?

The _____ sentence/paragraph/section is unified by metaphors of _____.

The style of the passage can best be characterized as _____.

"_____" signals a shift from _____ to _____.

The _____ paragraph employs which of the following?

The statement "_____" is best described as _____.

The use of "_____" instead of "_____" accomplishes which of the following?

In line _____ the author emphasizes "_____" because _____.

The use of "_____" suggests most strongly _____.

The major purpose of the word/phrase/statement "_____" is to make clear that _____.

By "_____", the speaker means/most probably means _____.

The mention of _____ is appropriate to the development of the argument because _____.

In the sentence/paragraph/section, the speaker seeks to draw attention to _____ by stressing _____.

In the context of the passage as a whole/the _____ paragraph, the word/phrase/sentence "_____" is best interpreted to mean _____.

In relation to _____, which of the following best describes the function of the word/phrase/sentence/paragraph?

The antecedent for "_____" (pronoun) is _____.

Which of the following best describes the word/phrase/sentence _____?

Which of the following is an example of "_____" mentioned in line _____?

All of the following qualities are present in the scene EXCEPT _____.

The subject of the verb "_____" is which of the following?

Questions about Logic and Sentence Construction

For these questions, you are asked to identify how words work together in groups. You are asked to analyze syntax, identify sentence construction, analyze relationships of sentences or phrases, identify logical fallacies, or determine patterns of exposition.

These questions usually appear in the following format:

The syntax of sentence/sentences _____ serves to _____.

All of the following antitheses may be found EXCEPT _____.

The relationship between _____ and _____ is explained primarily by the use of _____.

What is the function of the two (or three) words/phrases/clauses?

The author's discussion of _____ depends on which of the following?

The type of argument employed in _____ by _____ is _____.

The speaker describes _____ in an order described as _____.

The pattern of exposition exemplified in the passage is best described as _____.

Despite its length, the _____ sentence remains coherent chiefly because of its use of _____.

Questions about Inferences

For these questions, you are asked to draw conclusions based on context clues. You are asked to determine relationships or identify references. They usually appear as follows:

It can be inferred that _____ is/are _____.

It can be inferred from the description of _____ that _____ is _____.

It can be inferred that _____ refers to _____.

Questions about General Conclusions

For these questions, you are asked to predict outcomes and make inferences. You are asked to determine what the author would think about a certain subject, what the author wants us to do, or what the author would/would not advise us. Most of the questions have the following format:

The author believes that we should _____.

According to the author, _____ should _____ because _____.

Which of the following would the author be LEAST/MOST likely to encourage?

If one were to take the author's advice, one should _____.

After you read the question stems and underline or circle the significant nouns and verbs, read the passage carefully. Pay attention to the point of view (that literary device the author uses to invoke or employ a narrator), setting, characters, conflicts, etc. Underline well-chosen words or phrases, short sentences, significant details, irony, and descriptions that seem significant.

After you read the passage, go back to the questions. Read each question entirely and carefully, including the stem and the answer choices. Go to the passage to look for the answer.

You should "criss-cross" the literary landscape, reading the passage, or portions thereof, in searching for the correct answer to each question. Each reading or partial reading should produce for you a closer familiarity with detail and a better understanding. For example, after a first reading perhaps only plot, setting, and character relationships are clear to you. But after a second review, you may notice how the characters are developed, or what imagery the author has them employ consistently in their dialogue. After a third review, you may notice that the metaphors that the author uses are all drawn from nature, or from the military, or from industry. Why? What effect does it have on you to use them the way the author does? At each reading, something deeper comes to light. But you must look for it.

Answering Essay Questions

The essay section of the test is composed of three topics, for which you are given 1 hour and 45 minutes. Be conscious of the time: you should not take too long on one essay to the exclusion of the others, since this would force you to rush through the remaining topics.

The College Board will provide you with 12 sheets of lined paper for the essay section of the test. As with the time, divide this paper at your discretion. If your responses are brief or if your handwriting is very small, you may find that you do not fill these sheets. Throughout this chapter and during the practice tests, you should use lined 8½ x 11 in. paper with standard lines. To simulate test conditions, use only 12 pages for the essay section.

Essays on the English Language and Composition test are scored on a scale of 0 to 9 or 0 to 15 points, with the point count and standards being tailored to suit each essay question. More than one trained reader scores each paper. The previous scores are covered, so no one reader influences another. There can be up to as many as six readers. As you can see, the College Board takes pains to see that your good writing will be given careful consideration.

Strategies for Answering Essay Questions

Read the question carefully before you read the passage. Know what you are looking for before you read. As you read the question, underline the directions. Make sure you understand what you are looking for as you read. In the passage underline significant details, words with connotative meaning, reasons, logical structure, notable sentence beginnings or endings, unusual sentence structures, sentences that are noticeably short or long, vivid imagery, figures of speech, and words or phrases that may indicate the author's attitude.

The English Language and Composition essay answers are graded as "first draft" papers. You are not given enough time to do prewriting, rough draft, and final copy—prewriting and one draft are really all you have time for in a 30 minute time period. Therefore, prewriting—organizing in advance of writing, in which you decide on content and order of ideas—is critical to your success. Give yourself about 5-

10 minutes to read the essay question, write a working thesis sentence, and list 3-5 points in order of importance or logical development. The remaining time (15-20 minutes) should be spent writing, with 5 minutes to correct/revise and proofread.

You are pressed for time; therefore, you should never use long introductory or long concluding remarks. Long introductions and conclusions take valuable time away from your main argument. After all, you only have about 30 minutes to read the question, read the passage, plan your strategy, write your answer, and proofread/correct. Another argument against lengthy introduction and conclusions is that your central development will be shorter, and therefore most probably weaker in development. One or two sentences of introduction and conclusion are adequate.

Ideas should lead one to the other in a smooth, logical progression. Organization of ideas in prewriting and composing will depend on the type of essay, but organize before you write. The five-paragraph essay structure is adequate, as long as you truncate introduction and conclusion. Refer to the following chart for the format of this structure.

Paragraph Number	Type of Paragraph	What to Include
1	Thesis Paragraph	Introductory remarks, thesis
2	First Body Paragraph	Topic sentence containing first observation, then details and quotations bolstered and explained by elaboration
3	Second Body Paragraph	Development of second observation to prove thesis, same order as above
4	Third Body Paragraph	Development of third observation to prove thesis, same order as above
5	Conclusion	Summary of position in different words, observation about the topic

This format is apparent to the graders, and it may not get you a top score unless your structure is well disguised and you display a flair for ideas and control language to convey what you mean clearly and effectively.

Your essay should contain a restatement of the question close to the beginning, in the first three sentences. Your thesis sentence should be similar to or a close variation of this formula:

author's name + author's attitude/purpose + subject + devices.

Example: Hemingway's belief in the nobility of the struggle against nature in the short novel *The Old Man and The Sea* is achieved partly through the stark contrast between the single old man and the setting of the vast, unfathomable sea, where though alone, the old man nobly sets out on his quest to conquer the big fish.

Example: In "The Gettysburg Address" by Abraham Lincoln,
       [Title of work]   [author]

the ninth President uses the setting of the
        [device]

battlefield and the special jargon of democratic
        [device]

ideals ironically to promote a new idea of rebirth
        [thesis]

of government in the United States.

The elements of the formula can be re-arranged in any order comfortable for you, but leaving out one of the elements is not advised unless you are an advanced writer. Beginning with this thesis makes you focus on the essential problem and gives your essay a specific direction.

In your essay answer it is useful, but not necessary, to name the specific term ("metaphor," "inverted sentence," "parallelism"). Superior essay writers will, of course, know and use the basic devices of style in a smooth, mature manner. However, your essay answer must include specific examples in the form of short, direct quotations and your answer should explain.

Scoring Guidelines

Content counts much more than grammar, word choice, or spelling; however, seldom does an essay with even as few as three or four errors receive the top score. It is wise, therefore, to proofread and correct your writing before going on to the next topic. Recasting (rewording) some of your sentences is acceptable, but make sure your paper is not too messy and is legible. You must address the given task carefully; that is, you should not deviate from the topic or dwell too long on one point. You should attend to subtle nuances of language in your essay. The mediocre paper fails to identify and analyze subtleties of meaning. Quality papers recognize and respond to the emotional shadings of the topic. The scores are usually given as follows:

Scores of 9–8 These are superior essays. They have clear statement of position, thoughtful support, convincing examples, and stylistic maturity (sentence structure, diction, organization). Although there may be a few grammar or spelling errors, the author demonstrates a superior control of language.

Scores of 7–6 These are excellent essays. However, they have a thesis which lacks the specific and convincing proof of the superior essays. The author's writing style is less mature, and thus has occasional lapses of diction, tone, syntax, or organization. Although there may be errors of grammar and spelling, the author demonstrates an adequate control of language.

Scores of 5–4 These are mediocre, but adequate, essays. The thesis may not be quite clear, the argument not as well developed, and the organization not especially effective. There are some grammar and spelling errors. These essays will receive a score no higher than 4 if they show *any one* of the following:
   (a) oversimplify or overgeneralize the issues;
   (b) write only in general terms, ignoring fine distinctions;
   (c) fail to discuss the issue completely satisfactorily;
   (d) mismanage the evidence;
   (e) contain insufficient details;
   (f) fail to establish the importance to the writer;
   (g) treat only one aspect of a two-sided issue;
   (h) cite examples but fail to consider the consequences;
   (i) cite stylistic techniques but fail to explain the impact;
   (j) characterize the passage without analyzing the language.

Scores of 3–2 These are weak essays. They lack clear organization and adequate support, the writing style is simplistic, and there are frequent grammar and spelling errors.

Score of 1 These are poor essays. Although they may mention the question, they lack clarity, have little or no evidence, and contain consistent grammar and spelling errors. They are badly written, unacceptably brief, or off topic.

Essay Question Types

One type of question, often used in the past but one which has not appeared since the 1989 test, directs you to write a descriptive essay which will create a feeling or atmosphere or reveal your attitude toward the subject. For this essay you will be given specific instructions to describe a person or a place, or perhaps two incidents in a person's life, or perhaps two contrasting locations. Your essay must reveal your attitude toward that place or person, or must reveal the character of the person you describe, or must create an atmosphere for a location. Sometimes an essay of definition is used instead of the descriptive essay. You will be asked to define a term, or to elaborate on the distinctions between two words which are related in meaning but differ in connotative meaning (Man—Gentleman).

The essay should be a sterling example of "show, not tell." You should, for example, show your person barely hiding a smirk at someone who has just tripped, or give a quotation in which the character says something rather rude to another person, rather than just say that the character you are describing has a strange sense of humor that sometimes hurts others. Do not oversimplify your approach. The graders are looking for mature, not simplistic, writing. Descriptive writing should be spatially organized and contain no extraneous details which might detract from a unified overall impression. Essays of definition should be organized from least important to most important, or vice versa.

Another type of essay asks you to analyze the language used in a passage and to explain how the language achieves a certain effect. Do not oversimplify the author's position or attitude. Even if the essay is satirical in tone, take care not to exaggerate the tone and classify it as "bitter" or "biting" unless you are certain this is the author's intention. However, be aware that this extreme Juvenalian satire will never or quite rarely appear on the test. Remember, the makers of the test are looking for subtle gradations of analysis in your answer, and subtlety is difficult to achieve if you are analyzing a simplistic piece of literature, one with an obvious, one-sided, or "cut-and-dried" approach or tone.

Frequently, this question takes the form of two passages on the same topic but written in different styles and with different attitudes. Again, if you are asked to discuss the differences between two passages, do not oversimplify or overexaggerate the differences.

This question expects you to analyze the style of a passage. The question directs you to read the passage carefully. Then, you are instructed to write an essay that (1) analyzes the effect of the passage on the reader; or (2) defines the author's attitude toward his or her topic (usually, the AP test question will name the topic of the passage for you); or, (3) describes the rhetorical purpose of the passage; or (4) identifies the author's purpose or views and how he or she achieves that purpose or conveys those views.

A List of Typical Instructions

Below, you will find a list of the most common directions used for writing essays. Become familiar with these directions, since they have been used frequently on past exams.

- analyze the language and rhetorical devices; consider such elements as narrative structure, selection of detail, manipulation of language, and tone;

- analyze how the author uses juxtaposition of ideas, choice of details, and other aspects of style;

- analyze stylistic, narrative, and persuasive devices;

- analyze the figures of speech and syntax;

- consider word choice, manipulation of sentences, imagery, and use of allusions;

- consider the rhetorical devices such as arguments, assumptions, attitudes, and diction.

Don't let the wording intimidate you: "rhetoric" and "rhetorical devices" refer to word choice and such things as poetic devices; "diction" refers to word choice; "syntax" refers to sentence structure and placement of words within the sentence; "juxtaposition" refers to unlike ideas or details that appear side-by-side or in close proximity to each other.

Basically, this type of question asks you to examine (with attention to nuance) these stylistic devices:

WORD CHOICE
IMAGERY
FIGURES OF SPEECH
SELECTION OF DETAIL
SENTENCE STRUCTURE
TONE

"Word choice" or "diction" refers to individual words. "Imagery" refers to vivid pictures that appeal to the senses. "Figures of speech" refers to common devices, such as simile, allusion, alliteration, etc. "Selection of detail" is not exactly the same as word choice; rather, it is a significant piece of information about the character or location. "Sentence structure" or "syntax" is the arrangement of words in the sentence; sentence structure also includes types of sentences. "Tone" is the author's attitude toward the character, or location, and the author will use all of the devices above to generate that tone or attitude.

The question may ask you to consider these items in your answer:

NARRATIVE STRUCTURE
PERSUASIVE DEVICES
RHETORICAL DEVICES

"Narrative structure" refers to plot structure, or how the details are arranged. "Persuasive devices" refers to valid arguments the author uses, or perhaps logical fallacies. "Rhetorical devices" refers to imagery, word choice, figurative language, sentence structure.

The third type of question will give a quotation from a famous person. The quotation will present an assertion or an opinion which is arguable. You are asked to present a logical argument for or against the position or to defend, challenge, or qualify the position. The directions will tell you to include evidence from your observation, experience, or reading to defend your position.

Begin your essay with a statement of the author's opinion, or one to two sentences of introduction and then the author's opinion. Then, as your thesis, state that you agree or disagree with the author's position; or state that you agree or disagree with some portion of the author's position (and give some indication of which portion you would qualify).

AP
English Language & Composition

Chapter 5

Glossary of Literary and Rhetorical Terms

Abstract Language

Language describing ideas and qualities rather than observable or specific things, people, or places. The observable or "physical" is usually described in concrete language.

Ad hominem

Latin for "against the man." When a writer personally attacks his or her opponents instead of their arguments.

Allegory

A story, fictional or nonfictional, in which characters, things, and events represent qualities or concepts. The interaction of these characters, things, and events is meant to reveal an abstraction or a truth. These characters, etc. may be symbolic of the ideas referred to.

Alliteration

The repetition of initial identical consonant sounds. Or, vowel sounds in successive words or syllables that repeat.

Allusion

An indirect reference to something (usually a literary text) with which the reader is supposed to be familiar. Allusion is often used with humorous intent, to establish a connection between writer and reader, or to make a subtle point.

Ambiguity

An event or situation that may be interpreted in more than one way. Also, the manner of expression of such an event or situation may be ambiguous. Artful language may be ambiguous. Unintentional ambiguity is usually vagueness.

Analogy

An analogy is a comparison to a directly parallel case. When a writer uses an analogy, he or she argues that a claim reasonable for one case is reasonable for the analogous case.

Anaphora

Repetition of a word, phrase, or clause at the beginning of two or more sentences in a row. This is a deliberate form of repetition and helps make the writer's point more coherent.

Anecdote

A brief recounting of a relevant episode. Anecdotes are often inserted into fictional or nonfictional texts as a way of developing a point or injecting humor.

Annotation

Explanatory notes added to a text to explain, cite sources, or give bibliographical data.

Antithesis

A balancing of two opposite or contrasting words, phrases, or clauses.

Assonance

Repetition of a vowel sound within two or more words in close proximity.

Asyndeton

Commas used (with no conjunction) to separate a series of words. The parts are emphasized equally when the conjunction is omitted; in addition, the use of commas with no intervening conjunction speeds up the flow of the sentence. Asyndeton takes the form of X, Y, Z as opposed to X, Y, and Z.

Authority

Arguments that draw on recognized experts or persons with highly relevant experience are said to rest on authoritative backing or authority. Readers are expected to accept claims if they are in agreement with an authority's view.

Backing

Support or evidence for a claim in an argument.

Balance

Construction in which both halves of the sentence are about the same length and importance.

Begging the Question

Often called circular reasoning, begging the question occurs when the believability of the evidence depends on the believability of the claim.

Causal Relationship

In causal relationships, a writer asserts that one thing results from another. To show how one thing produces or brings about another is often relevant in establishing a logical argument.

Chiasmus

Arrangement of repeated thoughts in the pattern of X Y Y X. Chiasmus is often short and summarizes a main idea.

Common Knowledge

Shared beliefs or assumptions are often called common knowledge. A writer may argue that if something is widely believed, then readers should accept it.

Concrete Language

Language that describes specific, observable things, people or places, rather than ideas or qualities.

Connotation

Rather than the dictionary definition, the associations suggested by a word. Implied meaning rather than literal meaning or denotation.

Consonance

Repetition of a consonant sound within two or more words in close proximity.

Conventional

Following certain conventions, or traditional techniques of writing. An overreliance on conventions may result in a lack of originality. The five-paragraph theme is considered conventional.

Cumulative

Sentence which begins with the main idea and then expands on that idea with a series of details or other particulars.

Deconstruction

A critical approach that debunks single definitions of meaning based on the instability of language. The deconstructionist re-examines literary conventions in light of a belief that deconstruction "is not a dismantling of the structure of a text, but a demonstration that it has already dismantled itself."

Diction

Word choice, particularly as an element of style. Different types and arrangements of words have significant effects on meaning. An essay written in academic diction would be much less colorful, but perhaps more precise than street slang.

Didactic

A term used to describe fiction or nonfiction that teaches a specific lesson or moral or provides a model of correct behavior or thinking.

Dramatic Irony

When the reader is aware of an inconsistency between a fictional or nonfictional character's perception of a situation and the truth of that situation.

Either-Or Reasoning

When the writer reduces an argument or issue to two polar opposites and ignores any alternatives.

Elliptical

Sentence structure which leaves out something in the second half. Usually, there is a subject-verb-object combination in the first half of the sentence, and the second half of the sentence will repeat the structure but omit the verb and use a comma to indicate the ellipted material.

Emotional Appeal

When a writer appeals to an audience's emotions (often through pathos) to excite and involve them in the argument.

Epigraph

A quotation or aphorism at the beginning of a literary work suggestive of theme.

Equivocation

When a writer uses the same term in two different senses in an argument.

Ethical Appeal

When a writer tries to persuade the audience to respect and believe him or her based on a presentation of image of self through the text. Reputation is sometimes a factor in ethical appeals, but in all cases the aim is to gain the audience's confidence.

Example

An individual instance taken to be representative of a general pattern. Arguing by example is considered reliable if examples are demonstrably true or factual as well as relevant.

Explication

The act of interpreting or discovering the meaning of a text. Explication usually involves close reading and special attention to figurative language.

Exposition

Background information provided by a writer to enhance a reader's understanding of the context of a fictional or nonfictional story.

False Analogy

When two cases are not sufficiently parallel to lead readers to accept a claim of connection between them.

Fiction

A product of a writer's imagination, usually made up of characters, plot, setting, point of view, and theme. Fiction is often described as lies told with the consent of the reader.

Figurative Language

A word or words that are inaccurate literally, but describe by calling to mind sensations or responses that the thing described evokes. Figurative language may be in the form of metaphors or similes, both non-literal comparison. Shakespeare's "All the world's a stage" is an example of non-literal, figurative language (metaphor, specifically).

Freight-train

Sentence consisting of three or more very short independent clauses joined by conjunctions.

Generalization

When a writer bases a claim upon an isolated example or asserts that a claim is certain rather than probable. Sweeping generalizations occur when a writer asserts that a claim applies to all instances instead of some.

Hyperbole

Conscious exaggeration used to heighten effect. Not intended literally, hyperbole is often humorous.

Image

A word or words, either figurative or literal, used to describe a sensory experience or an object perceived by the senses. An image is always a concrete representation.

Imagery

The use of images, especially in a pattern of related images, often figurative, to create a strong, unified sensory impression.

Inversion

Variation of the normal word order (subject first, then verb, then complement) which puts a modifier or the verb as first in the sentence. The element that appears first is emphasized more than the subject.

Irony

When a reader is aware of a reality that differs from a character's perception of reality (dramatic irony). The literal meaning of a writer's words may be verbal irony.

Logic

An implied comparison resulting when one thing is directly called another. To be logically acceptable, support must be appropriate to the claim, believable and consistent.

Metaphor

A comparison of two things, often unrelated. A figurative verbal equation results where both "parts" illuminate one another. I.A. Richards called the literal term in a metaphor the "tenor" and the figurative term the "vehicle."

Mood

An atmosphere created by a writer's word choice (diction) and the details selected. Syntax is also a determiner of mood because sentence strength, length, and complexity affect pacing.

Moral

The lesson drawn from a fictional or nonfictional story. A heavily didactic story.

Negative-positive

Sentence that begins by stating what is not true, then ending by stating what is true.

Non-sequitur

Latin for "it does not follow." When one statement isn't logically connected to another.

Objectivity

A writer's attempt to remove himself or herself from any subjective, personal involvement in a story. Hard news journalism is frequently prized for its objectivity, although even fictional stories can be told without a writer rendering personal judgment.

Onomatopoeia

The use of a word whose pronunciation suggests its meaning. "Buzz," "hiss," "slam," and "pop" are frequently used examples.

Oversimplification

When a writer obscures or denies the complexity of the issues in an argument.

Oxymoron

A rhetorical antithesis. Juxtaposing two contradictory terms, like "wise fool" or "eloquent silence."

Paradox

A seemingly contradictory statement which is actually true. This rhetorical device is often used for emphasis or simply to attract attention.

Parallelism

Sentence construction which places in close proximity two or more equal grammatical constructions. Parallel structure may be as simple as listing two or three modifiers in a row to describe the same noun or verb; it may take the form of two or more of the same type of phrases (prepositional, participial, gerund, appositive) that modify the same noun or verb; it may also take the form of two or more subordinate clauses that modify the same noun or verb. Or, parallel structure may be a complex blend of single-word, phrase, and clause parallelism all in the same sentence.

Parody

An exaggerated imitation of a serious work for humorous purposes. The writer of a parody uses the quirks of style of the imitated piece in extreme or ridiculous ways.

Pathos

Qualities of a fictional or nonfictional work that evoke sorrow or pity. Over-emotionalism can be the result of an excess of pathos.

Periodic

Sentence that places the main idea or central complete thought at the end of the sentence, after all introductory elements.

Persona

A writer often adopts a fictional voice (or mask) to tell a story. Persona or voice is usually determined by a combination of subject matter and audience.

Personification

Figurative language in which inanimate objects, animals, ideas, or abstractions are endowed with human traits or human form.

Point of View

The perspective from which a fictional or nonfictional story is told. First-person, third-person, or omniscient points of views are commonly used.

Polysyndeton

Sentence which uses *and* or another conjunction (with no commas) to separate the items in a series. Polysyndeton appears in the form of X and Y and Z, stressing equally each member of the series. It makes the sentence slower and the items more emphatic than in the asyndeton.

Post hoc, ergo propter hoc

Latin for "after this, therefore because of this." When a writer implies that because one thing follows another, the first caused the second. But sequence is not cause.

Red Herring

When a writer raises an irrelevant issue to draw attention away from the real issue.

Refutation

When a writer musters relevant opposing arguments.

Repetition
Word or phrase used two or more times in close proximity.

Rhetoric
The art of effective communication, especially persuasive discourse. Rhetoric focuses on the interrelationship of invention, arrangement, and style in order to create felicitous and appropriate discourse.

Satire
A work that reveals a critical attitude toward some element of human behavior by portraying it in an extreme way. Satire doesn't simply abuse (as in invective) or get personal (as in sarcasm). Satire targets groups or large concepts rather than individuals.

Sarcasm
A type of verbal irony.

Simile
A figurative comparison of two things, often dissimilar, using the connecting words "like" or "as."

Straw Man
When a writer argues against a claim that nobody actually holds or is universally considered weak. Setting up a straw man diverts attention from the real issues.

Style
The choices in diction, tone, and syntax that a writer makes. In combination they create a work's manner of expression. Style is thought to be conscious and unconscious and may be altered to suit specific occasions. Style is often habitual and evolves over time.

Symbol
A thing, event, or person that represents or stands for some idea or event. Symbols also simultaneously retain their own literal meanings.

Syntactic Fluency
Ability to create a variety of sentence structures, appropriately complex and/or simple and varied in length.

Syntactic Permutation
Sentence structures that are extraordinarily complex and involved. Often difficult for a reader to follow.

Theme
The central idea of a work of fiction or nonfiction, revealed and developed in the course of a story or explored through argument.

Tone

A writer's attitude toward his or her subject matter revealed through diction, figurative language, and organization on the sentence and global levels.

Tricolon

Sentence consisting of three parts of equal importance and length, usually three independent clauses.

Unity

A work of fiction or nonfiction is said to be unified if all the parts are related to one central idea or organizing principle. Thus, unity is dependent upon coherence.

Verbal Irony

When the reader is aware of a discrepancy between the real meaning of a situation and the literal meaning of the writer's words.

AP

English Language & Composition

Practice Test I

AP Examination in English Language & Composition

Test I

Section 1

TIME: 60 Minutes
60 Questions

(Answer sheets appear in the back of this book.)

DIRECTIONS: Rephrase each of the following sentences according to the directions given, and choose the response that best corresponds to the necessary changes to the original sentence. Keep the meaning of the new sentence as close to the original as possible, maintaining natural phrasing, the requirements of standard written English, and logical and concise construction.

---

1.   A fund set up by a local philanthropist who died some 30 years ago maintains the park's playground facilities and carefully tended playing fields.
      Change <u>maintains</u> to <u>are maintained</u>.

   (A)   for funding   (D)   by funds

   (B)   funding for   (E)   which is funded

   (C)   by a fund

2.   Virgil wrote verse copiously in many genres, but derives most of his fame as the author of *The Aeneid.*
      Omit <u>but</u>.

   (A)   to derive   (D)   who derived

   (B)   having derived   (E)   while deriving

   (C)   although he derives

3. In that state, the law requires that a knowing accomplice be treated no differ-
    ently from the assailant who pulls the trigger.
    Begin with <u>In that state the law treats</u>.

    (A) requiring   (D) accomplice no differently

    (B) requirement   (E) knowing assailant

    (C) accomplice who

4. Subsequent references to the man are absent; this has always been considered
    puzzling and conspicuous.
    Begin with <u>The absence</u>.

    (A) the man has always   (D) the man considered

    (B) references have always   (E) the man puzzled

    (C) puzzling has always

5. Hashing remains unpopular despite its time efficiency; it employs the prin-
    ciple of putting something where you'll remember you put it, instead of where
    it "belongs," and is arguably the most disorganized way to organize computer
    data.
    Begin with <u>Hashing, which employs</u>.

    (A) and argues   (D) because arguments

    (B) because it is   (E) although arguments

    (C) because it argues

6. The visual sphere of a white-tailed deer is limited by the range of motion of its
    head, which cannot turn up, leaving it blind to hunters in tree-stands.
    Begin with <u>A white-tailed deer is blind</u>.

    (A) limiting range

    (B) limited ranging

    (C) although its visual sphere

    (D) because its visual sphere

    (E) despite its visual sphere

Questions 7–16 are based on the following passage. Read the passage carefully before choosing your answers.

THE Number of Souls in *Ireland* being usually reckoned one Million and a half; of these I calculate there may be about Two hundred Thousand Couple whose Wives are Breeders; from which Number I subtract thirty thousand Couples, who are able to maintain their own Children; although I apprehend
5   there cannot be so many, under *the present Distresses of the Kingdom*, but this being granted, there will remain an Hundred and Seventy Thousand Breeders. I again subtract Fifty Thousand, for those Women who miscarry, or whose Children die by Accident, or Disease, within the Year. There only remain an Hundred and Twenty Thousand Children of poor Parents, annually born:
10   The Question therefore is, How this Number shall be reared, and provided for? Which, as I have already said, under the present Situation of Affairs, is utterly impossible, by all the Methods hitherto proposed: For we can *neither employ them in Handicraft* or *Agriculture*, we neither build Houses, (I mean in the Country) nor cultivate Land: They can very seldom pick up a Livelyhood
15   by *Stealing* until they arrive at six Years old; except where they are of towardly Parts; although, I confess, they learn the Rudiments much earlier; during which Time, they can, however, be properly looked upon only as Probationers; as I have been informed by a principal Gentleman in the County of *Cavan*, who protested to me, that he never knew above one or two Instances under the
20   Age of six, even in a Part of the Kingdom *so renowned for the quickest Proficiency in that Art.*

I AM assured by our Merchants, that a Boy or a Girl before twelve Years old, is no saleable Commodity; and even when they come to this Age, they will not yield above Three Pounds, or Three Pounds and half a Crown at most, on
25   the Exchange; which cannot turn to Account either to the Parents or the Kingdom; the Charge of Nutriment and Rags, having been at least four Times that Value.

I SHALL now therefore humbly propose my own Thoughts, which I hope will not be liable to the least Objection.

30   I HAVE been assured by a very knowing *American* of my Acquaintance in
      London; that a young healthy Child, well nursed, is, at a Year old, a most
      delicious, nourishing, and wholesome Food; whether *Stewed, Roasted, Baked,*
      or *Boiled*; and, I make no doubt, that it will equally serve in a *Fricasie*, or
      Ragoust.

35   I DO therefore humbly offer it to *publick Consideration,* that of the Hundred
      and Twenty Thousand Children, already computed, Twenty thousand may be
      reserved for Breed; whereof only one Fourth Part to be Males; which is more
      than we allow to *Sheep, black Cattle,* or *Swine*; and my Reason is, that these
      Children are seldom the Fruits of Marriage, *a Circumstance not much regarded by*
40   *our Savages*; therefore, *one Male* will be sufficient to serve *four Females.* That the
      remaining Hundred thousand, may, at a Year old, be offered in *Sale to the*
      Persons of Quality and *Fortune,* through the Kingdom; always advising the Mother
      to let them suck plentifully in the last Month, so as to render them plump, and
      fat for a good Table. A Child will make two Dishes at an Entertainment for
45   Friends; and when the Family dines alone, the fore or hind Quarter will make a
      reasonable Dish; and seasoned with a little Pepper or Salt, will be very good
      Boiled on the fourth Day, especially in *Winter.*

      I HAVE reckoned upon a Medium, that a Child just born will weigh
      Twelve Pounds; and in a solar Year, if tolerably nursed, encreaseth to twenty
50   eight Pounds.

      I GRANT this Food will be somewhat dear, and therefore *very proper for*
      Landlords; who, as they have already devoured most of the Parents, seem to
      have the best Title to the Children.

      INFANTS Flesh will be in Season throughout the Year; but more plentiful
55   in *March,* and a little before and after: For we are told by a grave Author, an
      eminent *French* Physician, that *Fish being a prolifick Dyet,* there are more
      Children born in *Roman Catholick Countries* about Nine Months after Lent
      than at any other Season: Therefore reckoning a Year after *Lent,* the Markets
      will be more glutted than usual; because the Number of *Popish Infants,* is, at
60   least three to one in this Kingdom; and therefore it will have one other Collat-
      eral Advantage, by lessening the Number of *Papists* among us.

      I HAVE already computed the Charge of nursing a Beggar's Child (in
      which List I reckon all *Cottagers, Labourers,* and Four fifths of the *Farmers*) to
      be about two Shillings *per Annum,* Rags included; and I believe, no Gentleman
65   would repine to give Ten Shillings for the *Carcase of a good fat Child*; which, as

I have said, will make four Dishes of excellent nutritive Meat, when he hath only some particular Friend, or his own Family, to dine with him. Thus the Squire will learn to be a good Landlord, and grow popular among his Tenants; the Mother will have Eight Shillings net Profit, and be fit for Work until she
70   produceth another Child.

7.   The phrase "I GRANT this Food will be somewhat dear, and therefore *very proper for Landlords*; who, as they have already devoured most of the Parents, seem to have the best Title to the Children" (lines 51–53) does all of the following EXCEPT

(A)   understates the cost of the "Food."

(B)   reverses the metaphor which dominates the passage.

(C)   sarcastically indicts the children's parents.

(D)   reveals the speaker's attitudes toward landlords and tenants in a seeming aside.

(E)   suggests persons who may play a role in giving the children better outcomes to their lives.

8.   Throughout the passage, poor children and their parents are metaphorically described using images of

(A)   urban decay.   (D)   scientific analysis.

(B)   animal husbandry.   (E)   religious rituals.

(C)   business transactions.

9.   The "very knowing *American*" (line 30) is most probably

(A)   a scientist studying in London.

(B)   an Irish expatriate living in America.

(C)   a Native American.

(D)   an American physician.

(E)   an American chef serving in a London household.

10.   What effect does the construction of the argument in lines 1–47 have upon the reader?

(A)   Its seemingly rational progression makes the startling proposal even more jarring.

(B)   The emphasis upon "Souls" (line 1) initiates an atmosphere of religious reverence.

(C)   The references to animal breeding in the first and fifth paragraphs detract from the passage's main point.

(D)   The use of census-like statistics before the proposal confuses the issue and makes the reader more suseptible to persuasion.

(E)   The emphatic first person opening of each paragraph except the first underscores the speaker's reasonableness.

11.   The antecedent of "many" (line 5) is

(A)   "Children" (line 4).   (D)   "Wives" (line 3).

(B)   "Number" (line 3).   (E)   "Couples" (line 4).

(C)   "Souls" (line 1).

12.   Which of the following can be inferred to be the intent of the passage?

I.   To rebuke landlords for their callousness

II.   To force a reexamination of other proposals

III.   To offer a measured solution to a crisis

IV.   To build the speaker's reputation as a civic-minded person

(A)   I only   (D)   I, II, and III only

(B)   I and II only   (E)   I, II, III, and IV

(C)   III and IV only

13.   Stylistically, the passage may best be described as

(A)   philosophical.   (D)   hortative.

(B)   lyrical.   (E)   satirical.

(C)   scientific.

14.   The speaker's use of "Breeders" (line 3) as a predicate adjective for "Wives"

(A)   depersonalizes the women.

(B)   praises the women's fertility.

(C)   describes the women's occupation.

(D)   distinguishes the women from the men.

(E)   criticizes the women for having children.

15. The phrase "I SHALL now therefore humbly propose my own Thoughts, which I hope will not be liable to the least Objection" (lines 28–29) is an example of

(A) hyperbole.

(B) oxymoron.

(C) understatement.

(D) metaphor.

(E) digression.

16. In the context of the passage as a whole, the references to women as "Breeders" and children as a "saleable Commodity" (line 23) serve as

(A) digressions from the course of the argument.

(B) statements of fact.

(C) summaries of the argument.

(D) omens of the proposal to come.

(E) objections to the proposal itself.

Questions 17–22 are based on the following passage. Read the passage carefully before choosing your answers.

UNDER the strange nebulous envelopment, wherein our Professor has now shrouded himself, no doubt but his spiritual nature is nevertheless progressive, and growing: for how can the "Son of Time," in any case, stand still? We behold him, through those dim years, in a state of crisis, of transition: his mad

5 Pilgrimings, and general solution into aimless Discontinuity, what is all this but a mad Fermentation; wherefrom, the fiercer it is, the clearer product will one day evolve itself.

Such transitions are ever full of pain: thus the Eagle when he moults is sickly; and, to attain his new beak, must harshly dash-off the old one upon rocks. What

10 Stoicism soever our Wanderer, in his individual acts and motions, may affect, it is clear that there is a hot fever of anarchy and misery raging within; coruscations of which flash out: as, indeed, how could there be other? Have we not seen him disappointed, bemocked of Destiny, through long years? All that the young heart might desire and pray for has been denied; nay, as in the last worst instance, offered

15 and then snatched away. Ever an "excellent Passivity"; but of useful, reasonable Activity, essential to the former as Food to Hunger, nothing granted: till at length, in this wild Pilgrimage, he must forcibly seize for himself an Activity, though useless, unreasonable. Alas, his cup of bitterness, which had been filling drop by drop, ever since that first "ruddy morning" in the Hinterschlag Gymnasium, was at

20 the very lip; and then with that poison-drop, of the Towngood-and-Blumine business, it runs over, and even hisses over in a deluge of foam.

He himself says once, with more justice than originality: "Man is, properly speaking, based upon Hope, he has no other possession but Hope; this world of his is emphatically the Place of Hope." What, then, was our Professor's
25 possession? We see him, for the present, quite shut-out from Hope; looking not into the golden orient, but vaguely all round into a dim copper firmament, pregnant with earthquake and tornado.

17. All of the following name the main character of the passage EXCEPT

   (A) our Wanderer.   (D) our Professor.

   (B) the Eagle.   (E) the "Son of Time" (line 3).

   (C) he/him.

18. Which phrase best summarizes the speaker's intent in examining this stage of the main character's life?

   (A) "Such transitions are ever full of pain" (line 8)

   (B) "Have we not seen him disappointed, bemocked of Destiny, through long years" (lines 12–13)

   (C) "there is a hot fever of anarchy and misery raging within" (line 11)

   (D) "what is all this but a mad Fermentation; wherefrom, the fiercer it is, the clearer product will one day evolve itself" (lines 5–7)

   (E) "We see him, for the present, quite shut-out from Hope" (line 25)

19. The accumulative painfulness of this time for the main character is illustrated primarily by the use of

   (A) metaphors.   (D) oxymoron.

   (B) digressions.   (E) onomatopoeia.

   (C) hyperbole.

20. What is the function of the clause introduced by "nay" in line 14?

   (A) It negates the clause that precedes it.

   (B) It contradicts the clause that precedes it.

   (C) It intensifies the clause that precedes it.

(D)   It restates the clause that precedes it.

(E)   It downplays the clause that precedes it.

21.   It can be inferred that the speaker considers the statement "Man is, properly speaking, based upon Hope, he has no other possession but Hope; this world of his is emphatically the Place of Hope" (lines 22–24) to be

(A)   a simile.   (D)   an epiphany.

(B)   a quotation.   (E)   a platitude.

(C)   a metaphor.

22.   "Coruscations" (line 11) can best be defined as

(A)   boils.   (D)   blocks.

(B)   threads.   (E)   scars.

(C)   sparks.

Questions 23–34 are based on the following passage. Read the passage carefully before choosing your answers.

It was late at night, and a fine rain was swirling softly down, causing the pavements to glisten with hue of steel and blue and yellow in the rays of the innumerable lights. A youth was trudging slowly, without enthusiasm, with his hands buried deep in his trousers' pockets, toward the downtown places where
5   beds can be hired for coppers. He was clothed in an aged and tattered suit, and his derby was a marvel of dust-covered crown and torn rim. He was going forth to eat as the wanderer may eat, and sleep as the homeless sleep. By the time he had reached City Hall Park he was so completely plastered with yells of "bum" and "hobo," and with various unholy epithets that small boys had
10   applied to him at intervals, that he was in a state of the most profound dejection. The sifting rain saturated the old velvet collar of his overcoat, and as the wet cloth pressed against his neck, he felt that there no longer could be pleasure in life. He looked about him searching for an outcast of highest degree that the two might share miseries. But the lights threw a quivering glare over
15   rows and circles of deserted benches that glistened damply, showing patches of wet sod behind them. It seemed that their usual freights had fled on this night to better things. There were only squads of well-dressed Brooklyn people who swarmed toward the Bridge.

20   The young man loitered about for a time and then went shuffling off down Park Row. In the sudden descent in style of the dress of the crowd he felt relief, and as if he were at last in his own country. He began to see tatters that matched his tatters. In Chatham Square there were aimless men strewn in front of saloons and lodging houses, standing sadly, patiently, reminding one vaguely of the attitudes of chickens in a storm. He aligned himself with these men, and turned
25 slowly to occupy himself with the flowing life of the great street.

    Through the mists of the cold and storming night, the cable cars went in silent procession, great affairs shining with red and brass, moving with formidable power, calm and irresistible, dangerful and gloomy, breaking silence only by the loud fierce cry of the gong. Two rivers of people swarmed along the
30 sidewalks, spattered with black mud, which made each shoe leave a scar-like impression. Overhead elevated trains with a shrill grinding of the wheels stopped at the station, which upon its leg-like pillars seemed to resemble some monstrous kind of crab squatting over the street. The quick fat puffings of the engines could be heard. Down an alley there were sombre curtains of purple
35 and black, on which street lamps dully glittered like embroidered flowers.

    A saloon stood with a voracious air on a corner. A sign leaning against the front of the doorpost announced: "Free hot soup tonight." The swing doors snapping to and fro like ravenous lips, made gratified smacks as the saloon gorged itself with plump men, eating with astounding and endless appetite,
40 smiling in some indescribable manner as the men came from all directions like sacrifices to a heathenish superstition.

    Caught by the delectable sign, the young man allowed himself to be swallowed. A bartender placed a schooner of dark and portentous beer on the bar. Its monumental form upreared until the froth a-top was above the crown of
45 the young man's brown derby.

    "Soup over there, gents," said the bartender, affably. A little yellow man in rags and the youth grasped their schooners and went with speed toward a lunch counter, where a man with oily but imposing whiskers ladled genially from a kettle until he had furnished his two mendicants with a soup that was
50 steaming hot and in which there were little floating suggestions of chicken. The young man, sipping his broth, felt the cordiality expressed by the warmth of the mixture, and he beamed at the man with oily but imposing whiskers, who was presiding like a priest behind an altar. "Have some more, gents?" he inquired of the two sorry figures before him. The little yellow man accepted
55 with a swift gesture, but the youth shook his head and went out, following a

man whose wondrous seediness promised that he would have a knowledge of cheap lodging houses.

23. The description of the main character's hat as "a marvel of dust-covered crown and torn rim" (line 6) utilizes which of the following?

    (A)   Metaphor   (D)   Synecdoche

    (B)   Oxymoron   (E)   Ellipsis

    (C)   Alliteration

24. The first paragraph establishes an atmosphere of

    (A)   uncertain experimentation.   (D)   social harmony.

    (B)   open hostility.   (E)   quiet dignity.

    (C)   profound squalor.

25. It can be inferred that the sentence "He was going forth to eat as the wanderer may eat, and sleep as the homeless sleep" (lines 6–7) is

    (A)   a straightforward portrayal of the main character's actions.

    (B)   an idealistic imagining of the main character's actions.

    (C)   a fantastic description of the minor character's actions.

    (D)   an understated retelling of the main character's actions.

    (E)   a realistic portrait of the minor character's actions.

26. The taunts that children shout at the main character parallel which of the following?

    (A)   The hat with a "dust-covered crown and torn rim" (line 6)

    (B)   The streets that "glisten with hue of steel and blue and yellow" (line 2)

    (C)   The "downtown places where beds can be hired for coppers" (lines 4–5)

    (D)   The "sifting rain" (line 11) that soaks through the main character's coat

    (E)   The "deserted benches that glistened damply" (line 15)

27. The use of "unholy epithets" in line 9 rather than "curse words"

    (A)   calls attention to the irreverence of the jeering boys.

    (B)   downplays the effects of the taunts upon the main character.

    (C)   highlights the religious atmosphere that dominates the passage.

(D) emphasizes the speaker's sarcastic tone.

(E) emphasizes the clash between the main character's idealization of himself as homeless and the gritty reality.

28. What are the "usual freights" (line 16) and their bearers?

(A) "Well-dressed Brooklyn people" (line 17) and the bridge

(B) Trees and "patches of wet sod" (lines 15–16)

(C) Homeless persons and benches

(D) Shadows and streetlamps

(E) Passengers and ferrys

29. The speaker's use of "descent" in line 20 is particularly appropriate because it

(A) parallels a lowering of the weather conditions.

(B) prepares the reader for the unexpected appearance of derelicts.

(C) echoes the main character's movement downward from uptown/comfort to downtown/poverty.

(D) reveals the speaker's condemnation of derelicts.

(E) mirrors the deterioration of the surrounding cityscape.

30. The description of the "cable cars" (line 26) in paragraph three is remarkable for its

I.   use of personification.

II. parallel structure.

III. inverted syntax.

IV. use of onomatopoeia.

(A) I only

(B) II only

(C) III and IV only

(D) I and IV only

(E) I, II, III, and IV

31. The descriptions of the people in the background of paragraphs one, two, and three

(A) are united by water imagery.

(B) are highly individualized.

(C) are progressively opposite in focus.

(D)   are lacking in concrete imagery.

(E)   are developed through animalism.

32.   The fourth paragraph is unified by

(A)   a paradox.   (D)   hyperbole.

(B)   colloquial diction.   (E)   a conceit.

(C)   terse sentence structure.

33.   Which of the following best describes the speaker's attitude toward drinking establishments?

(A)   They prey upon potential customers' weaknesses.

(B)   They are legitimate business operations.

(C)   They should be located only in lower-class neighborhoods.

(D)   They show responsibility by serving food with alcohol.

(E)   They should restrict business hours to evenings.

34.   All of the following antitheses are found in the passage EXCEPT

(A)   uptown and downtown.

(B)   working-class comfort and lower-class poverty.

(C)   confidence and resignation.

(D)   sacredness and blasphemy.

(E)   darkness and light.

Questions 35–44 are based on the following passage. Read the passage carefully before choosing your answers.

The house of fiction has in short not one window, but a million—a number of possible windows not to be reckoned, rather; every one of which has been pierced, or is still pierceable, in its vast front, by the need of the individual vision and by the pressure of the individual will. These apertures, of dissimilar
5   shape and size, hang so, all together, over the human scene that we might have expected of them a greater sameness of report than we find. They are but windows at the best, mere holes in a dead wall, disconnected, perched aloft; they are not hinged doors opening straight upon life. But they have this mark of their own that at each of them stands a figure with a pair of eyes, or at least
10   with a field-glass, which forms, again and again, for observation, a unique

instrument, insuring to the person making use of it an impression distinct from every other. He and his neighbours are watching the same show, but one seeing more where the other sees less, one seeing black where the other sees white, one seeing big where the other sees small, one seeing coarse where the

15 other sees fine. And so on, and so on; there is fortunately no saying on what, for the particular pair of eyes, the window may <u>not</u> open; "fortunately" by reason, precisely, of this incalculability of range. The spreading field, the human scene, is the "choice of subject"; the pierced aperture, either broad or balconied or slitlike and low-browed, is the "literary form"; but they are, singly

20 or together, as nothing without the posted presence of the watcher—without, in other words, the consciousness of the artist. Tell me what the artist is, and I will tell you of what he has *been* conscious. Thereby I shall express to you at once his boundless freedom and his "moral" reference.

35. The "house of fiction" (line 1) is

(A) a symbol that represents the meeting place of authors.

(B) a conceit that unifies the passage.

(C) a metaphor that portrays the genre.

(D) a simile that describes fiction as a structure.

(E) a concrete image that names a literary dynasty.

36. What is the function of the quotation marks surrounding "choice of subject" (line 18) and "literary form" (line 19)?

(A) They indicate that the speaker is using another author's ideas.

(B) They reveal the speaker's disgust with literary terminology.

(C) They are the speaker's appeal to authority.

(D) They emphasize the major points of the speaker's argument.

(E) They set the generic critical labels apart from the more expansive field of human experience and structure the author has to choose from.

37. The phrase "they are not hinged doors opening straight upon life" (line 8) implies that

(A) fiction does not directly mirror life.

(B) works of fiction are windows not doors.

(C) fiction presents twisted versions of life.

    (D)   fictional works are not easily created.

    (E)   each example of fiction has its own individuality.

38.   What is the antecedent of "they" in line 6?

    (A)   Windows (line 7)

    (B)   Apertures (line 4)

    (C)   Holes (line 7)

    (D)   Need (line 3) and pressure (line 4)

    (E)   Eyes (line 9)

39.   The shifts in point of view from "we" (lines 5–6) to "he" (line 12) to "I" (line 22) has which of the following effects?

    (A)   The shifts indicate the speaker's distinguishing himself/herself from the critics who inhabit the house of fiction.

    (B)   The shifts symbolize the speaker's alienation from the genre.

    (C)   The movement from group to individual parallels the movement from the group "house of fiction" (line 1) to individual "figure with a pair of eyes" (line 9).

    (D)   The movements separate the readers from the authors.

    (E)   The shifts reveal the inconsistencies in the speaker's argument.

40.   Which of these phrases contains an example of antithesis?

    (A)   "These apertures, of dissimilar shape and size, hang so, all together, over the human scene" (lines 4–5)

    (B)   "They are but windows at the best, mere holes in a dead wall, disconnected, perched aloft; they are not hinged doors" (lines 6–8)

    (C)   "…at each of them stands a figure with a pair of eyes, or at least with a field-glass" (lines 9–10)

    (D)   "…one seeing more where the other sees less, one seeing black where the other sees white, one seeing big where the other sees small, one seeing coarse where the other sees fine" (lines 12–15)

    (E)   "…they are, singly or together, as nothing without the posted presence of the watcher" (lines 19–20)

41.   Which of the following does the speaker consider to be the most important element in the "house of fiction"?

(A) The "figure with a pair of eyes" (line 9)

(B) The "apertures" (line 4)

(C) The "hinged doors" (line 8)

(D) The "human scene" (line 5)

(E) The "spreading field" (line 17)

42. It may be inferred from the connotations of windows being "pierced" in the "house of fiction" (lines 1–4) that

(A) individual works of fiction are merely tiny components of the larger genre.

(B) the windows are merely decorative and have no practical function in the house.

(C) the literary canon resists new works of fiction.

(D) the writer needs special tools and techniques to create fiction.

(E) the writer bends fiction to his/her vision rather than bending his vision to predetermined strictures of fiction.

43. The speaker apparently believes that the distinctiveness of a work of fiction

(A) is directly correlated to the subject matter.

(B) is determined by the literary form.

(C) is dependent upon the individuality of the author.

(D) is subject to the dictates of the author's contemporaries.

(E) is immaterial to the construction of the "house of fiction."

44. The syntax of the sentence in lines 21–22 presents an example of

(A) parallelism. (D) hyperbole.

(B) chiasmus. (E) ellipsis.

(C) alliteration.

Questions 45–60 are based on the following passage. Read the passage carefully before choosing your answers.

After considering the historic page, and viewing the living world with anxious solicitude, the most melancholy emotions of sorrowful indignation have depressed my spirits, and I have sighed when obliged to confess, that either

nature has made a great difference between man and man, or that the civilization which has hitherto taken place in the world has been very partial. I have
turned over various books written on the subject of education, and patiently
observed the conduct of parents and the management of schools; but what has
been the result?—a profound conviction that the neglected education of my
fellow-creatures is the grand source of the misery I deplore; and that women,
in particular, are rendered weak and wretched by a variety of concurring
causes, originating from one hasty conclusion. The conduct and manners of
women, in fact, evidently prove that their minds are not in a healthy state; for,
like the flowers which are planted in too rich a soil, strength and usefulness are
sacrificed to beauty; and the flaunting leaves, after having pleased a fastidious
eye, fade, disregarded on the stalk, long before the season when they ought to
have arrived at maturity.—One cause of this barren blooming I attribute to a
false system of education, gathered from the books written on this subject by
men who, considering females rather as women than human creatures, have
been more anxious to make them alluring mistresses than affectionate wives
and rational mothers; and the understanding of the sex has been so bubbled by
this specious homage, that the civilized women of the present century, with a
few exceptions, are only anxious to inspire love, when they ought to cherish a
nobler ambition, and by their abilities and virtues exact respect.

In a treatise, therefore, on female rights and manners, the works which have
been particularly written for their improvement must not be overlooked; especially when it is asserted, in direct terms, that the minds of women are en-
feebled by false refinement; that the books of instruction, written by men of
genius, have had the same tendency as more frivolous productions; and that, in
the true style of Mahometanism, they are treated as a kind of subordinate
beings, and not as a part of the human species, when improveable reason is
allowed to be the dignified distinction which raises men above the brute creation, and puts a natural sceptre in a feeble hand.

Yet, because I am a woman, I would not lead my readers to suppose that I
mean violently to agitate the contested question respecting the quality or inferiority of the sex; but as the subject lies in my way, and I cannot pass it over
without subjecting the main tendency of my reasoning to misconstruction, I
shall stop a moment to deliver, in a few words, my opinion.—In the government of the physical world it is observable that the female in point of strength
is, in general, inferior to the male. This is the law of nature, and it does not
appear to be suspended or abrogated in favour of woman. A degree of physical

superiority cannot, therefore, be denied—and it is a noble prerogative! But not
content with this natural pre-eminence, men endeavour to sink us still lower,
merely to render us alluring objects for a moment; and women, intoxicated by
the adoration which men, under the influence of their senses, pay them, do
45 not seek to obtain a durable interest in their hearts, or to become the friends of
the fellow creatures who find amusement in their society.

45. The terms "the historic page" (line 1) and "the living world" (line 1) are
synonymous with

(A) fiction and reality.   (D) past and present.

(B) books and specimens.   (E) antiques and contemporaries.

(C) page and globe.

46. The speaker's description of her own manner as filled with "anxious solicitude" and "the most melancholy emotions of sorrowful indignation [which]
have depressed my [her] spirits" (lines 2–3) is notable for its

(A) emphatic repetitiveness.   (D) bitter irony.

(B) pointed brevity.   (E) delicate understatement.

(C) controlled wittiness.

47. Which of the following assumptions can be made about the speaker's original
conclusion that "either nature has made a great difference between man and
man, or that the civilization which has hitherto taken place in the world has
been very partial" (lines 3–5)?

(A) The speaker does not decide between the two propositions.

(B) The speaker eventually concludes that nature has created man unequal.

(C) The speaker determines that civilization has rendered man unequal.

(D) The speaker asserts that both nature and civilization have created man
unequal.

(E) None of the above.

48. Rhetorically, the passage as a whole can best be described as

(A) deliberative.   (D) analytical.

(B) judicial.   (E) expository.

(C) panegyric.

49. The speaker's study of "the historic page" (line 1), "the living world" (line 1), books on education, parents, schools, and other works on women has which of the following effects?

    I.   It reveals the speaker's lack of confidence in her theories.

    II. It portrays the speaker as a rational and thorough researcher.

    III. It provides the reader with the basis of the speaker's conclusions.

    IV. It lends authority to the speaker's own work.

    (A) I only   (D) I, II, and III only

    (B) II only   (E) II, III, and IV only

    (C) II and III only

50. In the first paragraph the main point of the argument, the unnatural inequality of women, is introduced by

    (A) an ellipsis.   (D) a rhetorical question.

    (B) a metaphor.   (E) a proverb.

    (C) a paradox.

51. What is the "one hasty conclusion" (line 11) which has resulted in reduced status for women?

    (A) Women have been undereducated.

    (B) The minds of women are weak.

    (C) Women inspire love rather than respect.

    (D) Women peak before they reach maturity.

    (E) Women's roles are "wife" and "mother."

52. All of the following can be inferred about the speaker's female contemporaries EXCEPT

    (A) their very actions prove that their minds' cultivation has been neglected.

    (B) as women, they are other than human.

    (C) their education makes them better suited as idolized lovers than effective mothers.

    (D) they receive little or no respect.

    (E) they have been educated primarily by males.

53. The description of women's minds as "not in a healthy state" (line 12) is expanded using

(A)   a conceit.   (D)   a parable.

(B)   a metaphor.   (E)   a pun.

(C)   a simile.

54. Which of the following phrases contains an oxymoron?

(A)   "the most melancholy emotions of sorrowful indignation have depressed my spirits" (lines 2–3)

(B)   "like the flowers which are planted in too rich a soil, strength and usefulness are sacrificed to beauty" (lines 13–14)

(C)   "One cause of this barren blooming I attribute to a false system of education" (lines 16–17)

(D)   "men who...have been more anxious to make them alluring mistresses than affectionate wives and rational mothers" (lines 18–20)

(E)   "improveable reason is allowed to be the dignified distinction which raises men above the brute creation" (lines 30–32)

55. The alliteration occurring in lines 11–16 has the effect of

(A)   linking the behavior resulting from, the cause of, and the ultimate effect of the unequal status of women.

(B)   digressing from the main point of the argument.

(C)   contradicting the description contained in the simile that precedes it.

(D)   downplaying the role unequal treatment has forced upon women.

(E)   joining the simile to the concept it seeks to describe.

56. Despite its length, the sentence that makes up the second paragraph maintains coherence through

(A)   parallel syntax.

(B)   compound sentence structure.

(C)   repetition of key phrases.

(D)   strings of prepositional phrases.

(E)   complex sentence structure.

57. Who has made the assertions in lines 25–32?

    (A) The authors of works "which have been particularly written for their [women's] improvement" (lines 24–25)

    (B) The speaker of the passage

    (C) Other female authors

    (D) "Men of genius" (lines 27–28)

    (E) Men who "have been more anxious to make them [women] alluring mistresses than affectionate wives and rational mothers" (lines 18–20)

58. It can be inferred that lines 33–38 function as

    I. an assuaging of the fear of radical reformation.

    II. a presentation of the speaker as builder of a rational argument.

    III. an example of woman as other than "enfeebled by false refinement" (lines 26–27).

    IV. a disclaimer of any involvement in the struggle for the betterment of women.

    (A) I only   (D) I, II, and III only

    (B) I and II only   (E) I, II, III, and IV

    (C) I and IV only

59. Whom would the speaker most probably blame for the unequal status of women?

    (A) Men

    (B) Women

    (C) Men and women

    (D) Authors of works intended for women's education

    (E) Parents

60. The overall style of the passage can best be described as

    (A) humorous and light.   (D) formal and complex.

    (B) colloquial and unstructured. (E) urbane and ironic.

    (C) florid and pedantic.

Section 2

TIME: 1 Hour and 45 Minutes
3 Essay Questions

Question 1 (Suggested time—35 minutes.) This question is one-third of the total essay score.

Examine the following passage by Edgar Allen Poe. Then write an essay that defines and discusses the effect of the selection on the reader. Pay particular attention to how the writer uses syntax, diction, imagery, tone, and argument to produce that effect.

> For the most wild yet most homely narrative which I am about to pen, I neither expect nor solicit belief. Mad indeed would I be to expect it, in a case where my very senses reject their own evidence. Yet, mad am I not—and very surely do I not dream. But tomorrow I die, and today I would unburden my soul. My immediate purpose is to place before the world, plainly, succinctly, and without comment, a series of mere household events. In their consequences, these events have terrified—have tortured—have destroyed me. Yet I will not attempt to expound them. To me, they have presented little but horror—to many they will seem less terrible than baroque. Hereafter, perhaps, some intellect may be found which will reduce my phantasm to the commonplace—some intellect more calm, more logical, and far less excitable than my own, which will perceive, in the circumstances I detail with awe, nothing more than an ordinary succession of very natural causes and effects.

CONTINUE TO QUESTION 2 >

Question 2 (Suggested time—35 minutes.) This question is one-third of the total essay score.

The passages below represent early and later drafts of a poem. Write a well-organized essay in which you discuss the probable reasons for the writer's additions and deletions and the ways in which those revisions change the effect of the poem.

Early Draft

My hope was one, from cities far
Nursed on a lonesome heath:
Her lips were red as roses are,
Her hair a woodbine wreath.

She lived among the untrodden ways
Besides the springs of Dove,
A maid whom there were none to praise,
And very few to love;

A violet by a mossy stone
Half-hidden from the eye!
Fair as a star when only one
Is shining in the sky!

And she was graceful as the broom
That flowers by Carron's side;
But slow distemper checked her bloom,
And on the Heath she died.

Long time before her head lay low
Dead to the world was she:
But now she's in her grave, and Oh!
The difference to me!

Later Draft

She dwelt among th' untrodden ways
Beside the springs of Dove,
A Maid whom there were none to praise
And very few to love.

A Violet by a mossy stone
Half-hidden from the Eye!
—Fair, as a star when only one
Is shining in the sky!

She *liv'd* unknown, and few could know
When Lucy ceas'd to be;
But she is in her Grave, and Oh!
The difference to me.

CONTINUE TO QUESTION 3

Question 3 (Suggested time—35 minutes.) This question is one-third of the total essay score.

Our use of language differs depending upon the manner or conditions in which it is used. Our language may differ in use of syntax, inflection, vocabulary and pronunciation, dependent on circumstances.

Write an essay describing the differences in the language you would use in two different circumstances—a conversation with a friend and a job interview, for example. Your essay should indicate what purposes the differences in your use of language serve.

EXAM IS FINISHED

AP Examination in English Language & Composition

TEST I

ANSWER KEY

Section 1

1.	**(C)**	21.	**(E)**	41.	**(A)**
2.	**(C)**	22.	**(C)**	42.	**(E)**
3.	**(D)**	23.	**(B)**	43.	**(C)**
4.	**(A)**	24.	**(A)**	44.	**(B)**
5.	**(B)**	25.	**(B)**	45.	**(D)**
6.	**(D)**	26.	**(D)**	46.	**(A)**
7.	**(C)**	27.	**(E)**	47.	**(C)**
8.	**(B)**	28.	**(C)**	48.	**(A)**
9.	**(C)**	29.	**(C)**	49.	**(E)**
10.	**(A)**	30.	**(B)**	50.	**(D)**
11.	**(E)**	31.	**(A)**	51.	**(B)**
12.	**(B)**	32.	**(E)**	52.	**(B)**
13.	**(E)**	33.	**(A)**	53.	**(C)**
14.	**(A)**	34.	**(D)**	54.	**(C)**
15.	**(C)**	35.	**(B)**	55.	**(A)**
16.	**(D)**	36.	**(E)**	56.	**(A)**
17.	**(B)**	37.	**(A)**	57.	**(B)**
18.	**(D)**	38.	**(B)**	58.	**(D)**
19.	**(A)**	39.	**(C)**	59.	**(C)**
20.	**(C)**	40.	**(D)**	60.	**(D)**

Detailed Explanations of Answers

Test I

Section 1

1. **(C)** The rephrased sentence reads: **The park's playground facility and carefully tended playing fields are maintained by a fund set up by a local philanthropist who died some 30 years ago.** (C) is the correct answer because "by a fund" introduces the dependent clause as it was originally constructed. (A) is incorrect because to say the park is maintained "for funding" is to say the park generates funds, where the original says the park is supported by a fund. (B) is incorrect because "for" requires as a prepositional object what must instead by the subject of "are maintained." (D) is incorrect because "funds" indicates more than one source for the financial support, contrary to the original. (E) is incorrect because "is" does not accommodate the compound subject.

2. **(C)** The rephrased sentence reads: **Virgil wrote verse copiously in many genres, although he derives most of his fame as author of *The Aeneid.*** (C) is the correct answer because only "although" provides the sense of contradicting ideas conveyed by "but." (A) is incorrect because "to derive" does not introduce any form of clause. (B) is incorrect because it lacks the negation of "but." (D) is incorrect because, again, it lacks the negation of "but." (E) is incorrect because, finally, it lacks the negation of "but."

3. **(D)** The rephrased sentence reads: **In that state, the law treats a known accomplice no differently than the assailant who pulls the trigger.** (D) is the correct answer because when the action of treatment is given directly to "law," "be treated" is simply removed from that part of the original sentence. (A) is incorrect because the verb "to require" is omitted because of the direct action of "the law treats." (B) is incorrect because "requirement" as a noun is redundant in a sentence about the "law." (C) is incorrect because "knowing accomplice" is more concise than "accomplice who knowingly...." (E) is incorrect because "knowing assailant" is a completely different issue from the one dealt with in the original sentence.

4. **(A)** The rephrased sentence reads: **The absence of subsequent references to the man has always been considered puzzling and conspicuous.** (A) is the correct answer because "has always" agrees with the tense and number for the subject "absence." (B) is

incorrect because the subject is singular, "absence," disqualifying the plural "have." (C) is incorrect because "puzzling" should follow the verb "has always been considered." (D) is incorrect because the sentence is passive, disqualifying the active "considered." (E) is incorrect; "puzzled" disrupts the parallel structure of the original's "puzzling and conspicuous" because "conspicuous" does not easily lend itself to an active verb form.

5. **(B)** The rephrased sentence reads: **Hashing, which employs the principle of putting something where you will remember where you put it, remains unpopular because it is the most disorganized way to organize computer data.** (B) is the correct answer because in this sentence you are meant to see a causal relationship between the clauses; "because it is" contains the needed "because" and successfully introduces the "arguably the most…" clause with "it is." (A) is incorrect because it lacks "because." (C) is incorrect because the method does not engage in the action of arguing, but is argued about. (D) is incorrect because while being potentially workable it could not be as concise as (B). (E) is incorrect because the relationship is not negative, but causal.

6. **(D)** The rephrased sentence reads: **A white-tailed deer is blind to hunters in trees because its visual sphere is limited by the range of motion of its head, which cannot turn up.** (D) is the correct answer because the clauses have a causal relationship, which is brought out in the new construction, requiring "because." (A) is incorrect because "range" is not affected by the new construction. (B) is incorrect because, again, "range" is not affected by the new construction. (C) is incorrect because the relationship between the clauses is not negative, but causal. (E) is incorrect because, again, the relationship between the clauses is causal, not negative.

7. **(C)** (A) is correct because the invaluable life of a child is understatedly appraised as "somewhat dear" (line 51). (B) is also correct because the passage's dominant metaphor is that of parents raising their infants as food for the wealthy: here the parents are being "devoured" (line 52). (D) and (E) are correct, and (C) is incorrect because the landlords are sarcastically indicted. They have financially "eaten up" the parents and can be held responsible for the ends of their children.

8. **(B)** While the monetary mechanics of buying and selling a child for food (C) are mentioned and scientific jargon briefly used (D), (B), "animal husbandry," is the best answer. The wives/mothers are referred to as "Breeders" and the children as "a most delicious, nourishing and wholesome Food" (lines 31–32) when cooked in ways associated with cuts of animal meats (lines 32–34). Lines 35–40 compare ratios of human males and females to those found among domesticated animal herds. Children are described as if they were holiday turkeys, with instructions for fattening them and calculating the number of persons they will serve. Images of a dying, unstable city [urban decay, (A)], or religious rivals (E) are not found in the passage.

9. **(C)** (C) and (E) may seem correct because of the references to means of cooking in lines 32–34, but (C) is the best choice because a person who has experience eating

children must be a savage, stereotypically an "uncivilized" native inhabitant of any non-European country. There is no indication, such as mention of experiments or scientific terminology, that this person is a scientist (A). Being an acquaintance of the speaker, whose nationality is unclear, does not necessarily make one Irish (B). The paragraph lacks any clues of medicine or medical treatments that might name the person "physician" (D).

10. **(A)** The argument in these lines moves from a statement of a problem to a refutation of previously suggested solutions. Evidence to support a new remedy (the shocking revelation of the "American") is followed by this new proposal. The juxtaposition of such a frightening suggestion with such logical order shows the proposal in heightened horrific relief; therefore, (A) is correct. "Souls" [line 1, (B)] is simply a synonym for "persons"; moreover, no other religious sentiments or principles follow. (D) is incorrect because the author is using statistics to introduce and clarify his idea, not to befuddle his reader. References to animal breeding (C) and first person openings (E) occur but do not have the effects given.

11. **(E)** The speaker is calculating the number of fertile "Couples" and subtracts 30,000 who can afford the upkeep of their children (although there cannot be "so many" because of the economic situation). The "couples" are numbered, not the "children" (A). "Number" (B) is incorrect because its own antecedent is "200,000 Couple" (line 2). "Souls" (C) is equal to the total number of persons in Ireland and not the subtracted "many." "Wives" (D) is incorrect because it is only a component of the "many" couples.

12. **(B)** III and IV may appear correct: the author creates a satiric speaker who leads the reader to expect a plausible solution suggested by a rational, concerned citizen. The terrifying and definitively unmeasured proposal shatters these initial illusions. The author's actual appraisal of the landlords as uncaring (I), and even responsible for much of the problem of poverty, is revealed in lines 51–53 (they financially "devoured" parents and are best suited nonmetaphorically to consume their children), lines 62–63 (cottagers and farmers have beggars' status), and lines 68–69 (the landlord will learn that being good to his tenants means giving them financial assistance). The previous proposals (lines 12–14) have seemed impossible; juxtaposed with such an improbable idea as raising children for food, they accrue new reasonableness and possibility (II).

13. **(E)** Stylistically the passage is neither philosophical (A); lyrical [(B), expressing the writer's thoughts and sentiments, usually poetically]; scientific (C); or hortative [(D), earnestly urging a specific course of action]. It is satirical [(E), sarcastically and ironically exposing vice or folly].

14. **(A)** The best answer is (A); the animalistic connotations of "Breeders" dehumanizes the women. The speaker is so removed from these persons that no emotions toward them, such as those in choices (B) and (E) are present. The women are not given

any special status over that of the men (C); they are simply singled out as the actual producers of children. The speaker does not blame or chastise the women for bearing children, (D) but the landlords for impoverishing these children.

15. **(C)**   The proposal which follows these lines is likely to cause explosive reactions far beyond the understated "least Objection" (line 29). It does not contain exaggeration (A), seemingly opposite but apt terms (B), or an implied comparison (D). The phrase signals the coming of the main point of the argument rather than a distraction from it (E).

16. **(D)**   Under an argument whose logical progression seems to suggest the coming of a rational proposal, these references are warning flags. While couched in nonemotional language, they imply that people can be bought and sold as animals. The "knowing American" (line 30) adds the concept of children as food. If the reader has missed this direction so far, letting the argument's rational layout sweep over him/her, the speaker "humbly" hammers it home. (A) and (E) are incorrect because the references are key elements of the argument, not digressions from or objections to it. Children as food of breeder mothers are not actual occurrences (B) but the speaker's "invention." The argument has not been fully introduced; therefore, these terms cannot be summarizing it (C).

17. **(B)**   The main character is named "our Professor" (line 1), "the Son of Time" (line 3), and "our Wanderer" (line 10). Choice (B), "the Eagle" (line 8), is incorrect because it is the subject of a metaphor that describes the transitional state the main character is in, not the character himself. The main character is also called "he/him" [choice (C)]. (B) is therefore the proper choice, since it is the only incorrect answer.

18. **(D)**   The speaker intends to show that this turbulent time is necessary for the formation of the main character's self; the more chaotic it is, the more composed the person who emerges from it. Choices (A), (B), (C), and (E) are incorrect because each describes this period of the main character's life but does not indicate why the speaker considers it worth examining.

19. **(A)**   The subject's life thus far is extensively compared to a cup overflowing with bitterness (lines 18–21). (B) is incorrect because the subject's pain is the focal point, not an aside from another topic. There is no overstatement of the pain [(C), hyperbole] or description using seemingly contradictory terms [(D), oxymoron]. There are no descriptive words which imitate sounds [(E), onomatopoeia].

20. **(C)**   This clause offers the more intense "last worst instance" (line 14) of having one's desires denied. (C) is the best choice because the "nay" clause relates and emphasizes its predecessor. (A) and (B) misinterpret "nay" as a strict negative rather than as a corrective pause before a restatement. (D) merely restates without emphasizing. (E) is incorrect because it lists the opposite effect.

21. **(E)** The speaker qualifies this statement as having "more justice than original-ity" (line 22), implying that while solemnly delivered and true it is still a common observation (E), "platitude." (A) and (C) are incorrect because there is no comparison being made in the statement. The statement is not attributed to another person and therefore cannot be considered a quotation (B). The statement is commonplace and thus cannot have come as a sudden revelation [(D), epiphany].

22. **(C)** Contextually, coruscations "flash" out, making "sparks" (C) the best definition. "Boils" (A) and "scars" (E) may seem to be consequences of an illness ("fever," line 11), but they would form over time and not flash out suddenly. "Threads" (B) and "blocks" (D) are not supported by contextual evidence.

23. **(B)** This description calls a "marvel" a wonderful thing; this joining of seem-ingly contradictory terms is an oxymoron. The hat is not being compared to something else; therefore, (A), "metaphor," is incorrect. There is no deliberate repetition of initial consonants ("covered" does not alliterate with "crown" because it is part of the compound adjective "dust-covered," beginning with "d," (C). (D) is the substitution of a part for whole; it is incorrect because the hat is named and described in its entirety. No words are omitted from the description, making ellipsis (E) incorrect.

24. **(A)** The main character is "going forth to eat as the wanderer may eat, and sleep as the homeless sleep" (lines 6–7) and is "searching for an outcast of the highest degree" (line 13), implying that he is attempting to "try out" the role of a homeless person (A). Although the main character is labeled "bum" and "hobo" (lines 8–9), these names are only taunts by children and lack "open hostility" (B). The main character's clothing is ragged and somewhat dusty but not repulsively so; (C) is therefore incorrect. The taunts of the children highlight social differences and leave the main character "in a state of the most profound dejection" (line 10); there is neither harmony (D) nor dignity (E).

25. **(B)** The use of "going forth" and "wanderer," both carrying connotations of a quest, give a sanitized, unrealistic picture of homelessness (B). (A) is wrong because the sentence creates an unrealistic fantasy of the main character's projected actions. The sentence pertains to the main character's actions; (C) and (E) are therefore incorrect. The romanticized description precedes the actual events: (D) is incorrect because it claims that the description is downplayed and after the fact.

26. **(D)** The taunts parallel the "sifting rain" (line 11) because they "[plaster]" (line 8) the main character, metaphorically penetrating his spirit as the rain literally penetrates his coat. (A), (B), (C), and (E) are incorrect because they remain in the background and have no direct effect upon the main character.

27. **(E)** (E) is correct because the main character initially envisions his homelessness as a "wanderer's" quest but is actually faced with hardship and degradation. The boys' shouts are "unholy epithets" to his idealizing ears. (A) is incorrect because there is no

reason why the boys should show respect to a derelict. The raising of common profanity to "unholy epithets" heightens, rather than downplays, its effect; (B) is, consequently, incorrect. (C) is wrong because the atmosphere that prevails is one of quiet despair. The speaker's tone is not bitter and ironic (D).

28. **(C)** The answer (C) is located in the two preceding sentences (lines 13–16): the main character is searching for a homeless person but finds the benches "deserted," "their usual freights had fled" (lines 15–16). (A) is incorrect because the people and bridge occur in the sentence following the "freights" and could not possibly be their antecedents. (B), (D), and (E) are wrong because trees, shadows, passengers, and ferries are not mentioned or implied in the passage.

29. **(C)** The main character has literally descended from uptown to downtown and figuratively fallen into the lowly state of poverty. (A) is incorrect because there is no change from fair to foul weather—it has been miserably raining from the beginning of the passage. (D) is wrong because the speaker uses a neutral tone in discussing the homeless. The physical surroundings are not described as worsening (E).

30. **(B)** The description is unified by parallel pairs of adjectives (II): the background night is "cold and storming" (line 26), the cable cars are "shining with red and brass" (line 27), "calm and irresistible" (line 28), and "dangerful and gloomy" (line 28). The inanimate cable cars are not given human attributes (I, personification). Although this sentence contains many descriptive clauses, the main clause follows the usual "subject (cable cars) precedes verb (went)" format, making inverted syntax (III) incorrect. The cable car's gong sounds, but it is not described in terms that mimic this noise (IV, onomatopoiea).

31. **(A)** All three paragraphs describe background crowds as water (A). They "[swarm] toward the Bridge" (line 17), are the "flowing life of the great street" (line 25), and are "two rivers…[swarming] along the sidewalks" (lines 29–30). The descriptions create a faceless mass of water, containing no individuals (B). (C) is incorrect because the descriptions share a common focus, water. The descriptions focus upon the image of water, a physical thing rather than an abstraction (D). (E) relies upon a misinterpretation of "swarm" as insectlike behavior.

32. **(E)** Each sentence of this paragraph describes the saloon as a hungry monster luring prey, building an extended metaphor [conceit, (E)]. Paradox (A), a seemingly impossible but true statement, does not occur. The speaker's choice of words is not common and lowly [colloquial, (B)]. Only the first sentence is relatively short, making (C) incorrect. The description does not rely upon overexaggeration [hyperbole, (D)].

33. **(A)** The speaker describes the saloon as a monster luring impoverished men inside with promises of free soup. (B) connotes approval or at least ambivalence; the

monster image, however, connotes evil and disapproval. The scene at the saloon occurs in a lower-class area and during the evening, but this is only background information and not symbolic and condemning placement (C) and (E). There is no indication that the soup is served to counteract the effect of alcohol (D).

34. **(D)**   (D) relies upon a misreading of "unholy epithets" (line 9): there is nothing sacred about a homeless man or blasphemous about cursing boys. The main character moves uptown to downtown (A) and through the realms of the working class and the impoverished (B). The purposeful homeward-bound "well-dressed Brooklyn people" (line 17) is juxtaposed with the patient loitering of the homeless [(C), confidence and resignation]. The light of the street lamps penetrates the evening's darkness (E).

35. **(B)**   (B) is a better answer than (C) because the metaphor of fiction as a house is extended and expanded throughout the passage (conceit). Authors who write fiction are figuratively gathered in the "house of fiction," but they do not literally meet in an actual place (A). (D) is incorrect because there is no comparison using "like" or "as." The image is concrete, but it does not pertain to any particular group of authors (E).

36. **(E)**   The quotation marks indicate that the framed terms are not the speaker's own: the speaker prefers "the spreading field, the human scene" (lines 17–18) to the narrow "choice of subject" and the multifaceted "pierced aperture" (line 18) to "literary form" (E). (A) is incorrect because the speaker applies these labels to his/her own terminology but does not attribute them to a specific author. The speaker may prefer his/her own terminology, but there is no negative emotion toward the labels (B). The quotation marks do not give authoritative weight to the labels (C). (D) is incorrect because the terms in quotation marks are not the speaker's but generic labels he expands upon.

37. **(A)**   A door that would open "straight upon life" would directly reveal life: fictional works are not such doors and do not strictly imitate life (A). (A) is a better answer than (B) because (B) interprets the phrase literally, not as the metaphor it is. (C) is incorrect because it relies upon a misinterpretation of "not…opening straight." There are no contextual references to the making of fiction (D). (E) is incorrect because it refers to the sentence which follows this phrase and introduces additional information.

38. **(B)**   "Apertures" (openings) precedes "they" and is synonymous with its predicate "windows" (B). (A) and (C) are incorrect because they follow "they" and are its predicates. "Need" and "pressure" (D) describe the formation of the windows, not the windows themselves. "Eyes" (E) follows "they" and cannot be its antecedent.

39. **(C)**   The shifts in point of view from "we" to "I" mimics the description of fiction that moves from building/genre housing all authors to each watcher at a window with an individual perspective (C). (A) is incorrect because the "house of fiction" contains authors, not their critics. The speaker neither affirms nor denies that he/she is a writer of fiction, making (B) incorrect. The use of "we" draws readers in and allies them with,

rather than alienating them from, the speaker's perspective (D). The argument moves logically from house to windows to individual perspective, making (E) incorrect.

40. **(D)**   (D), with its parallel pairs of contrasting words, exemplifies antithesis. There are no such contrasts in the other four choices. Shape and size (A), windows and doors (B), eyes and field-glass (C), and singly and together (E) are not opposites.

41. **(A)**   The speaker states that human scene/choice of subject and window/literary form are nothing without the "consciousness of the artist" (line 21). (B) and (D) are consequently incorrect. (E) is incorrect because it is synonymous with (D). Hinged doors (C) are dismissed because they do not have the same function as the windows.

42. **(E)**   Piercing connotes forceful action: force an author directs toward the "house of fiction" to make his work part of it (E). (A) and (B) are incorrect because they misinterpret piercing as making holes for jewelry, and contradict the speaker's emphasis upon the importance of windows and the "watcher" behind them. There is no evidence that established authors reject or fight new works (C). The windows are created by "the need of the individual vision and by the pressure of the individual will" (lines 3–4), not by any special implements (D).

43. **(C)**   The speaker states "tell me what the artist is, and I will tell you of what he has been conscious" (lines 21–22), implying that the individuality of the work comes from its author's own distinct character (C). The subject and form [(A) and (B)] cannot give the work its individuality without the author's "posted presence" (line 20). (D) is incorrect because there is no mention of an author's contemporaries in the passage. The passage details the shaping of fiction by the individual author and his work and thus affirms their importance; (E) is consequently incorrect.

44. **(B)**   The sentence contains a chiasmus (B), a reversal of grammatical structures:

> "[you] tell me
> I will tell you."

(A) is incorrect because there is no repetition of similarly constructed clauses. "Alliteration" (C), the repetition of initial consonants, is not present. There is no exaggeration [hyperbole, (D)] or omission of easily understood words [ellipsis, (E)].

45. **(D)**   The conclusion the speaker makes from reviewing these items, nature has created men unequal or civilization "which has hitherto taken place" (lines 4–5), indicates that they are the past and the present. (A), (B), and (C) rely upon misinterpretations of "page," each assuming that page is literally part of a book. (D) misreads "historic" as "old" and "aged."

46. **(A)** The speaker emphasizes the depths of her concern by stacking words with the same meanings, such as "anxious" with "solicitude" (meaning "anxiety") and "melancholy" (meaning "sadness") with "sorrowful" and "depressed." The description is neither short (B) nor lessened (E). (C) is incorrect because the speaker is not attempting to be cleverly amusing. The rest of the paragraph makes it clear that the speaker is not mockingly describing her feelings with their opposites [irony, (D)].

47. **(C)** The speaker's subsequent affirmation that "the neglected education of my fellow creatures is the grand source of the misery I deplore" (lines 8–9) makes it clear that she believes that civilization (C), not nature (B), is responsible for man's inequality. (A), (D), and (E) are consequently incorrect.

48. **(A)** The passage is "deliberative" because the speaker seeks to persuade the reader of the injustice of the inequality of women. It is not "judicial" (B) because it is neither accusing nor defending. "Panegyric" (C) is incorrect because the passage does not praise or blame. (D) and (E) are incorrect because the passage's rhetorical purpose is not analyzing or explaining.

49. **(E)** (I) is incorrect [and thus (A) and (D)] because the speaker strongly states that it is her "profound conviction" (line 8) that education creates inequality among men. The speaker's study indicates the sources for her ideas (III) and extensive research (II), both of which give greater weight to her own conclusions (IV); (E) (II, III, and IV only) is thus the correct answer.

50. **(D)** The speaker's main point, that lack of education leads to inequality, particularly of women, is the speaker's answer to the question "what has been the result" (lines 7–8). "Ellipsis" (A) is incorrect because no words are omitted in the introduction. There is no comparison being made (B). "A paradox" (C) would involve a seemingly contradictory yet true statement. The sentences which precede this point do not contain "a proverb" (E), a statement of a general truth.

51. **(B)** Mention of the "one hasty conclusion" is followed by the admission that the behavior of women would prove that their minds are unhealthy. (A) is subsequently explained as a cause of the behavior that indicates a weakened mind. (C) and (D) are given as results of women's undereducation rather than the cause of their inequality. (E) is incorrect because these are the roles the speaker would have for women if their status were not reduced and their roles prescribed as "alluring mistresses" (line 19).

52. **(B)** (A), (C), (D), and (E) are listed in lines 9–23 as consequences and examples of women's undereducation. (B), women are less than human (see lines 29–32), is the speaker's summary of this treatment women receive rather than their natural state.

53. **(C)** Using "like," women are compared to flowers, fragile and short-lived (C), "simile." "Metaphor" (B) is incorrect because the comparison is explicit. "Conceit" (A) and "parable" (D) are both extended forms of metaphor. There is no play on words, making "pun" (E) incorrect.

54. **(C)** "Barren blooming" (C) is an oxymoron combining the seemingly contradictory terms of sterility and fertility. (A) is incorrect because sorrow and indignation are not opposites. (B), (D), and (E) also lack a pairing of apparent opposites.

55. **(A)** The alliterated f's join the "flaunting leaves" (line 14) of female coquettishness, the "fastidious eye" (lines 14–15) of male admiration, and the subsequent "fade" (line 15) of the only skill woman has been led to cultivate. (B), (C), and (E) are incorrect because the alliterative phrase is part of the simile that expands upon the speaker's description of the origin of the inequality of women. The phrase draws attention to, rather than downplays, the unequal treatment of women, making (D) incorrect.

56. **(A)** An independent clause ["In a treatise…must not be overlooked" (lines 24–25)] is followed by two parallel dependent clauses, each beginning with "when" ["when it is asserted…" (line 26) and "when improveable reason is allowed…" (lines 30–31), (A)]. In addition, the first adverbial clause contains three parallel clauses introduced by "that." (B) is incorrect because the sentence does not contain more than one independent clause. Each of the dependent clauses makes a new point without repetition (C). While there are a number of prepositional phrases, they are not strung directly together (D) but interspersed throughout the passage. The sentence is complex (E), containing one independent and a number of dependent clauses, but (A) is a better answer because it specifically describes the type of complex structure.

57. **(B)** All three of these points assert the inequality of women, the main point of the speaker. (A), (D), and (E) are incorrect because all three groups are described as contributing to this inequality rather than countering it. There is no reference to other female authors (C) in the passage.

58. **(D)** The speaker asserts that she will not "violently…agitate" (line 34) for women's equality (I) but will face the issue to prevent her argument from being misunderstood (line 36, II). A woman who could argue so calmly and logically would obviously counteract her contemporaries' decorative education (III). (IV) misreads "I would not lead my reader to suppose that I mean violently to agitate the contested question" (lines 33–34): the speaker does not deny agitation itself, only violent agitation.

59. **(C)** Each of these persons has a contributory role in the unequal status of women—men, parents, and authors as miseducators and women as so flattered by admiration that they prefer to receive love rather than respect (lines 21–23). (C) is the best answer because it is the most inclusive.

60. **(D)** (D) is correct because the passage's diction is formal and its syntax complex. The passage takes its subject very seriously, making (A) incorrect. (B) is incorrect because the passage is just the opposite of colloquial (common speech) and unstructured. The speaker is not blatantly parading book learning (C) nor sarcastically adopting a stance in order to ridicule it (E).

Student Response to Essay Question 1:

The main effect of this passage is to foster in readers an anticipation of the horror that will be found in what otherwise might be considered "everyday" events which will be described in the following pages.

It is fitting that the author chooses to create this tone of fearful anticipation by juxtaposing the promise of extraordinary emotional impact with the images and reality of seemingly ordinary descriptions ("household events"). In the first line, the author portrays a dichotomy in the phrase, "most wild yet most homely." The passage goes on to directly state that "mere household events" have "terrified—have tortured—have destroyed me." Here he reemphasizes the surprising conversion of the everyday into the extraordinary by saying that these events are horrible to him, yet they may seem little more than frivolous exaggerations ("*baroques*") to others. Finally, he states that some day, the extraordinary events he is about to chronicle may be interpreted by others "more logical" as "commonplace"—an oblique reference to possible madness.

Referring to himself as "mad" instead of insane, anticipating that others might think his story will be "*baroque*" instead of simply elaborate, and claiming that what he has experienced might be a "phantasm" instead of a misinterpretation, are intentional word choices designed to create in readers a feeling that they are about to enter a world in which what is real is always open to question—by the author as well as the reader. Others might not see what he has seen, or draw the same conclusions. Poe is, in effect, defining the lines of argument in which he participates ("Mad indeed would I be...mad I am not") and—he seems to hope—his readers will participate as well.

Repetition and anticipation of the horrible is also seen in Poe's cryptic statement that "to-morrow I die, and today I would unburden my soul." This comment and others in the passage (that he would be mad for the author to think that others will believe him), both motivates readers to continue and indicates to them that they will have to decide whether or not the story's author is mad—whether or not the commonplace events that he will be describing constitute a "phantasm" most extraordinary.

Analysis of Student Response to Essay Question 1:

The student's response has addressed the main challenge of the question *(an analysis of the effect of the passage on the reader),* and each of its elements: syntax *(the arrangement and interrelationship of words in sentences),* diction *(the use, choice, and arrangement of words in writing),* imagery *(mental images, collectively),* and tone (defined as a prevailing mood). The response is delivered with attention to words and phrases from the text and with appropriate interpretations or restatements. The responder also succeeds in defining the central argument Poe implies exists within the writer of the passage, and by extension, the same one he hopes will engage the reader (i.e., is he mad?). The essay itself is delivered in a compact and economic whole in which the conclusion echoes the themes raised in the conclusion. For all these reasons, the essay deserves a 5.

Student Response to Essay Question 2:

Through stringent use of deletion, the poet turns a somewhat rambling, unfocused poem into a tightly-knit, moving memorial to a lost love. The later draft is superior because it lacks the physical descriptions of the subject that the earlier draft gives us, creating a mystical aura around the subject.

The first and fourth stanzas that were deleted in the later draft of the poem paint a vivid picture of the nameless dead woman. We learn that her hair was a "woodbine wreath," her lips were "red as roses are," and that she was "graceful." This description happens even though the narrator of the poem states that she was a "maid whom there were none to praise" (line 9). If there were none to praise her, who is it that is doing this praising? The writer must have realized this contradiction, solving the problem by deleting the descriptive passages.

The later draft veils the subject in mystery, so that it does indeed seem that there were none to praise her. All that we learn of the subject is that she was "Fair." It becomes impossible for the reader to create a mental image of the subject, making it apparent that her existence was a solitary one. To avoid the possibility that the reader might not feel sympathy for the "she" of the early draft, the poet makes up for the lack of physical description by giving the subject a name, "Lucy." This use of the proper noun allows the reader to believe that the subject of the poem was a real, living person, since we all identify ourselves and others by our names. Since the "she" now has a name, "Lucy," we can identify her in this way, without needing the contradictory physical description provided in the early draft.

In the early draft, we learn how the subject died, "slow distemper checked her bloom" (15). This is an unnecessary detail, and in the later draft, all that we know is that Lucy "ceas'd to be" (10). This lack of detail as to her means of death adds to the mysterious quality of the hardly known Lucy. The shorter length of the later draft shows that even the narrator of the poem did not have much to say about Lucy's physical being. This allows for her to be portrayed as otherwordly, like an angel.

In addition to the deletions, the poet changes some of the wording of the poem. In the first stanza of the later draft, "dwelt" replaces "lived" from the earlier draft. "Liv'd" is than inserted in the final stanza to emphasize (note the italics) that the important thing about Lucy's life was not where she lived, but that she lived "unknown." This leads to the final idea that this poem is giving her something that she did not have when alive. In death she is now known, because of this poem eulogizing her. Another small change that the poet made is the capitalization of the word "Eye" in the later version. This shows that Lucy was hidden not only from the eye of one person, but from a universal "Eye," maybe even the "Eye" of God. The poet calls Lucy a "Maid" and a "Violet" in both drafts, but it is only in the final draft that these words are capitalized. This capitalization serves to portray Lucy as the perfect embodiment of all "Maids" and "Violets" by turning the nouns of the early draft into proper nouns that could only be describing Lucy.

The later draft of this poem is superior to the earlier draft because all extraneous detail has been removed, resulting in a concise poem that gives Lucy an ethereal quality. Since the reader cannot know who Lucy is, the final couplet has a much stronger dramatic effect in the later version. The narrator says that now that Lucy is no longer living, "Oh!/The difference to me" (11-12). The speaker of the poem is the only one who really knew Lucy, and the reader can sense the feeling of aloneness that the speaker is left with upon the death of his solitary love.

Analysis of Student Response to Essay Question 2:

This essay provides a strong and clear thesis that addresses all parts of the question. It persuasively argues that the poet's deletions serve to create a more concise, moving poem. In addition, the essay discusses some of the more subtle, less obvious changes that the author made in the passages, revealing a strong understanding of the finer points of the language.

The thesis is persuasively developed in the second, third, and fourth paragraphs of this essay. These paragraphs show why the lack of descriptive language in the final draft of the poem make it a stronger poem. The second paragraph illustrates that by removing physical description from the poem, the poet is following the internal logic of what he has written.

The third paragraph of the essay shows the importance of the introduction of a proper noun in the later draft by showing an awareness that a name can function as a non-physical way to show identity. The fourth paragraph further strengthens the central thesis by revealing that the shorter length of the final draft better serves the purpose of portraying the subject of the poem as ethereal and mysterious.

The essay is presented in a well-organized manner. The fifth paragraph addresses some of the small differences between the two passages, logically drawing on arguments made earlier in the essay, concerning proper nouns, to further solidify an already strong argument.

The final paragraph returns to the central thesis. This paragraph clearly illustrates the importance that the removal of all "extraneous detail" plays in making the later draft stronger than the earlier draft. The final paragraph also shows that the final couplet of the revised poem creates a stronger dramatic effect, by clearly showing that the poet's anguish over Lucy's death is a solitary anguish.

Student Response to Essay Question 3:

The language I would use in talking to a friend would certainly be different than the language I would use during a job interview. My purposes in both cases would contrast a great deal, and this would be reflected in the ways I spoke. In talking with a friend, I would be informal and not very concerned with such things as showing off my vocabulary or using correct grammar, and I would be more inclined to use slang terms.

My pronunciation and inflection would reflect the common ways that my friends and I speak, reflecting my desire to be casual and "cool." During a job interview I would speak in a more formal vein, to show my potential employer that I am mature and have a firm grasp of the English language.

In talking with a friend, I would be more prone to use phrases drawn from popular culture that we are both aware of. For example, I might say "That's cool," or "That sucks," to make a reference to a popular show on MTV, instead of using such stock phrases as "I like that" or "I'm not fond of that." I would know that my friends and I are members of a group by using such language, since we all know the jokes. I would never use such language during a job interview. Instead I would speak in the clearest language possible in an attempt to show my potential employer that I am intelligent. If s/he were to ask me what I think of school, I wouldn't chuckle and say dismissively, "Sometimes it's cool and sometimes it sucks." I would reflect for a few seconds, and then reply in full sentences, pointing out both the positive and negative aspects of my school—"I enjoy Shakespeare immensely, especially "Macbeth," but I find chemistry quite challenging sometimes."

In talking with friends I would be more prone to use certain words and phrases, such as "hey," "like," and "you know," in ways that are both unconventional and grammatically incorrect. Upon greeting a friend I would probably address him or her by saying, "Hey man, what's up?" The use of "hey" implies a certain amount of casualness and familiarity, as it is a short monosyllable that rolls off the tongue effortlessly. I would say "man" regardless of the sex of the addressee since among my friends we all understand "man" is an informal way of saying "friend." The final part of my phrase of greeting would be pronounced as one word "whazup." Furthermore my inflection would not rise at the end of this phrase, it would be more of a statement than a question.

In talking with my friends I would pepper my vocabulary with words that have no set meaning on their own, such as "like." "Like" functions as an intensifier, "He was, like, so gone," with emphasis on "like," would imply that the person of whom I was speaking was very, very drunk. I would consciously resist such usage of "like" during a job interview since it is not grammatically correct and it would also show a lack of respect if I were to address my potential employer as if he were one of my peers.

When greeting my interviewer, I would clearly say, in an even tone, "Hello, it's nice to meet you." I would follow this by questioning "How are you?" with a rise in my voice to show that I really want to know how this person is doing. I would continue throughout the interview in this way, being sure that I used my vocabulary in a conventional, intelligent way. I would also make certain that I employed proper grammar during my interview to show my potential employer that I am both respectful and smart.

My use of language among friends would be casual, informal and idiosyncratic, reflecting these same qualities in our relationships. I would speak properly and formally during a job interview to make a positive impression on the interviewer, to show him or her that I am an intelligent human being who is capable of communicating clearly and effectively with all people.

Analysis of Student Response to Essay Question 3:

This well-written essay expertly contrasts the different ways in which one might use language, dependent on circumstances. The opening paragraph clearly states the different purposes that language would serve during a job interview and during a conversation with a friend.

The essay goes on to describe how a conversation with a friend would draw from the vernacular of popular culture. The essay gives concrete examples of such phrases, as well as pointing out that the purpose of using them is to form a group identity in which friends feel at ease with each other.

The essay proceeds in a logical way to describe why such language would not be proper during a job interview. The writer of this essay would want to be seen as intelligent during a job interview. The essay states that the way to do this is through the use of full sentences, conventional vocabulary, and correct grammar, of which examples of are then given.

The third, fourth, and fifth paragraphs of this essay contrast the use of pronunciation and inflection under the different circumstances. The essay cites many idiosyncrasies that would be used in talking with friends, and explains how pronouncing such phrases as "whazup" imply a certain amount of casualness and informality. The essay contrasts this by saying that it would be proper to use common pronunciation and inflection during a job interview, and provides examples of such pronunciation and inflection, as well as describing why it would be employed.

The final paragraph of this essay returns to its central thesis, clearly stating the reasons why one would use language in different ways in different circumstances, casual and informal when talking with friends to reflect a laid-back attitude, but formal and conventional during a job interview to express intelligence and respect.

AP
English Language & Composition

Practice Test II

AP Examination in English Language & Composition

Test II

Section 1

TIME: 60 Minutes
        60 Questions

(Answer sheets appear in the back of this book.)

DIRECTIONS: Rephrase each of the following sentences according to the directions given, and choose the response that best corresponds to the necessary changes to the original sentence. Keep the meaning of the new sentence as close to the original as possible, maintaining natural phrasing, the requirements of standard written English, and logical and concise construction.

---

1. "My term paper will analyze and evaluate Prohibition in terms of its ambitions, not the universally regretted outcome," said the student.
    Begin with <u>The student said that</u>.

    (A)   my term paper will have

    (B)   his term paper had

    (C)   his term paper would

    (D)   his term paper has

    (E)   the term paper were to have

2. The actor's reknown as the comic inspector obscures the respect he deserves for his earlier film career as a debonair romantic lead.
    Begin with <u>The actor is best known</u>.

    (A)   inspector, be he

    (B)   inspector, and so

    (C)   inspector, while obscuring

(D) inspector; obscuring

(E) inspector, but while

3. Should solar-powered automobiles become functionally and economically competitive with cars that burn fossil fuel, the entire gasoline industry would shut down, from refineries to local pumps.
Begin with If solar-powered automobiles become.

(A) should shut down

(B) will shut down

(C) will have shut down

(D) will result in the shut down

(E) shutting down would be

4. Most children ultimately fail to attain the idealized goals set for them by their vicariously ambitious parents.
Begin with Few children.

(A) will attain   (D) attain much

(B) attain   (E) attaining

(C) fail not to attain

5. The city's largest park is known as "Our Most Visible Public Disgrace"; it is a showcase for vandalism, prostitution, and drug commerce.
Begin with The label "Our Most…" adorns.

(A) park, a showcase   (D) park, the showcase is

(B) parks to be a showcase   (E) park as a showcase

(C) park, and a showcase

6. Haley's supposedly accidental encounter with Jim pushed him back into his tailspin.
Change pushed to but it pushed.

(A) encounter, and it was supposed

(B) encounter which was supposed

(C) encounter was supposedly

(D) encounter, supposedly

(E) encounter, despite the supposed

7. The perception of public officials by American citizens as dishonest and self-serving is fueled by government inefficiency and genuine ineptitude in fund allocations.
    Change <u>is fueled</u> to <u>fuel</u>.

    (A) perceptive   (D) citizens' perceptions

    (B) perceiving   (E) is perceived

    (C) and perceiving

8. The line stretched dauntingly around the building and meandered wearily along its length.
    Omit <u>and</u>.

    (A) which meandered   (D) which meandering

    (B) having meandered   (E) while meandering

    (C) meandering

9. The hikers were condemned to a slow death when the avalanche obliterated the trails linking them to civilization.
    Begin with <u>The avalanche</u>.

    (A) condemns   (D) for the hikers

    (B) condemned the hikers   (E) the hikers' slow death

    (C) of the hikers

10. The afternoon seemed to stretch endlessly, despite the wonderful time everyone was having.
    Begin with <u>Everyone was having</u>.

    (A) despite the afternoon   (D) yet stretched

    (B) despite stretching   (E) seemingly endless

    (C) yet the afternoon

11. "Our cross-country trek brought us into contact with many relatives whom we rarely see," mentioned Paul.
    Begin with <u>Paul mentioned that</u>.

    (A) would bring them

    (B) had brought them

    (C) would have brought them

    (D) brought them

    (E) brought us

12. The director strove single-mindedly to pack the house over the week of repeat performances by using sensationalistic gimmicks, rather than pursuing such goals as the actors' realizations of their roles or the wardrobe's thematic continuity.
Begin with <u>Such goals as</u>.

    (A) the director, striving

    (B) the director striving

    (C) the director, who strove

    (D) the director, who instead strove

    (E) pursued, the director

13. Should America convert to government revenue collection based solely on income tax, the simplification of budget calculation would boggle the mind of every politician.
Begin with <u>If America converts</u>.

    (A) should boggle   (D) will result in the boggling

    (B) will boggle   (E) boggling would be

    (C) will have boggled

14. Most of a guppy's numerous offspring cannot be expected to achieve maturity.
Begin with <u>Few of</u>.

    (A) can achieve   (D) can be expected

    (B) can expect or achieve   (E) expect much

    (C) expect maturity

15. The family doctor's gruff, apparently undeliberated diagnosis proved correct after several months of visits to various contradicting specialists.
Change <u>proved</u> to <u>but it proved</u>.

    (A) diagnosis, and it was

    (B) diagnosis was

    (C) diagnosis which was

    (D) diagnosis, apparently

    (E) diagnosis, although apparently

DIRECTIONS: This section of the test consists of selections from literary works and questions on their use of language. After reading each passage or poem, choose the best answer to each question and blacken the corresponding oval on the answer sheet.

Questions 16–32 are based on the following passage. Read the passage carefully before choosing your answers.

A   "Is this the end?

B   O Life, as futile, then, as frail!

C   What hope of answer or redress?"

A cloudy day: do you know what that is in a town of iron-works? The sky sank down before dawn, muddy, flat, immoveable. The air is thick, clammy with the breath of crowded human beings. It stifles me. I open the window, and, looking out, can scarcely see through the rain the grocer's shop opposite,
5   where a crowd of drunken Irishmen are puffing Lynchburg tobacco in their pipes. I can detect the scent through all the foul smells ranging loose in the air.

The idiosyncrasy of this town is smoke. It rolls sullenly in slow folds from the great chimneys of the iron-foundries, and settles down in black, slimy pools on the muddy streets. Smoke on the wharves, smoke on the dingy boats,
10 on the yellow river,—clinging in a coating of greasy soot to the house-front, the two faded poplars, the faces of the passersby. The long train of mules, dragging masses of pig-iron through the narrow street, have a foul vapor hanging to their reeking sides. Here, inside, is a little broken figure of an angel pointing upward from the mantel-shelf; but even its wings are covered with
15 smoke, clotted and black. Smoke everywhere! A dirty canary chirps desolately in a cage beside me. Its dream of green fields and sunshine is a very old dream,—almost worn out, I think.

From the back-window I can see a narrow brick-yard sloping down to the river-side, strewed with rain-butts and tubs. The river, dull and tawny-colored,
20 (*la belle rivière!*) drags itself sluggishly along, tired of the heavy weight of boats and coal-barges. What wonder? When I was a child, I used to fancy a look of

weary, dumb appeal upon the face of the negro-like river slavishly bearing its burden day after day. Something of the same idle notion comes to me to-day, when from the street-window I look on the slow stream of human life creeping

25 past, night and morning, to the great mills. Masses of men, with dull, besotted faces bent to the ground, sharpened here and there by pain or cunning; skin and muscle and flesh begrimed with smoke and ashes; stooping all night over boiling caldrons of metal, laired by day in dens of drunkenness and infamy; breathing from infancy to death an air saturated with fog and grease and soot,

30 vileness for soul and body. What do you make of a case like that, amateur psychologist? You call it an altogether serious thing to be alive: to these men it is a drunken jest, a joke,—horrible to angels perhaps, to them commonplace enough. My fancy about the river was an idle one: it is no type of such a life. What if it be stagnant and slimy here? It knows that beyond there waits for it

35 odorous sunlight,—quaint old gardens, dusky with soft, green foliage of apple-trees, and flushing crimson with roses,—air, and fields, and mountains. The future of the Welsh puddler passing just now is not so pleasant. To be stowed away, after his grimy work is done, in a hole in the muddy graveyard, and after that,—*not* air, nor green fields, nor curious roses.

40 Can you see how foggy the day is? As I stand here, idly tapping the window-pane, and looking out through the rain at the dirty back-yard and the coalboats below, fragments of an old story float up before me,—a story of this old house into which I happened to come to-day. You may think it is a tiresome story enough, as foggy as the day, sharpened by no sudden flashes of pain or plea-

45 sure.—I know: only the outline of a dull life, that long since, with thousands of dull lives like its own, was vainly lived and lost: thousands of them,—massed, vile, slimy lives, like those of the torpid lizards in yonder stagnant water-butt.— Lost? There is a curious point for you to settle, my friend, who study psychology in a lazy, *dilettante* way. Stop a moment. I am going to be honest. This is what I

50 want you to do. I want you to hide your disgust, take no heed to your clean clothes, and come right down with me,—here, into the thickest of the fog and mud and foul effluvia. I want you to hear this story. There is a secret down here, in this nightmare fog, that has lain dumb for centuries: I want to make it a real thing to you. You, Egoist, Pantheist, or Arminian, busy in making straight paths

55 for your feet on the hills, do not see it clearly,—this terrible question which men here have gone mad and died trying to answer. I dare not put this secret into words. I told you it was dumb. These men, going by with drunken faces and brains full of unawakened power, do not ask it of Society or of God. Their lives

ask it; their deaths ask it. There is no reply. I will tell you plainly that I have a
60 great hope; and I bring it to you to be tested. It is this: that this terrible dumb
question is its own reply; that it is not the sentence of death we think it, but,
from the very extremity of its darkness, the most solemn prophecy which the
world has known of the Hope to come. I dare make my meaning no clearer, but
will only tell my story. It will, perhaps, seem to you as foul and dark as this thick
65 vapor about us, and as pregnant with death; but if your eyes are free as mine are
to look deeper, no perfume-tinted dawn will be so fair with promise of the day
that shall surely come.

16. What is the function of the epigraph that opens the passage?

(A) It makes it clear that the passage which follows is a retrospective of the
speaker's life.

(B) It establishes a mood of despair and hopelessness.

(C) It lends authority to the speaker's work by quoting another writer.

(D) It sets the scene as that of a preapocalyptic society.

(E) It comments critically upon the speaker's work.

17. The opening sentence of the passage (line 1) does all of the following EX-
CEPT

(A) draw the reader into the passage.

(B) directly address the reader.

(C) challenge the reader's knowledge and experience.

(D) reveal to the reader the speaker's lack of knowledge about her subject
matter.

(E) imply that the reader belongs to a different world than that being
described here.

18. It can be inferred that "Lynchburg tobacco" (line 5) is

(A) the preferred brand of Irishmen.

(B) detrimental to its smokers' health.

(C) a particularly inferior brand.

(D) obtainable at the "grocer's shop" (line 4).

(E) a scent pleasing to the speaker.

19. The sentence "Smoke...passersby" (lines 9–11) contains which of the following?

    (A) An ellipsis   (D) Alliteration

    (B) A metaphor   (E) Abstract imagery

    (C) Metonymy

20. Which of the following best describes what the "little broken figure of an angel" (line 13) represents?

    (A) The poverty that extends even into the homes of the inhabitants of the ironworks town

    (B) The irreverence that prevails in the speaker's home

    (C) The smoke that invades every aspect of ironworks town life

    (D) The grime of ironworks town life that weighs down even dreams of an afterlife

    (E) The sincere piety of the speaker

21. The aside "(*la belle rivière*)" (line 20) can best be interpreted as

    (A) an ironical description.

    (B) a nostalgic memory.

    (C) a pedantic display of the speaker's education.

    (D) a humorous comment.

    (E) a redundant characterization.

22. A "dirty canary" (line 15) with its "dream of green fields and sunshine" (line 16) and the river that "drags itself sluggishly along, tired of the heavy weight of boats and coal-barges" (lines 20–21) are examples of

    (A) metaphor.   (D) hyperbole.

    (B) personification.   (E) assonance.

    (C) oxymoron.

23. The expository technique of the third paragraph (lines 18–39) is best described as

    (A) cause and effect.   (D) question and answer.

    (B) chronological order.   (E) comparison/contrast.

    (C) classification.

24. The relationship between the rivers and men (paragraph 3)

    I.   crosses the characteristics of water and humans.

    II.   comparatively implies that the town's workers are slaves.

    III.   gives superior status to the river.

    IV.   dehumanizes the worker.

    (A)   I only   (D)   II, III, and IV only

    (B)   II and III only   (E)   I, II, III, and IV

    (C)   III only

25. The speaker assumes that the reader's attitude toward the ironworks laborer is one of

    (A)   sympathy.   (D)   antipathy.

    (B)   defensiveness.   (E)   ignorance.

    (C)   clinical observation.

26. A "Welsh puddler" (line 37) is most probably

    (A)   a grave digger.   (D)   a street cleaner.

    (B)   an ironworks employee.   (E)   a bartender.

    (C)   a hand on a coal barge.

27. In line 36, "air, and fields, and mountains" parallel yet contrast with

    (A)   "fog and grease and soot" (line 29).

    (B)   "skin and muscle and flesh" (lines 26–27).

    (C)   "soul and body" (line 30).

    (D)   "*not* air, nor green fields, nor curious roses" (line 39).

    (E)   "quaint old gardens, dusky with soft, green foliage of apple-trees, and flushing crimson with roses" (lines 35–36).

28. The antecedent of "it" (line 53) is

    (A)   "this nightmare fog" (line 53).

    (B)   "this story" (line 52).

    (C)   the "foul effluvia" (line 52).

    (D)   the "secret down here" (line 52).

    (E)   "this terrible question" (line 55).

29. Considering the passage as a whole, the "terrible question which men here have gone mad and died trying to answer" (lines 55–56) can best be identified as:

(A) How can the life of the ironworks town laborer be bettered?

(B) What is the meaning of life?

(C) How can the pollution from the ironworks be lessened?

(D) What is the responsibility of the upper to the lower classes?

(E) Why are the workers Western Europeans?

30. The speaker's characterization of the reader as "Egoist, Pantheist, or Arminian, busy in making straight paths for [his/her] feet on the hills, [does] not see it clearly" (lines 54–55) implies that

(A) the reader, absorbed in ordering his/her own life according to various doctrines, cannot fully comprehend the struggle for meaning in life.

(B) the reader is a landowner making civic improvements without regard to the concerns of ironworks town inhabitants.

(C) the reader seeks meaning in a materialistic existence.

(D) the reader, relying on psychology and its terminology, would scientifically order life.

(E) as a foreigner, the reader is only briefly and dispassionately trekking through the ironworks town.

31. It can be inferred that the speaker believes that

(A) human existence is pointless.

(B) social reform is imminent.

(C) afterlife is the ultimate hope.

(D) men live more desperate lives than women.

(E) educated persons experience life differently than factory workers.

32. The speaker's story is most probably

(A) a bitter life lived without redress.

(B) an example of a terrible life ending with an anticipated unearthly reward.

(C) a retelling of his/her own life in the ironworks town.

(D) a futuristic tale of life to come in the ironworks town.

(E) a fantasy transporting the pampered reader into the ironworks employee's role.

Questions 33–45 are based on the following passage. Read the passage carefully before choosing your answers.

I then inquired for the person that belonged to the petticoat; and, to my great surprise, was directed to a very beautiful young damsel, with so pretty a face and shape, that I bid her come out of the crowd, and seated her upon a little crock at my left hand. "My pretty maid," said I, "do you own yourself to
5 have been the inhabitant of the garment before us?" The girl I found had good sense, and told me with a smile, "That notwithstanding it was her own petticoat, she should be very glad to see an example made of it; and that she wore it for no other reason, but that she had a mind to look as big and burly as other persons of her quality; that she had kept out of it as long as she could, and till
10 she began to appear little in the eyes of all her acquaintance; that if she laid it aside, people would think she was not made like other women." I always give great allowances to the fair sex upon account of the fashion, and therefore was not displeased with the defense of the pretty criminal. I then ordered the vest, which stood before us to be drawn up by a pulley to the top of my great hall,
15 and afterwards to be spread open by the engine it was placed upon, in such a manner, that it formed a very splendid and ample canopy over our heads, and covered the whole court of judicature with a kind of silken rotunda, in its form not unlike the cupola of St. Paul's. I entered upon the whole cause with great satisfaction, as I sat under the shadow of it.

20 The counsel for the petticoat was now called in, and ordered to produce what they had to say against the popular cry which was raised against it. They answered the objections with great strength and solidity of argument, and expatiated in very florid harangues, which they did not fail to set off and furbelow (if I may be allowed the metaphor) with many periodical sentences
25 and turns of oratory. The chief arguments for their client were taken, first, from the great benefit that might arise to our woolen manufactory from this invention, which was calculated as follows: the common petticoat has not above four yards in the circumference; whereas this over our heads had more in the semidiameter; so that by allowing it twenty-four yards in the circumfer-
30 ence, the five millions of woolen petticoats, which (according to Sir William Petty) supposing what ought to be supposed in a well-governed state, that all petticoats are make of that stuff, would amount to thirty millions of those of the ancient mode. A prodigious improvement of the woolen trade! and what could not fail to sink the power of France in a few years.

35 To introduce the second argument, they begged leave to read a petition of the rope-makers, wherein it was represented, that the demand for cords, and the price of them, were much risen since this fashion came up. At this, all the company who were present lifted up their eyes into the vault; and I must confess, we did discover many traces of cordage which were interwoven in the
40 stiffening of the drapery.

A third argument was rounded upon a petition of the Greenland trade, which likewise represented the great consumption of whalebone which would be occasioned by the present fashion, and the benefit which would thereby accrue to that branch of the British trade.

45 To conclude, they gently touched upon the weight and unwieldiness of the garment, which they insinuated might be of great use to preserve the honor of families.

These arguments would have wrought very much upon me (as I then told the company in a long and elaborate discourse), had I not considered the great
50 and additional expense which such fashions would bring upon fathers and husbands; and therefore by no means to be thought of till some years after a peace. I further urged, that it would be a prejudice to the ladies themselves, who could never expect to have any money in the pocket, if they laid out so much on the petticoat. To this I added, the great temptation it might give to
55 virgins, of acting in security like married women, and by that means give a check to matrimony, an institution always encouraged by wise societies.

33. The argument takes the form of

(A) a question and answer session.

(B) a trial.

(C) a confession.

(D) a sermon.

(E) a debate.

34. The girl "began to appear little in the eyes of all her acquaintance" (line 10)

(A) in girth and social standing.

(B) in size and wealth.

(C) in body and mind.

(D)   in waist and undergarment.

(E)   in weight and education.

35.   The girl's statement in lines 6–11 can best be interpreted as

(A)   the actions of a slave to fashion.

(B)   the scheme of a social climber.

(C)   the tricks of an underweight woman.

(D)   the response of a sensible woman pressured by social dictates.

(E)   the rantings of a condemned woman.

36.   The "vest" of line 13 is

(A)   a garment.   (D)   a jacket.

(B)   a petticoat.   (E)   a robe.

(C)   an umbrella.

37.   All of the following are present in the sentence in lines 13–18 EXCEPT

(A)   hyperbole.   (D)   metaphor.

(B)   simile.   (E)   humor.

(C)   oxymoron.

38.   The description of the argument of the counsel for the petticoat (lines 21–25) parallels

(A)   the petticoat itself.

(B)   the formality of the inquiry.

(C)   the complexity of the woolen industry.

(D)   the "power of France" (line 34).

(E)   the good sense of the owner of the petticoat.

39.   The observation that the production of large petticoats "could not fail to sink the power of France in a few years" (line 34) is

(A)   an understatement of the might of fashion.

(B)   a hyperbolic statement.

(C)   a declaration of war.

(D)   an economic statistic.

(E)   an egotistical boast.

40.   The "petition of the Greenland trade" (line 41) was most likely issued from

(A)   petticoat makers.   (D)   whalers.

(B)   carvers.   (E)   shipowners.

(C)   merchants.

41.   Why would petticoats, such as the one being examined in the passage, "be of great use to preserve the honor of families" (lines 46–47)?

(A)   Ladies would be able to dress as fashion demands women of their station should.

(B)   Families would exhibit their wealth through their clothing.

(C)   A bulky petticoat could not be easily removed during illicit love affairs.

(D)   The size of the petticoat would prevent young ladies from being kidnapped.

(E)   Demeaning small places could not be entered by ladies wearing large petticoats.

42.   The final point of the speaker's judgment against the petticoat (lines 54–56)

(A)   assents to the concluding point of the counsels' argument.

(B)   turns the concluding point of the counsels' argument against itself.

(C)   opposes the concluding point of the counsels' argument.

(D)   is not linked to the concluding point of the counsels' argument.

(E)   is weakened by the concluding point of the counsels' argument.

43.   Who/what can best be identified as the passage's criminal?

(A)   The girl who owned the petticoat

(B)   Society

(C)   Fashion

(D)   "Persons of her quality" (line 9)

(E)   The petticoat

44. Both the defense of the petticoat and the speaker's reply are primarily structured as

    (A) appeals to authority.   (D) patriotic arguments.

    (B) appeals to emotion.   (E) ethical appeals.

    (C) economic appeals.

45. The style of the passage taken as a whole can best be described as

    (A) gently satiric.   (D) colloquially informal.

    (B) bitterly ironic.   (E) pedantically formal.

    (C) wryly humorous.

Questions 46–51 are based on the following passage. Read the passage carefully before choosing your answers.

We laymen have always been intensely curious to know—like the cardinal who put a similar question to Ariosto—from what sources that strange being, the creative writer, draws his material, and how he manages to make such an impression on us with it and to arouse in us emotions of which, perhaps, we
5 had not even thought ourselves capable. Our interest is only heightened the more by the fact that, if we ask him, the writer himself gives us no explanation, or none that is satisfactory; and it is not at all weakened by our knowledge that not even the clearest insight into the determinants of his choice of material and into the nature of the art of creating imaginative form will ever help to make
10 creative writers of *us*.

If we could at least discover in ourselves or in people like ourselves an activity which was in some way akin to creative writing! An examination of it would then give us a hope of obtaining the beginnings of an explanation of the creative work of writers. And, indeed, there is some prospect of this being
15 possible. After all, creative writers themselves like to lessen the distance between their kind and the common run of humanity; they so often assure us that every man is a poet at heart and that the last poet will not perish till the last man does.

Should we not look for the first traces of imaginative activity as early as in
20 childhood? The child's best-loved and most intense occupation is with his play or games. Might we not say that every child at play behaves like a creative writer, in that he creates a world of his own, or, rather, rearranges

the things of his world in a new way which pleases him? It would be wrong
to think he does not take that world seriously; on the contrary, he takes play
25 very seriously and he expends large amounts of emotion on it. The opposite
of play is not what is serious but what is real. In spite of all the emotion with
which he cathects his world of play, the child distinguishes it quite well from
reality; and he likes to link his imagined objects and situations to the tangible and visible things of the real world. This linking is all that differentiates
30 the child's "play" from "fantasying."

46. What is the effect of the speaker's use of "we"?

   (A) It separates the speaker and his/her colleagues from the reader.

   (B) It involves the reader in the search for, yet distinguishes him/her from,
        the creative writer.

   (C) It creates a royal and authoritative persona for the speaker.

   (D) It makes the speaker the stand-in for all men.

   (E) It unites speaker, reader, and creative writer.

47. What is the antecedent of "it" (line 7)?

   (A) "explanation" (line 6)   (D) "impression" (line 4)

   (B) "fact" (line 6)   (E) "insight" (line 8)

   (C) "interest" (line 5)

48. Which of the following statements would the speaker be most likely to DIS-
     AGREE with?

   (A) A layperson cannot become a creative writer by studying the writer's
        methods.

   (B) All men are writers at heart.

   (C) Creative writers are fundamentally different from nonwriters.

   (D) Children understand the distinction between imagination and reality.

   (E) The creative writer at work mirrors the child in play.

49. "Cathects" (line 27) can best be defined as

   (A) constructs.   (D) discourages.

   (B) distances.   (E) destroys.

   (C) fantasizes.

50. The structure of the passage can best be described as

    (A) an initial paragraph that introduces an idea and two paragraphs that digress from that idea.

    (B) a series of paragraphs that answer the questions with which they begin.

    (C) a series of questions ascending in their inability to be answered.

    (D) paragraphs whose length or brevity parallel their depth or narrowness of inquiry.

    (E) sentences that grow in structural complexity.

51. It can be inferred that the speaker believes that creative writing is

    (A) an opposite of childhood play.

    (B) unrelated to childhood play.

    (C) a continuation of childhood play.

    (D) the destiny of every man due to his play as a child.

    (E) similar to the fantasizing of childhood play.

Questions 52–60 are based on the following passage. Read the passage carefully before choosing your answers.

In failing thus to state plainly and unequivocally the legitimate demands of their people, even at the cost of opposing an honored leader, the thinking classes of American Negroes would shirk a heavy responsibility,—a responsibility to themselves, a responsibility to the struggling masses, a responsibility
5 to the darker races of men whose future depends so largely on this American experiment, but especially a responsibility to this nation,—this common Fatherland. It is wrong to encourage a man or a people in evil-doing; it is wrong to aid and abet a national crime simply because it is unpopular not to do so. The growing spirit of kindliness and reconciliation between the North
10 and South after the frightful differences of a generation ago ought to be a source of deep congratulation to all, and especially to those whose mistreatment caused the war, but if that reconciliation is to be marked by the industrial slavery and civic death of those same black men, with permanent legislation into a position of inferiority, then those black men, if they are
15 really men, are called upon by every consideration of patriotism and loyalty to oppose such a course by all civilized methods, even though such opposition involves disagreement with Mr. Booker T. Washington. We have no

right to sit silently by while the inevitable seeds are sown for a harvest of disaster to our children, black and white.

20   First, it is the duty of black men to judge the South discriminatingly. The present generation of Southerners are not responsible for the past, and they should not be blindly hated or blamed for it. Furthermore, to no class is the indiscriminate endorsement of the recent course of the South toward Negroes more nauseating than to the best thought of the South. The South is not
25   "solid"; it is a land in the ferment of social change, wherein forces of all kinds are fighting for supremacy; and to praise the ill the South is to-day perpetrating is just as wrong, as to condemn the good. Discriminating and broadminded criticism is what the South needs,—needs it for the sake of her own white sons and daughters, and for the insurance of robust, healthy mental and
30   moral development.

To-day even the attitude of the Southern whites toward the blacks is not, as so many assume, in all cases the same; the ignorant Southerner hates the Negro, the workingmen fear his competition, the money-makers wish to use him as a laborer, some of the educated see a menace in his upward de-
35   velopment, while others—usually the sons of the masters—wish to help him to rise. National opinion has enabled this last class to maintain the Negro common schools, and to protect the Negro partially in property, life, and limb. Through the pressure of the money-makers, the Negro is in danger of being reduced to semi-slavery, especially in the country districts; the work-
40   ingmen, and those of the educated who fear the Negro, have united to disfranchise him, and some have urged his deportation; while the passions of the ignorant are easily aroused to lynch and abuse any black man. To praise this intricate whirl of thought and prejudice is nonsense; to inveigh indiscriminately against the South is unjust; but to use the same breath in prais-
45   ing Governor Aycock, exposing Senator Morgan, arguing with Mr. Thomas Nelson Page, and denouncing Senator Ben Tillman, is not only sane, but the imperative duty of thinking black men.

It would be unjust to Mr. Washington not to acknowledge that in several instances he has opposed movements in the South which were unjust to the
50   Negro; he sent memorials to the Louisiana and Alabama constitutional conventions, he has spoken against lynching, and in other ways has openly or silently set his influence against sinister schemes and unfortunate happenings. Notwithstanding this, it is equally true to assert that on the whole the distinct

impression left by Mr. Washington's propaganda is, first, that the South is
55 justified in its present attitude toward the Negro because of the Negro's degradation; secondly, that the prime cause of the Negro's failure to rise more
quickly is his wrong education in the past; and, thirdly, that his future rise
depends primarily on his own efforts. Each of these propositions is a dangerous
half-truth. The supplementary truths must never be lost sight of: first, slavery
60 and race-prejudice are potent if not sufficient causes of the Negro's position;
second, industrial and common-school training were necessarily slow in plant-
ing because they had to await the black teachers trained by higher institu-
tions,—it being extremely doubtful if any essentially different development
was possible, and certainly a Tuskegee was unthinkable before 1880; and,
65 third, while it is a great truth to say that the Negro must strive and strive
mightily to help himself, it is equally true that unless his striving be not simply
seconded, but rather aroused and encouraged, by the initiative of the richer
and wiser environing group, he cannot hope for great success.

52. Which of the following phrases contains examples of euphemism and understatement?

   (A) "[T]he thinking classes of American Negroes would shirk a heavy re-
        sponsibility,—a responsibility to themselves, a responsibility to the strug-
        gling masses, a responsibility to the darker races of men whose future
        depends so largely on this American experiment" (lines 2–6).

   (B) "The growing spirit of kindliness and reconciliation between the North
        and South after the frightful differences of a generation ago ought to be
        a source of deep congratulation to all, and especially to those whose
        mistreatment caused the war" (lines 9–12).

   (C) "The present generation of Southerners are not responsible for the past,
        and they should not be blindly hated or blamed for it" (lines 20–22).

   (D) "The South is not 'solid'; it is a land in the ferment of social change,
        wherein forces of all kinds are fighting for supremacy" (lines 24–26).

   (E) "[S]lavery and race-prejudice are potent if not sufficient causes of the
        Negro's position" (lines 59–60).

53. The terms "industrial slavery and civic death" (line 13)

   I.   condemn the potential postwar status of blacks.

   II. echo the prewar condition of blacks.

   III. contradict the "spirit of kindliness and reconciliation" (line 9).

IV. define the "position of inferiority" (line 14) that may be brought about by law.

(A) I only

(D) I, II, and III only

(B) I and II only

(E) I, II, III, and IV

(C) III and IV only

54. The creation and result of a state of inequality between blacks and whites are summarily described using

(A) legalistic jargon.

(B) a dichotomy between South and North.

(C) a simile likening this state to bondage.

(D) an agricultural metaphor.

(E) personification.

55. In the first sentence of the passage (lines 1–7), "themselves" (line 4) parallels all of the following EXCEPT

(A) "the struggling masses" (line 4).

(B) "the darker races of men" (line 5).

(C) "this American experiment" (lines 5–6).

(D) "this nation" (line 6).

(E) "this common Fatherland" (lines 6–7).

56. Structurally, the relationship between the second and third sentences of paragraph three (lines 36–43) and the first (lines 31–35) can best be described as

(A) a linear progression of ideas. (D) a parallel series of ideas.

(B) an inversion of ideas. (E) a jumbled flow of ideas.

(C) a repetition of ideas.

57. It can be inferred that the persons named in the last sentence of the third paragraph (lines 42–47) are

(A) one supporter and three opponents of political and social empowerment for blacks.

(B) one governor, two senators, and a businessman.

(C) politicians united in their attempts to disenfranchise blacks.

(D)   one black and three white politicians.

(E)   the "ignorant Southerners" of lines 32 and 42.

58.   What is the effect of "propaganda" in line 54?

(A)   It clarifies Mr. Washington's ideas.

(B)   It politicizes Mr. Washington's ideas.

(C)   It broadcasts Mr. Washington's ideas.

(D)   It derides Mr. Washington's ideas.

(E)   It praises Mr. Washington's ideas.

59.   Rhetorically, the final paragraph is structured as

(A)   an argument and its summation.

(B)   a defense and an attack.

(C)   an opposing argument and a rebuttal.

(D)   a prosecution and a defense.

(E)   a eulogy and an excoriation.

60.   The passage's purpose can be characterized as

(A)   eulogistic.   (D)   expository.

(B)   exhortative.   (E)   satiric.

(C)   judicial.

Section 2

TIME: 1 Hour and 45 Minutes
3 Essay Questions

Question 1 (Suggested time—35 minutes.) This question is one-third of the total essay score.

Our perceptions of the world around us are influenced by our feelings and conditions in life. Imagine that you are looking out of a window. Describe the view from this window at two different times, employing vivid descriptive detail to make clear the differences in your states of mind.

CONTINUE TO QUESTION 2

Question 2 (Suggested time—35 minutes.) This question is one-third of the total essay score.

The naturalist and explorer John Muir has left us a journal of his life and thoughts that is brimming with insight and brilliance. Analyze the following passage for its diction, tone, and syntax. How are these elements well suited to the theme of this passage?

There is love of wild nature in everybody, an ancient mother-love ever showing itself whether recognized or no, and however covered by cares and duties.

In God's wildness lies the hope of the world—the great fresh unblighted, unredeemed wilderness. The galling harness of civilization drops off, and the wounds heal ere we are aware.

I am often asked if I am not lonesome on my solitary excursions. It seems so self-evident that one cannot be lonesome where everything is wild and beautiful and busy and steeped with God that the question is hard to answer—seems silly.

In the mountains, free, unimpeded, the imagination feeds on objects immense and eternal.

To the Indian mind all nature was instinct with deity. A spirit was embodied in every mountain, stream, and waterfall.

—From *John of the Mountains: The Unpublished Journals of John Muir.* Ed. Linnie Marsh Wolfe.

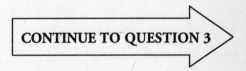

CONTINUE TO QUESTION 3

Question 3 (Suggested time—35 minutes.) This question is one-third of the total essay score.

Analyze the following passage from Thoreau's *Walden*. How does the diarist craft his description so that it not only explores symbols of rebirth, but supports the description by the use of effective elements of style, sound, and syntax as well? How is form related to content in Thoreau's passage, entitled "The Green Blade"?

The brooks sing carols and glees to the spring. The marsh hawk, sailing low over the meadow, is already seeking the first slimy life that awakes. The sinking sound of melting snow is heard in all dells, and ice dissolves apace in the ponds. The grass flames up on the hillsides like a spring fire, as if the earth sent forth an inward heat to greet the returning sun; not yellow but green is the color of its flame. The symbol of perpetual youth, the grass-blade, like a long green ribbon, streams from the sod, checked indeed by the frost, but anon pushing on again, lifting its spear of last year's hay with the fresh life below. It grows as steadily as the rill oozes out of the ground. It is almost identical with that, for in the growing days of June, when the rills are dry, the grass blades are their channels, and from year to year the herds drink at this perennial green stream and the mower draws from it betimes their winter supply. So our human life but dies down to its root, and still puts forth its green blade to eternity.

—From *Walden, "The Green Blade."*

EXAM IS FINISHED

AP Examination in English Language & Composition

TEST II

ANSWER KEY

Section 1

1.	(C)	21.	(A)	41.	(C)
2.	(A)	22.	(B)	42.	(B)
3.	(B)	23.	(E)	43.	(E)
4.	(B)	24.	(E)	44.	(C)
5.	(A)	25.	(C)	45.	(A)
6.	(C)	26.	(B)	46.	(B)
7.	(D)	27.	(D)	47.	(C)
8.	(C)	28.	(D)	48.	(B)
9.	(B)	29.	(B)	49.	(A)
10.	(C)	30.	(A)	50.	(B)
11.	(B)	31.	(C)	51.	(C)
12.	(D)	32.	(B)	52.	(B)
13.	(B)	33.	(B)	53.	(E)
14.	(D)	34.	(A)	54.	(D)
15.	(B)	35.	(D)	55.	(C)
16.	(B)	36.	(B)	56.	(B)
17.	(D)	37.	(C)	57.	(A)
18.	(C)	38.	(A)	58.	(D)
19.	(A)	39.	(B)	59.	(C)
20.	(D)	40.	(D)	60.	(B)

Detailed Explanations of Answers

Test II

Section 1

1. **(C)** The rephrased sentence reads: **The student said that his term paper would analyze and evaluate Prohibition in terms of its ambitions, not the universally regretted outcome.** (C) is the correct answer because "he would" is the third-person equivalent of "I will" in reference to an uncertain future action. (A) is incorrect because "that" cannot introduce a quotation and therefore "my" is inappropriate. (B) is incorrect because the past tense is inappropriate. (D) is incorrect because the present tense in inappropriate. (E) is incorrect because it is hopelessly wordy and probably inaccurate.

2. **(A)** The rephrased sentence reads: **The actor is best known as the comic inspector, but he deserves respect for his earlier film career as a debonair romantic lead.** (A) is the correct answer because the sentence will be more fluid with a compound complex structure. (B) is incorrect because "and" undermines the contradiction inherent in the original sentence. (C) is incorrect because "while" refers back to "reknown," which is no longer in the sentence. (D) is incorrect because a semicolon is an inappropriate separation of an apparently dependent clause. (E) is incorrect because "but" and "while" do not work together.

3. **(B)** The rephrased sentence reads: **If solar-powered automobiles become functionally and economically competitive with cars that burn fossil fuel, the entire gasoline industry will shut down, from refineries to local pumps.** (B) is the correct answer because should-would becomes if-will. (A) is incorrect because this is temporal logic, not moral logic. (C) is incorrect because "will have" is a different temporal tense. (D) is incorrect because it is too wordy compared with option (B). (E) is incorrect because it implies a possibility but not the certainty of the original.

4. **(B)** The rephrased sentence reads: **Few children attain the idealized goals set for them by their parents.** (B) is the correct answer because it is the opposite of "fail to attain" while being consistent in its tense. (A) is incorrect because "will" limits the original meaning to future goals, omitting past goals and parents. (C) is incorrect because it is wordy and ornate. (D) is incorrect because "much" exaggerates the original

meaning. (E) is incorrect because "-ing" prevents "attain" from being the main verb of the sentence.

5. **(A)** The rephrased sentence reads: **The label "Our Most Visible Public Disgrace" adorns the city's largest park, a showcase for vandalism, prostitution, and drug commerce.** (A) is the correct answer because it successfully replaces the linking verb equality of the original sentence with an appositive. Also, appositives are often the most handy way to employ a metaphor. (B) is incorrect because the infinitive "to be" in this context needs to be activated by a verb like "causes" or "forces." The verb "adorns" does not serve this function. (C) is incorrect because "and" sets up a parallel structure requiring "showcase" to be in an independent clause. No verb is provided for such a new clause. (D) is incorrect because "showcase is" is a literal treatment of what is meant to be a metaphor. The word "is" also begins a new independent clause making the sentence a run-on. (E) is incorrect because, through the metaphor, the park is a showcase, not "in a showcase."

6. **(C)** The rephrased sentence reads: **Haley's encounter was supposedly accidental, but it pushed Jim back into his tailspin.** (C) is the correct answer because it is the only sentence to put "encounter" in the subject; "but it pushed" absolutely requires a new independent clause to precede it. (A) is incorrect because "encounter" ends the first clause and therefore cannot be the subject. (B) is incorrect because it separates "encounter" from the verb it needs to be the subject ("supposed") with "which," a word that introduces a dependent clause. (D) is incorrect because "supposedly" is an adverb when the clause requires "supposed" as a verb. (E) is incorrect because, like (B), "encounter" is separated from "supposed" by a word that introduces a dependent clause, "despite."

7. **(D)** The rephrased sentence reads: **Government inefficiency and genuine ineptitude in fund allocations fuel citizen's perceptions of public officials as dishonest and self-serving.** (D) is the correct answer because only (D) retains "perception" as a noun; "fuel" needs a noun as a direct object, namely the same one that was the subject of "is fueled" in the original sentence. This is a passive to active conversion. (A) is incorrect because "perceptive" is an adjective. (B) is incorrect because "perceiving" is a verb. (C) is incorrect because "and" is an unnecessary conjunction. (E) is incorrect because "perceived" is in the past tense.

8. **(C)** The rephrased sentence reads: **The line stretched dauntingly around the building, meandering wearily along its length.** (C) is the correct answer because it introduces a successful dependent clause version of the original clause. (A) is incorrect because it must follow "line" and interrupts the flow of the sentence. (B) is incorrect because it implies a sequence that was not in the original sentence. (D) is incorrect because "which" is extraneous. (E) is incorrect because "while" is extraneous.

9. **(B)** The rephrased sentence reads: **The avalanche condemned the hikers to a slow death when it obliterated the trails linked to civilization.** (B) is the correct answer because it is the proper transition to an active sentence with "hikers" changing from subject to direct object. (A) is incorrect because "condemns" is the present tense, not the simple past tense of the original sentence. (C) is incorrect because "hikers" cannot be the direct object from within a prepositional phrase. (D) is incorrect because "for" is also a preposition. (E) is incorrect because "hikers" cannot be the direct object as a possessive adjective.

10. **(C)** The rephrased sentence reads: **Everyone was having a wonderful time, yet the afternoon seemed to stretch endlessly.** (C) is the correct answer because it smoothly preserves the original construction of the "afternoon" clause by using "yet," a conjunction synonym of the preposition "despite." (A) is incorrect because it requires the awkward phrase "seeming to stretch endlessly." (B) is incorrect because the sequence "despite stretching" puts "afternoon" in the position of direct object of stretching, unlike the original where it had an active construction. (D) is incorrect because "stretched" is not equivalent to "seemed to stretch." (E) is incorrect because it omits "stretched," which had an odd note of effort in the original sentence and must not be left out.

11. **(B)** The rephrased sentence reads: **Paul mentioned that the cross-country trek had brought them into contact with many relatives whom they rarely see.** (B) is the correct answer because it properly shifts the point of view from "us" to "them" and shifts the verbal tense from simple past to distant past, "had brought." The action "to bring" was in the past tense in the original sentence, and the action "to mention" was also in the past tense. Without the insulating quotations, it must be observed that "to bring" is further past than "to mention." (A) is incorrect because "would" is a conditional when the event actually has occurred. (C) is incorrect because, again, "would" is a conditional. (D) is incorrect because "brought" is simple past and can occur only when the verb "to bring" precedes "to mention." (E) is incorrect because "us" incorrectly retains the quotation's point of view.

12. **(D)** The rephrased sentence reads: **Such goals as the actor's realizations of their roles or the wardrobe's thematic continuity were not pursued by the director, who instead strove single-mindedly to pack the house over a week of repeat performances by using sensationalist gimmicks.** (D) is the correct answer because the former independent clause "strove…gimmicks" is properly subordinated into the dependent clause opener "who"; "instead" tips the balance between (D) and (C) because it implies the direct replacement of ideas that the original had in its use of "rather than." (A) is incorrect because the "-ing" ending is an awkward transition into this dependent clause. It usually introduces a clause that refers back to the subject. (B) is incorrect because if the "-ing" were correct, it would need the comma found in answer (A). (C) is incorrect because it fails to create the antithesis between the two motives that was implied in the original sentence. (E) is incorrect because although such a construction is potentially

possible the sentence would require a conjunction between these two independent clauses.

13. **(B)** The rephrased sentence reads: **If America converts to government revenue based solely on income tax, the simplification of budget calculation will boggle the mind of every politician.** (B) is the correct answer because it is a should-would to if-will conversion. (A) is incorrect because "should" is a moral conditional. (C) is incorrect because "will have boggled" is a past tense. (D) is incorrect because it is wordy and backward. (E) is incorrect because "would" does not apply in the "if" construction.

14. **(D)** The rephrased sentence reads: **Few of a guppy's numerous offspring can be expected to reach maturity.** (D) is the correct answer because it is simply the reverse of "cannot be expected." (A) is incorrect because it omits the verb "to expect." (B) is incorrect because it wrongly converts the infinitive "to achieve" to a direct action. (C) is incorrect because it omits "to achieve." (E) is incorrect because "much" is a quantitative reference with no place in this context.

15. **(B)** The rephrased sentence reads: **The family doctor's diagnosis was gruff and apparently undeliberated, but it proved correct after several months of visits to various contradicting specialists.** (B) is the correct answer because "but it proved" sets up the second half of the sentence as independent, and "but" as the conjunction requires the former subject to become another entire independent clause; "diagnosis was" allows the former subject adjectives to be predicate adjectives in a linking verb independent clause. (A) is incorrect because "diagnosis" is the subject and needs a verb. (C) is incorrect because "which" interferes with subject-verb structure. (D) is incorrect because it omits the verb for "diagnosis." (E) is incorrect because it omits the verb.

16. **(B)** The epigraph describes life as "futile" and "frail" and altogether hopeless, creating an aura of despair (B). (A) is incorrect because it misreads "end" (line A) as "death" rather than the highest attainable standard of living. Because the source of the quoted epigraph is unclear, it carries no particular weight (C). (D) would also misread "end" as "the end of the world"; furthermore, there is no indication in the passage which follows that this society is awaiting annihilation. Taking the passage as a whole, it is clear that the despairing statement of the epigraph is in agreement with, rather than contrary to (E), the speaker's attitudes.

17. **(D)** The speaker brings the reader into the passage (A) by directly asking him/her "do you know…"(B), and by immediately providing the answer makes it clear that the reader could not possibly have firsthand knowledge [(C) and (E)] of life in an ironworks. (D) is incorrect because it misinterprets the intent of the question; the speaker's swift and detailed response indicates that information is not actually sought from the audience.

18. **(C)** The speaker implies that Lynchburg tobacco is inferior (C) by having it smoked by men who are loitering, drunken, and, as a result of these states, assumably poor. The smoking of this tobacco by this group does not imply that all Irishmen smoke it or even that these particular men prefer it to other brands (A). There is no suggestion of tobacco's effect upon its smokers (B). One cannot assume that the smokers bought their tobacco at the grocer's shop simply because they are loitering outside it (D). Rather than being pleasing, the scent of the tobacco must be particularly noxious to be distinguishable "through all the foul smells ranging loose in the air" (line 6) (E).

19. **(A)** The sentence omits several easily understood words (A), such as a verb in the main clause ("smoke [lies] on the...") and the preposition "to" (preceding "the two faded poplars" and "the faces"). There is no comparison being implied (B) or descriptive substitution of a part for a whole [(C), metonymy]. Alliteration (D) is incorrect because there is no repetition of initial consonants. The imagery of this sentence is decidedly concrete, making (E) incorrect.

20. **(D)** "Pointing upward" (line 14), the angel symbolizes heavenly afterlife; such hope, however, is "broken" and dirtied by the ironworks soot (D). Although the angel is broken, it does not indicate that its owner lives a life of deprivation (A). The soot that covers the angel is atmospheric rather than an intentional dishonoring (B); the statue's spot on the mantle may even be a place of honor. The smoke (C) does not need to be symbolically portrayed—it is literally described as omnipresent. Display of an angel figurine is not an indication of religious fervor (E). In addition, it is unclear if the house and its contents are the speaker's own.

21. **(A)** The "dull and tawny-colored" (line 19) river is mockingly described as its opposite, a beautiful river (A). The beautiful river cannot possibly be a wistful, yearning memory (B) since the speaker later describes the river of her childhood as tired and overburdened (line 20). Neither here, nor elsewhere in the passage, is the speaker seeking arrogantly to display "book learning" (C); in fact, the speaker is sharing knowledge from life experience. The comment is not amusing (D)—it is bitterly mocking. The river is first described as dirty and slow: a second depiction of it as beautiful cannot possibly be repetitious (E).

22. **(B)** Both descriptions attribute human characteristics, dreaming and weariness, to an animal or inanimate object [(B), personification]. "Metaphor" (A) is incorrect because there is no comparison being made in these specific phrases. There is no joining of seemingly opposite terms, making "oxymoron" (C) incorrect. Neither phrase is overly exaggerated [(D), hyperbole]. "Assonance" (E), repetition of vowel sounds in words with differing initial consonants, is not present here.

23. **(E)** This paragraph compares and contrasts (E) the river and the ironworks laborer, both "working" slavishly, but one bearing hope of a better future. The paragraph does not present a series of actions or occurrences and their consequences (A).

The narration is not chronological (B) because the speaker moves from present to past to present to future. There is no ordering of terms or things by groups or classes (C). (D) misinterprets the questions in lines 30–31 and 34: they are rhetorical, and the speaker expects no answers.

24. **(E)** The river is given the human sensation of weariness (line 20), and man is dehumanized by being given the river's status of "stream...creeping past" (lines 24–25) (I, II). The speaker implies that the workers are slaves (III) by describing the river as "negro-like...slavishly bearing its burden day after day" (lines 22–23) and subsequently noting that "something of the same idle notion comes to [him/her] today" when viewing the routine of the worker. The river ultimately has the higher status (IV) because it will pass on to a better "life," whereas the laborer will simply go slavishly on until his death (lines 37–39).

25. **(C)** The speaker anticipates the reader's reaction to be what an "altogether serious thing to be alive" (line 31), a coldly detached remark (C). This projected response is not one of shared feelings (A) or contempt (D). There is no sign that the speaker considers the reader to be fending off an anticipated attack (B). The reader seems to have some understanding of the seriousness of the laborer's situation, making (E) incorrect.

26. **(B)** By analogy, "Welsh puddler" is one out of the "masses of men" who labor in the ironworks (line 25). The river is compared to the human masses, then it is contrasted with an individual member. (A) relies upon a misreading of lines 36–39; the grave is the puddler's end, not his place of occupation. (C), (D), and (E) all misinterpret puddler as having to do with liquid.

27. **(D)** The phrases in line 36 and in (D) are parallel in structure, being set off by dashes and organized as a series of three; the former phrase, however, is an expected destination while the latter is the opposite of an ultimate end point. Although they are tripartite in structure, (A) and (B) are not contextually related to the phrase in line 36. (C) and (E) do not have the tripartite structure necessary for parallelism.

28. **(D)** The antecedent of "it" can be found by dropping the descriptive subordinate clauses and joining the independent clauses in lines 52–54: "there is a secret down here.... I want to make it a real thing to you." The "nightmare fog" (A) is part of a prepositional phrase that describes the secret's location and not the thing that is to be made real. This "story" (B) reveals the secret. While the reader may not have yet experienced it firsthand, "foul effluvia" (C) is already a real thing. The "terrible question" (E) is the secret, but it follows "it" and thus cannot be its antecedent.

29. **(B)** The very lives and deaths of the workers (lines 57–59) are lives so terrible and hopeless and deaths so unremarkable that they ask, "What is the point of existence?" (B). In order for (A) to be correct there would have to be suggestions for concrete reform, rather than abstract promises "of the day that shall surely come" (lines 66–67). Pollution (C) is

indeed a problem, but it is a backdrop to the problems of the workers. While it is implied that the reader is of higher socioeconomic status than the worker, there is no blame given or responsibility attributed for the condition of the workers (D). The workers are variously described as Irish and Welsh, but the question of their ethnicity is irrelevant (E).

30. **(A)**   Egoism, Pantheism, and Arminianism are respectively self-worship, nature worship, and a theology opposed to predestination. They are all systems of belief and by using such a system the reader seeks to make his/her own way through life without seeing "it" (the "secret"/"question," inferentially the meaning of life) (A). (B) mistakenly takes the concept of making paths literally. (C) is incorrect because there is no indication that the reader considers physical possessions to be the key to life. Harkening back to the speaker's comment of "amateur psychologist" (lines 30–31), (D) misinterprets "Egoism" as the scientific jargon of Freudianism. (E) confuses "Arminian" with Armenian and also interprets "paths" as literal places for walks.

31. **(C)**   The speaker states that the question answers itself and is "the most solemn prophecy…of the Hope to come" (lines 62–63); in addition, the story to be told "will be so fair with promise of the day that shall surely come" (lines 66–67). These phrases indicate that there is a reason for human life [ruling out (A)], and their religious connotations imply that this reason is a "life" after human toil (C). The predicted relief is described in vague and religious terms, not in socioeconomic language (B). Although only the terrible lives of men are described, the omission of women does not imply that they fare better (D). The reader, inferentially more educated than the worker, is "busy in making straight paths for his/her feet" (lines 54–55): he/she too is looking for a rationale for life, and by projecting [his/her] interest in the story about to be told, the speaker implies that afterlife will fulfill this goal (E).

32. **(B)**   The speaker describes the projected story as "the outline of a dull life, that long since…vainly lived and lost" (lines 45–46); its conclusion in the past ruling out (C), (D), and (E). (A) is incorrect because a hard life without remedy holds none of the hope the speaker foretells. Lines 64–68 imply that the story will be dark but will end with promise of otherworldly redress (B).

33. **(B)**   The argument is structured as "a trial" (B), with a defendant (the girl/petticoat) seated at a judge's left hand and counselors presenting arguments and petitions. While questions are asked and answered (A), the aforementioned persons and activities make "trial" a better answer. There is no admission of sin or error, making "confession" (C) incorrect. The argument is not a discourse on a religious or moral topic [sermon (D)]. Although the argument in front of the judge can be described as debating, the official term is a "trial." Therefore, (E) is incorrect.

34. **(A)**   Without the voluminous petticoat mandated by fashion, the girl would not be physically "big and burly as other persons of her quality" (lines 8–9) or, by implication, as "large" in social standing. (B), (C), and (E) are partially correct because

they name the first element of physical size. Their second elements, however, are incorrect: the girl's "quality" (line 9) depends more on social than monetary status (B), and her mental abilities [(C) and (E)] would not be indicated by her underwear. (D) takes up only the literal interpretation of "little," making the girl small because she lacks the proper underwear.

35. **(D)** The young lady dislikes the petticoat and put off wearing one until pressured by her slipping social reputation to don one (D). Her reluctance to immediately wear the garment indicates that she is not a slave to fashion (A). A social climber (B) would be so concerned about her reputation that she would quickly do what the ladies of quality do. (C) takes "little" (line 10) literally, assuming that the girl is actually physically undersized. The girl has yet to be blamed [versus being condemned, (E)], and in fact the judge seems pleased by her defense.

36. **(B)** A "vest" is "a garment" (A); "petticoat" (B) is a better answer, however, as it is the item being discussed, and its "big and burly" size matches the canopy-like description. There is no mention of any other article of clothing [(D) and (E)]. The vest is opened like "an umbrella" (C), but the displayed article is the focus of the passage and thus the petticoat.

37. **(C)** "Oxymoron" (C) is not present because this description of the petticoat does not contain a pairing of seemingly contradictory terms. The description of the petticoat is exaggerated (A) as forming a canopy over a "great hall" (line 14). Through a "simile" (B), its form is "not unlike [equaling 'like'] the cupola of St. Paul's" (line 18). Metaphorically (D), it is called a "canopy" and a "silken rotunda" (line 17). It is amusing (E) to think of a woman wearing an undergarment big enough to overspread a large room.

38. **(A)** The argument is described as great, solid, and heavily ornamented ["furbelowed…with many periodical sentences and turns of oratory," (lines 24–25)] like the petticoat (A) that spreads over the room. The argument is elaborate and decorated, but the ridiculous subject matter destroys any formality (B). The woolen industry would grow larger, but not necessarily more elaborate (C), with the production of such large petticoats. The "power of France" (D) would lessen, not grow and become more detailed. The statement which characterizes the girl's good sense (lines 5–11) is straightforward and plain, lacking elaborate devices or syntax (E).

39. **(B)** This remark grossly overstates (B) the effect that large petticoats would have on a rival economy. It exaggerates rather than understates (A) the impact of fashion upon the larger world. While the downfall of France is predicted as a side effect, the passage is concerned with the defense of the petticoat and not a direct economic attack (D). The statement may be a boast, but it is not self-aggrandizing (E) its speaker the counselor.

40. **(D)** The "Greenland trade" supports large petticoats because of the great amount of whalebone used therein; consequently, the members of this trade must be "whalers" (D). "Petticoat makers" (A) would use whalebone but would be more concerned with consumption of their garments than the materials for making them. "Carvers" (B), "merchants" (C), and "shipowners" (E) could deal in whalebone (or other goods). (D) is the best answer because whalers would be specifically and directly affected by the use of whalebone.

41. **(C)** The counsel can only insinuate (line 47) and not directly describe how the family's honor may be sullied; the petticoat must, consequently, prevent some extremely delicate matter, such as an adulterous or premarital affair (C). Dressing fashionably (A) and expensively (B) may preserve a family's social status, but not their honor. There is no information in the passage to suggest that dishonor results from being kidnapped (D) or from entering small rooms (E).

42. **(B)** The speaker's final point is linked to the counsels' [making (D) incorrect]: it asserts that the petticoat would remove any fear that a woman would be molested. The counsel would use this assertion in favor of wearing the petticoat, the speaker against (being secure from male assault makes seeking marriage for security unlikely). The speaker's point both assents to (A) and opposes (C) the counsels'; (B) is a better answer, however, because the speaker uses this point to make the opposite conclusion. The speaker's point is strengthened [rather than weakened, (E)] by being able to use the counsels' own ammunition against them.

43. **(E)** Although the speaker refers to the girl (A) as the "pretty criminal" (line 13), "the petticoat" (E) is the best choice for the criminal because it is the object whose merits are being debated. "Society" (B), "fashion" (C), and "persons of her quality" (D) are not being indicted; in fact, the speaker gives "great allowances to the fair sex upon account of the fashion" (line 12) and by inference the persons who dictate the styles.

44. **(C)** Both counsel and speaker concentrate on the large petticoat's effect upon the economy (C): boosting industry with increased consumption of raw materials or draining family fortunes. The counsels' argument seems logical (A), yet it ignores the expense and impracticality of the huge petticoat and raises it from mere underwear to economic savior. Neither argument appeals primarily to emotions (B) such as fear, love, or anger. An appeal to patriotism (D) occurs in the counsels' arguments but not in the speaker's. There is no appeal to moral duty (E) in either argument.

45. **(A)** Without rancor, the speaker is mildly ridiculing (A) the folly of sacrificing money and comfort for fashionably huge petticoats. The passage clearly and directly condemns such petticoats through the conclusions of the speaker/judge: it does not reach this judgment through irony's expression of meaning through an opposite point of view (B). The passage itself is funny with its underwear trial (C); "satiric" remains the better stylistic description, however, because the passage is poking fun at the petticoat and

intending to "reform" this fashion. The passage is not informal (D) because of its trial format and courtroom language, yet it is not replete with self-aggrandizing language (E).

46. **(B)** The speaker uses "we" to include the reader in the quest for understanding the creative writer (B). (A) is incorrect because the group that is "We laymen" (line 1) includes all persons but the creative writers. (C) incorrectly assumes that the speaker refers to him/herself with the royal "we" disregarding "laymen" (line 1), which defines "we" as plural. The speaker's "we" is not all-inclusive (D): it excludes the creative writer from the united speaker and reader.

47. **(C)** The antecedent is revealed by the sentence's parallel structure: the subject and verb of the second clause, "it is not at all weakened" (line 7), mirror that of the first, "our interest is only heightened" (line 5). "Explanation" (A) is incorrect because it is part of the dependent clause beginning with "that" (line 6). "Fact" (B) is the object of the preposition "by" (line 6). "Impression" [line 4, (D)] is too far removed from "it" to be its antecedent. "Insight" (E) follows, rather than precedes "it."

48. **(B)** The idea that "every man is a poet at heart" (line 17) clearly belongs to creative writers themselves: the speaker claims that comprehending the writer's methods of discovering and shaping his/her work will not enable a nonwriter to become a writer [(A), see paragraph one]. In lines 16–19 the speaker delineates a difference between writer and nonwriter by describing the writers' attempt to bring ordinary man closer (C). According to the speaker, "[in] spite of all the emotion with which he cathects his world of play, the child distinguishes it quite well from reality" [lines 26–28, (D)]. If "every child at play behaves like a creative writer" (lines 21–22), it follows that the business of creative writing parallels the play of childhood (E).

49. **(A)** The child concentrates and invests emotions in the creation of a "world of play" [line 27, (A)]. "Distances" (B) cannot define "cathects" because "in spite of" (line 26) taking such action upon his play world, the child distances ("distinguishes it quite well," line 27) from reality. The child seeks to link the occurrences of his/her created world with his/her real world; it consequently is not fantasized (C). The child's created world is his/her "most intense occupation" (line 20), and would thus not wish to discourage (D) or destroy (E) it.

50. **(B)** Each paragraph begins with a question and progresses to its answer (B): in one, how does the creative writer fashion a moving work? We cannot really understand or ourselves obtain this power; two, can we find in ourselves an activity similar to creative writing? This is possible. And three, is there creative activity in childhood? Yes, play is similar to creative writing. (A) is incorrect because paragraphs two and three continue the search for understanding of the process of creative writing begun in paragraph one. An answer to the third paragraph's question is given: none is offered to paragraph one's question, making (C) incorrect. Paragraphs one and three are relatively close in length; three, however, provides a detailed and longer answer to its question [discrediting (D)].

(E) is incorrect because paragraph three, which should have the most complex sentences (containing independent and dependent clauses), mainly contains simple, one subject/verb sentences.

51. **(C)** If a "child at play behaves like a creative writer" (lines 21–22), it follows that the writer behaves like a child at play; creative writing can consequently be considered to extend and expand the processes of childhood play (C). Paragraph three's establishment of the similarity of childhood and creative writing discredits (A) and (B). Although all men were once children at play, all men do not become creative writers (D); the speaker speaks for the nonwriting layman. (E) is incorrect because the speaker "differentiates the child's 'play' from 'fantasying' (lines 29–30).

52. **(B)** The "frightful differences of a generation ago" is a roundabout and mild way (a euphemism) of describing the Civil War, and "mistreatment" is an understated way of referring to the horror of slavery (B). (A) emphasizes, rather than downplays, the "responsibility." (C), (D), and (E) are incorrect because they are straightforward observations with deemphasis or inflation.

53. **(E)** Slavery and death were the lamentable pre-Civil War condition of blacks (I); using these terms to describe their possible business and social roles consequently condemns these roles (II). This precarious position for blacks would contradict the "kindliness and reconciliation" between North and South (III) by nearly restoring the state of affairs—slavery—over which they fought. The "reconciliation" would be "marked by industrial slavery and civic death" by means of "permanent legislation" (lines 13–14) and thus into "a position of inferiority" (line 14) (IV).

54. **(D)** The last sentence of the first paragraph makes a summation of this state, likening it to the sowing of seeds for an eventual "harvest of disaster" (lines 18–19) (D). Although the inequality is to be brought about by means of "legislation" (line 14), it is not described with the terminology of the legal profession (A). The division between South and North (B) remains in the past and is not brought forth to describe the current state of inequality. Blacks are described as potentially in "industrial slavery and civic death" (line 13); however, this comparison is not made using "like" or "as" [(C), simile]. "Personification" (E) is incorrect because no human characteristics are given to the inanimate state of inequality.

55. **(C)** "Themselves" is parallel to (A), (B), and (D) because all are preceded by "responsibility to." (E) also parallels "themselves" because it is synonymous with "this nation." (C) is incorrect because it is part of a dependent clause describing "the darker races of men" and the object of the preposition "on."

56. **(B)** The second and third sentences take the persons of the first sentence and present them in reverse order along with the results of their previously named fears (B). They do not progress forward, step-by-step, to new ideas (A). Although the second and

third repeat (C) the persons of the first sentence, they join them with new ideas, the results of the fears. The persons of the first sentence are presented in reverse (rather than the same) order and more complex subject/verb clauses, ruling out parallel structure (D). The ideas are given in an ordered pattern, rather than random order (E).

57. **(A)** The speaker commands black men to praise the first and move against the other men; given the advocation of equal status for blacks, one can assume that a man the speaker would praise would agree with this position, and a man condemned would disagree (A). The first man is called "Governor" and the second and fourth "Senator," but the third man's profession is not identified (B). Although all four men are by implication politicians, (C) is incorrect because the speaker would not praise one who sought to belittle blacks as he/she does the first man. Although the first man agrees while the others disagree with the speaker, their political positions are not indicative of their race (D). (E) cannot be correct because the first man is, as the speaker's praise implies, in favor of equal rights for blacks unlike an "ignorant Southerner."

58. **(D)** "Propaganda" carries negative connotations; calling Mr. Washington's ideas by this name consequently scorns them (D). It does not clearly relate these ideas [(A) and (C)] or admire (E) them. Mr. Washington's ideas can be characterized as political (B), but "derides" (D) is a better answer because it conveys the speaker's disapproval (indicated in lines 3–19).

59. **(C)** The speaker gives a summary of Mr. Washington's argument followed by the speaker's refutation of this argument (C). (A) is incorrect because the speaker answers rather than reiterates the opposing argument. While the speaker "attacks" Mr. Washington's argument, there is no defense (B), only a statement of the contrary position. (D) is incorrect because it restates (in reverse order) the terms of (B). There is neither praise of a dead person/idea or censuring (E).

60. **(B)** (B) is correct because the speaker is urging black men to take action to shoulder the responsibility of demanding equal status. The passage is not seeking to praise a dead person/idea [(A), eulogistic] or argue a case in a courtroom [(C), judicial]. Its primary purpose is not the giving of an explanation or a description (D). "Satiric" (E) is incorrect because the passage is not ridiculing and exposing vice or folly.

Student Response to Essay Question 1:

I am looking out at the world from my second floor bedroom window. I should not be sitting here wasting my time, not doing all of the things I should be. I can allow myself a short break from my obligations, though. The view from my window is beautiful. Directly across the street is a tree-filled park where children play on the swings and see-saws. The happy sounds of these children playing float across the street and reach my ears. I have so much to do now, but I am enjoying looking out my window. Some little kids are playing happily in the sandbox and on the slides with no other cares in the world.

There is a road between my window and the park. An old, blue Cadillac drives by with music blaring from its speakers, momentarily silencing the playing children. Many people are walking along the sidewalk, a mother pushing a baby carriage, a young couple holding hands, a man walking a small, black dog, my friends on their skateboards. I wonder why my friends are out hanging around when they should be home studying for final exams or the SAT's. I should be busy at work instead of sitting here looking out the window.

In addition to the park across the street I can see the front yard of my house. There is a large maple tree on my lawn. I can see a squirrel running around on the branches of this tree. The squirrel's nest is also visible from my room. As I watch, I notice that the squirrel is carrying twigs up to its nest. The squirrel is building its nest and preparing for the future. There is also a flower garden on my lawn that I can see. Purple crocuses and tulips are blooming in the garden. They are beautiful to look at. These flowers bloom every spring. Their sweet scent drifts up to my nose on a cool spring breeze. The sun is shining brightly in the cloudless sky. It is a lovely spring day and I am filled with hope, but I must get back to my work.

I am staring through my ice covered window at the cruel world outside. I have been sitting here for hours, just watching the emptiness outside. Across the street is a park. It is the middle of winter and the park is virtually empty. A cruel wind is blowing the swings around, as if to mock the children who play during the summer. Some pigeons hop around on the frozen ground, searching for a morsel of food. There is no one in the park today to feed them.

Between my window and the park there is a road. The road has been icy and treacherous all winter. Hardly a car drives by, except for the sand truck. I can hear it approaching now. The truck comes slowly up the street, dropping sand on the ice in the hopes of melting it, but the road will freeze up again overnight. The truck is gray, the same gray as the dark, unchanging sky that I see from my window. The sidewalk is as empty as the park. The only person who passes by is the homeless man who lives in the park. He carefully pushes his shopping cart along the sidewalk. He is bundled in layer upon layer of filthy brown clothes. I wonder how he survives in this cold harsh weather.

I can also see my front lawn from my window. A huge, leafless maple tree appears to be dead. During the summer, the tree seems full of life, sprouting green leaves and with squirrels running to and fro. But now the tree is stagnant, except for the thinner branches which are swaying violently in the wind. I can see the patch of dirt where the garden grows when it is warm outside. It is only a brown plot now, with a few dead stalks being the only reminder of life. I wish that I had something to do besides sit here and stare at this bleak empty, landscape. I am very bored though, so I think I will sit here for a few more hours.

Analysis of Response to Essay Question 1:

This essay displays a strong grasp of the ways in which language can be used to reveal different situations and circumstances. The essay employs vivid descriptive detail to portray two vastly different states of mind.

Both halves of the essay describe the same scene: a park across the street from the window, and the front lawn of the observer's house. The first half of the essay uses the beauty of early spring to vividly describe a hopeful outlook, while the second half expertly employs the cold dreariness of winter to portray an attitude of hopelessness.

The first section of the essay employs metaphors and descriptive language that clearly illustrate feelings of hope and joy. It is apparent through the details noted, the young couple holding hands, the squirrel building its nest, the blooming flowers, that the observer is identifying with these images metaphorically. S/he is looking forward to realizing some future potential.

In addition, the overall upbeat tone of the first part of the essay reflects the positive attitude and circumstances of the student looking out the window, as s/he busily prepares for the future.

The second part of this essay describing the same scene, but at a different time, uses stark, dreary imagery to illustrate a mood of despair. The view from the window is described as empty and frozen, perfectly reflecting the observer's mood. The gray mood portrayed in this part of the essay exemplifies that the writer is filled with dashed hopes; it is clear that s/he identifies with the starving pigeons and the freezing homeless man. The writer obviously knows how to use language metaphor, and detail to describe circumstances and states of mind.

Finally, the stark contrast between the two descriptive passages in this essay shows that the writer has a firm grasp of how to use language to expertly reflect disparate circumstances and situations.

Student Response to Essay Question 2:

This passage reveals that John Muir believed that all of nature was embodied with a wildness of spirit, and that mankind loves this wildness and should respect it—as Muir felt the "Indians" did, and as he felt "everybody" certainly would, because it is an "ancient mother-love," older than the "civilization" that inhibits our celebration of it ("galling harness of civilization drops off").

The selection is remarkable for its tone of freedom and expansiveness which is supported by the author's diction (the use, choice, and arrangement of words). In a little over 125 words, Muir has used words that are directly evocative of freedom nine times ("wild, wildness, unblighted, wilderness, solitary, free, unimpeded, immense, eternal"), as well as phrases and images that are traditionally associated with expansiveness ("galling harness...drops off, busy and steeped with God, mountain, stream, waterfall").

God and nature ("ancient mother-love") are synonymous in this passage, and are placed at some distance from those—such as the "Indians"—who had known this truth and had respected it. Muir portrays himself as one of the formerly "civilized" folk who had shaken off its destructive and jading influences and could now see as the "Indians" had—and as, he believes, "everybody" can once they realize that the "wilderness" is itself a liberating force which at the same time provides a rich diet ("feeds on") for the human imagination.

Thus, the theme of liberation is supported by appropriate diction, and is reinforced by the repetition of evocative words and phrases. The transcendence that Muir describes is further made attainable and placed within reasonable reach by his description of this element of Indian culture, and by his testimony that he himself has made the transition from stifling "civilization" to a reunion with his "ancient mother-love"—nature in its "unblighted...wilderness."

Analysis of Response to Essay Question 2:

The response has properly analyzed the Muir passage for diction, style, and syntax, and has provided details from the text that reinforce assertions. The responder has first identified the theme, then set forth a syntactic description of the passage, and concludes with a synthesis of how these elements are well suited to the theme of the passage. The key word here, which the responder recognizes as such, is "expansiveness," for this is the essence both of the language of the passage as well as the power of the promise of Muir's vision for "everybody" now under the "galling harness of civilization."

Student Response to Essay Question 3:

Thoreau's passage traces the changing of seasons by the use of symbols that are reinforced by an effective use of appropriate style, sound, and syntax as well.

The author begins his passage with the image of a hawk "seeking the first slimy life that awakes." The earth, therefore, is still asleep under winter's mantle, but already the "sinking sound of melting snow is heard in all dells" and the "ice dissolves." Almost immediately, grass "flames up"—the recognizable first arrival of spring, before flowers bloom and trees grow green with leaves.

Here Thoreau telescopes from an entire "hillside" down to "the grassblade" where his focus remains until the end of the passage. At once he announces it a "symbol of perpetual youth," and, using simile, says that "like a long green ribbon," it "streams from the sod," even though the change of seasons has not been complete: the frost still appears to "check" it, though it "push[es] on again."

The onomatopoeic "ess" sound throughout the entire passage is emphasized most in this first part of the passage (sing, carols, glees, marsh, sailing, seeking, first slimy, awakes, sinking sound, snow, dells, dissolves, apace, ponds, grass flames, etc.), perhaps to reinforce Thoreau's contention that the sound of spring is the hissing of an essential "spring fire" ("flames up like a spring fire," "green is the color of its flame").

The second half of the passage moves from June through the long ("perennial green") stretch of years (periodically checked by the "mower's" harvest) and outward to eternity, because neither oncoming winters nor the mower's seasonal reaping can destroy the roots of the grass blade—which "puts forth its green blade to eternity".

In these concluding lines are two opposing symbols: the grass, the "symbol of perpetual youth," and the "mower," which symbolizes, of course, both approaching winter and an individual's death. To synthesize and emphasize this, Thoreau concludes with the line, "So our human life but dies down to its root, and still puts forth its green blade to eternity." Thus, as the green blade of grass perenially grows from its roots to harvest, and then through the continuing cycles of nature into infinity, Thoreau believes that human lives move from birth through death and into eternity.

Analysis of Response to Essay Question 3:

This extensive response reflects the complex nature of Thoreau's passage, as well as the tightness with which form and content work together here to illustrate a truth of human and general nature. The responder has used a close reading of the text to illustrate the many elements of sound and style that are at work here, and has shaped the essay with attention to the overall argument: that the hope which springs eternal in the natural world operates in humanity's world as well.

AP

English Language & Composition

Practice Test III

AP Examination in English Language & Composition

Test III

Section 1

TIME: 60 Minutes
      60 Questions

(Answer sheets appear in the back of this book.)

> **DIRECTIONS:** Rephrase each of the following sentences according to the directions given, and choose the response that best corresponds to the necessary changes to the original sentence. Keep the meaning of the new sentence as close to the original as possible, maintaining natural phrasing, the requirements of standard written English, and logical and concise construction.

1. Landmark discoveries in astronomy eventually pushed religious scholars into interpreting certain biblical passages less and less literally. Change <u>pushed</u> to <u>forced</u>.

    (A)   to the interpretation of   (D)   to be interpreting

    (B)   with interpreting   (E)   into interpreting of

    (C)   to interpret

2. Although most consumers express concern for the environment in opinion polls, too few are willing to pay more for the safety constraints suggested by experts. Omit <u>Although</u>, use <u>but</u>.

    (A)   Most consumers express   (D)   but too few consumers

    (B)   Most express   (E)   but then too few

    (C)   but consumers are too willing

3. The new employee tried to make a good impression by proposing a more economical resource deployment system. Change <u>by proposing</u> to <u>with a suggestion</u>.

    (A) for more economical   (D) for a more economical

    (B) to deploy a system   (E) that is more economical

    (C) that resources

4. The real incendiary to the scandal was when the columnist implied that the "eye witnesses" behind Trader's conviction were compensated by the state prosecutor. Begin with <u>The columnist's</u>.

    (A) implication of   (D) implication that

    (B) implication having been   (E) implication concerning

    (C) implication because he

5. Lawrence is buying his way into people's confidence to gain enough backing to make a bid for office. Begin with <u>Buying</u>.

    (A) confidences, he is

    (B) confidences by which Lawrence is

    (C) confidences, so Lawrence is

    (D) confidences is how Lawrence is

    (E) confidences, Lawrence is

6. When you observe how the administrator treats female employees, you will see why so few ever work here longer than a year. Change <u>you will see</u> to <u>demonstrates</u>.

    (A) The adminstrator's treatment

    (B) The fact of the administrator's treatment

    (C) Due to the treatment

    (D) The administrator treating

    (E) On account of the administrator's treatment

7. The advertiser portrays its product as a catalyst for male-female social interaction, implying an end to loneliness is but a purchase away. Begin with <u>Portraying its product</u>.

    (A) will imply   (D) then interacts

    (B) implies   (E) will interact

    (C) have implied

8.   The theater company operates on a very limited budget and yet the perfor-
      mances never labor under frugality. Eliminate <u>and yet</u>.

      (A)   A very limited budget

      (B)   Although a very limited budget

      (C)   Although the theater company operates

      (D)   Despite a very limited budget

      (E)   Whereas the theater company operates

9.   Merging onto a busy highway requires you to match the speed of the flowing
      traffic and to pray the other motorists get out of the way. Insert <u>that</u> after
      <u>requires</u>.

      (A)   and prays   (D)   and to pray

      (B)   and praying   (E)   and pray

      (C)   and should pray

10.   In Shakespeare, perhaps the most demanding role to play is King Lear. Begin
      with <u>In Shakespeare, there is</u>.

      (A)   one demanding   (D)   most demanding in

      (B)   role than   (E)   more demanding

      (C)   role is

DIRECTIONS: This section of the test consists of selections from literary
works and questions on their use of language. After reading each passage or
poem, choose the best answer to each question and blacken the corresponding
oval on the answer sheet.

---

*Questions 11 - 24 are based on the following passage. Read the passage carefully
before choosing your answers.*

     Unjust laws exist: shall we be content to obey them, or shall we endeavor to
amend them, and obey them until we have succeeded, or shall we transgress
them at once? Men generally, under such a government as this, think that they
ought to wait until they have persuaded the majority to alter them. They think
5   that, if they should resist, the remedy would be worse than the evil. But it is
the fault of the government itself that the remedy *is* worse than the evil. *It*
makes it worse. Why is it not more apt to anticipate and provide for reform?

Why does it not cherish its wise minority? Why does it cry and resist before it is hurt? Why does it not encourage its citizens to be on the alert to point out its
10   faults, and *do* better than it would have them? Why does it always crucify Christ, and excommunicate Copernicus and Luther, and pronounce Washington and Franklin rebels?

If the injustice is part of the necessary friction of the machine of government, let it go, let it go: perchance it will wear smooth—certainly the machine
15   will wear out. If the injustice has a spring, or a pulley, or a rope, or a crank, exclusively for itself, then perhaps you may consider whether the remedy will not be worse than the evil; but if it is of such a nature that it requires you to be the agent of injustice to another, then, I say, break the law. Let your life be a counter-friction to stop the machine. What I have to do is to see, at any rate,
20   that I do not lend myself to the wrong which I condemn.

Under a government which imprisons any unjustly, the true place for a just man is also a prison. The proper place today, the only place which Massachusetts has provided for her freer and less desponding spirits, is in her prisons, to be put out and locked out of the State by her own act, as they have already put
25   themselves out by their principles. It is there that the fugitive slave, and the Mexican prisoner on parole, and the Indian come to plead the wrongs of his race should find them; on that separate, but more free and honorable, ground, where the State places those who are not *with* her, but *against* her—the only house in a slave State in which a free man can abide with honor. If any think
30   that their influence would be lost there, and their voices no longer afflict the ear of the State, that they would not be as an enemy within its walls, they do not know by how much more eloquently and effectively he can combat injustice who has experienced a little in his own person. Cast your whole vote, not a strip of paper merely, but your whole influence. A minority is powerless while
35   it conforms to the majority; it is not even a minority then; but it is irresistible when it clogs by its whole weight. If the alternative is to keep all just men in prison, or give up war and slavery, the State will not hesitate which to choose. If a thousand men were not to pay their tax-bills this year, that would not be a violent and bloody measure, as it would be to pay them, and enable the State
40   to commit violence and shed innocent blood. This is, in fact, the definition of a peaceable revolution, if any such is possible. If the tax-gatherer, or any other public officer, asks me, as one has done, 'But what shall I do?' my answer is, 'If you really wish to do anything, resign your office.' When the subject has refused allegiance, and the officer has resigned his office, then the revolution is

45 accomplished. But even suppose blood should flow. Is there not a sort of blood shed when the conscience is wounded? Through this wound a man's real manhood and immortality flow out, and he bleeds to an everlasting death. I see this blood flowing now.

11. In the second paragraph, the author refers to "the machine of government." How does this metaphor characterize the government as the author uses it?

   (A)   Efficient and reliable   (D)   Reparable

   (B)   Noisy and polluting   (E)   Labor-saving

   (C)   Single-minded and unfeeling

12. The opening paragraph poses a series of questions. What is the author's purpose?

   (A)   He states as questions the topics to be covered in the essay.

   (B)   He expects government officials to provide the reasons he seeks.

   (C)   He is satirically posing the questions to those with whom he disagrees.

   (D)   He is rhetorically stating what the government does and should not.

   (E)   He wants to polarize his readers between those who agree with him and those who do not.

13. In the passage, one goal of the speaker is to

   (A)   evoke the moral responsibility of the reader.

   (B)   encourage an armed rebellion.

   (C)   attract persecuted minorities to Massachusetts.

   (D)   promote a political party.

   (E)   reduce the tax burden.

14. The passage contains all of the following EXCEPT

   (A)   a proposal for peaceful protest.

   (B)   historical reference to other governments.

   (C)   criticism of specific persons.

   (D)   justification of bloodshed.

   (E)   unanswered questions.

15. Where is the "there" referred to in line 25?

    (A) Massachusetts   (D) Church

    (B) Prison   (E) The grave

    (C) Legislative building

16. Lines 34-36 are best restated as

    (A) a minority must maintain a difference from the majority, so it can disable the majority.

    (B) a minority is an important part of the majority, without which the majority would collapse under its own weight.

    (C) a majority exists only by actively contrasting the minority, and it is unconquerable when it acts in unison.

    (D) a minority remaining in silence brings injustice upon itself, which it could stand against with its voice and unified action.

    (E) a minority that complies to the will of the majority ceases to exist, but a minority that fully commits itself is unconquerable.

17. According to the passage, what should the tax-gatherer do?

    (A) Steal the state's funds   (D) Expect gunshots for greetings

    (B) Submit counterfeit money   (E) Sleep with one eye open

    (C) Quit his job

18. In lines 5-10, what is the antecedent of "it" and "its"?

    (A) Fault of the government   (D) Deceit of the government

    (B) Evil of the government   (E) Government

    (C) The governors

19. Contrast lines 19-20 with lines 21-22.

    (A) In lines 19-20, the author is content not to participate in injustice; but in lines 21-22, the existence of an injustice compels the author to give up his freedom in protest.

    (B) Lines 19-20 imply the author needs only react to what he sees; but lines 21-22 imply the author must react to all he knows.

    (C) Lines 19-20 advise neither a borrower nor a lender be; but lines 21-22 advise one to give up one's freedom for a man unjustly imprisoned.

    (D) In lines 19-20, the author implies it is enough to condemn injustice;

but in lines 21-22, the author says the only place for an honest man under a dishonest government is prison.

(E)   Lines 19-20 advise a man to circumvent the wrongs of his state; but lines 21-22 advise him to meet them at every sacrifice to himself.

20.   What does "cast your whole vote" (lines 33-34) mean?

(A)   Vote in every election, even the most local

(B)   Vote for the same party across the board

(C)   Run for office

(D)   Do everything you can to influence lawmaking

(E)   Vote as your conscience tells you

21.   It can be inferred from lines 22-25 that

(A)   the author has been unjustly imprisoned.

(B)   the author has a loved one who is unjustly imprisoned.

(C)   the author is either in prison or not in Massachusetts.

(D)   Massachusetts' prisons are overcrowded.

(E)   Massachusetts has banished citizens that the author feels are principled.

22.   What change in tone would occur if, in the series of questions in the first paragraph, "it" were replaced with "they"?

(A)   The paragraph would lose some of its impact.

(B)   The paragraph would be less condemning and more of a general complaint.

(C)   The paragraph would no longer lump all governments, past and present, into a convenient whipping post.

(D)   The paragraph would be more accusatory, showing greater dissent.

(E)   The paragraph would be more condescending, chastising a multitude instead of a single entity.

23.   Identify the stages of the discussion through the passage.

(A)   Question, answer, enact   (D)   Criticize, suggest, inspire

(B)   Goad, insult, attack   (E)   Argue, reason, propose

(C)   Taunt, imply, condemn

24. What assumption lies behind lines 36-37?

    (A) The state is a democracy.

    (B) "All just men" will act simultaneously.

    (C) The prisons will not be large enough.

    (D) The women will not bail out the men.

    (E) "All just men" are a significant number.

Questions 25 - 38 are based on the following passage. Read the passage carefully before choosing your answers.

If ye be thus resolved, as it were injury to think ye were not, I know not what should withhold me from presenting ye with a fit instance wherein to show both that love of truth which ye eminently profess and that uprightness of your judgement which is not wont to be partial to yourselves by judging
5   over again that order which ye have ordained *to regulate printing. That no book, pamphlet, or paper shall be henceforth printed, unless the same be first approved and licensed by such,* or at least one of such as shall be thereto appointed. I warn that this will be primely to the discouragement of all learning and the stop of truth, not only by disexercising and blunting our abilities in what we know
10 already, but by hindering and cropping the discovery that might be yet further made both in religious and civil wisdom.

I deny not, but that it is of greatest concernment in the church and commonwealth to have a vigilant eye how books demean themselves, as well as men; and thereafter to confine, imprison and do sharpest justice on them as
15 malefactors: for books are not absolutely dead things but do contain a potency of life in them to be active as that soul whose progeny they are; nay, they do preserve as in a vial the purest efficacy and extraction of that living intellect that bred them. I know they are as lively and as vigorously productive as those fabulous dragon's teeth and being sown up and down, may chance to spring
20 up armed men. And yet on the other hand unless wariness be used, as good almost kill a man as kill a good book; who kills a man kills a reasonable creature, God's image; but he who destroys a good book, kills reason itself, kills the image of God, as it were in the eye. Many a man lives a burden to the earth; but a good book is the precious life-blood of a master-spirit, embalmed
25 and treasured up on purpose to a life beyond life. 'Tis true, no age can restore a life, whereof perhaps there is no great loss; and revolutions of ages do not oft recover the loss of a rejected truth, for the want of which whole nations fare far

worse. We should be wary therefore what persecution we raise against the
living labours of public men, how we spill the seasoned life of man preserved
30   and stored up in books; since we see a kind of homocide may be thus committed, sometimes a martyrdom, and if it extend to the whole impression, a kind
of massacre, whereof the execution ends not in the slaying of an elemental life
but strikes at that ethereal and fifth essence, the breath of reason itself, slays an
immortality rather than a life.

35   Hear this revelation of the Apostle of Thessalonians: 'To the pure all things
are pure,' not only meats and drinks, but all kind of knowledge whether of
good or evil; the knowledge cannot defile, nor consequently the books, if the
will and conscience be not defiled. For books are as meats and viands are, some
of good, some of evil substance, and yet God in that unapocryphal vision, said
40   without exception, 'Rise Peter, kill and eat,' leaving the choice to each man's
discretion. Wholesome meats to a vitiated stomach differ little or nothing from
unwholesome, and best books to a naughty mind are not unapplyable to
occasions of evil. Bad meats will scarce breed good nourishment in the healthi-
est concoction; but herein the difference is of bad books, that they to a discreet
45   and judicious reader serve in many respects to discover, to confute, to forewarn
and to illustrate.

25. Which of the following is the grammatical antecedent of "them" in line 18?

(A)   Souls   (D)   Books

(B)   Authors   (E)   Children

(C)   Lives

26. The passage reads most like which of the following?

(A)   A letter   (D)   A rebuttal

(B)   A lesson   (E)   A sermon

(C)   A conversation

27. The author likens "killing" a book to killing a man. In what ways does the
author imply that the former is worse?

I.   Books live longer than men.

II.   Books, as objects, are free of sin.

III. Many men don't deserve to live.

(A)   I and III only.   (B)   I and II only.

(C) II and III only.   (D) All of the above.

(E) None of the above.

28. How does the author use "Rise Peter, kill and eat" to argue that printing should not be regulated?

(A) Just as Peter should strike down his own food, each man should destroy evil books.

(B) Just as God let Peter choose what meat to eat, men should be able to choose freely what to read.

(C) Just as Peter eats what he himself kills, men should read whatever books they find.

(D) Just as men need to hunt for edible food, the human mind needs the quest for truth and wisdom.

(E) Just as hunting has physical dangers, reading should have perils for the mind and soul.

29. The passage compares books to all of the following EXCEPT

(A) the image of God.   (D) reason.

(B) armed men.   (E) a vial of living intellect.

(C) a vault.

30. According to the passage, the regulation of printing will

(A) result in a ban on books.

(B) create a black market.

(C) discourage scientific discovery.

(D) suppress the word of God.

(E) inhibit the distribution of knowledge.

31. The author's tone in the passage's opening (lines 1-5) is

(A) scolding.   (D) pleading.

(B) sarcastic.   (E) agreeing.

(C) respectful.

32. In the second paragraph, the author shifts from one stance to another. That shift is from

(A)   agreement to warning.   (D)   acknowledgment to justification.

(B)   agreement to disagreement.   (E)   concern to wariness.

(C)   acknowledgment to denial.

33.   How does the author feel about censorship?

(A)   He is against it in every form.

(B)   It should only apply to blasphemous texts.

(C)   It should be determined by the church, not the state.

(D)   It should occur after the book exists, not before the book is first circulated.

(E)   It is a necessary evil.

34.   The sentence beginning "And yet on the other hand" (lines 20-23) serves primarily to

(A)   flatter the government officials being addressed.

(B)   introduce the author's departure from agreeing with them.

(C)   contradict the preceding part of the paragraph.

(D)   start an unrelated topic.

(E)   introduce the first metaphor.

35.   The author's argument would be more influential to a wider audience if he were to

(A)   quote prominent publishers.

(B)   include graphs and illustrations.

(C)   use puns and satire.

(D)   use historic examples instead of religious ones.

(E)   eliminate the transparently flattering introduction.

36.   The author's attitude toward the power of books in lines 24-25 is

(A)   envy.   (D)   respect.

(B)   suspicion.   (E)   hatred.

(C)   worship.

37.   What is the author's purpose in the repetition of the closing lines of the passage, ending with "to discover, to confute, to forewarn, and to illustrate"?

(A)   The author is emphasizing that reading is not man's only pasttime.

(B)   The author points out that there are more ways to learn than from books.

(C)   The author is emphasizing that readers are more socially active in general.

(D)   The author points out that reading is not passive, that men read and react according to their natures.

(E)   The author is emphasizing that all knowledge, good and evil, expands the experiences of men.

38.   The passage's longest sustained metaphor is that of books as

(A)   men.   (D)   mummies.

(B)   dragon's teeth.   (E)   reason itself.

(C)   meat.

Questions 39 - 52 are based on the following passage. Read the passage carefully before choosing your answers.

Prohibition was the world's first enactment, written by the finger of God in the Garden of Eden to keep the way of life, to preserve the innocence and character of man. But under the cover of the first night, "in the cool of the day," there crept into the Garden a brewer by the name of Beelzebub, who told
5 the first man that God was a liar; that he could sin and not die; that the prohibition law upon the tree of life was an infringement upon his personal liberty and that the law had no right to dictate what a man should eat or drink or wear. The devil induced Adam to go into rebellion against the law of God in the name of personal liberty, and from that hour dates the fall of man.

10 We are hearing something of that same argument in this campaign against the serpent drink, and not only on the part of the enemy. There are many good men who look upon prohibition as an assault upon the personal liberty of the citizen; but it seems to us they do not keep clear the issues involved in this fight. They are not personal at all.

15 Personal liberty is a matter of personal choice, of personal right to eat or to drink. No prohibitory law ever adopted or proposed attempts to interfere with that right. It does not seek to compel a man to abstain; it does not say that he ought not, must not, or dare not drink. It passes only upon the social right of trade, traffic and sale. Whether a man drinks or abstains is entirely his own
20 affair, so long as he does not poison himself, compel society to cure him, support him when he is unable to take care of himself, lock him up when he is

dangerous to be at large, bury him at the public expense when he is a corpse, or interfere with the personal liberty of others when he is exercising his own.

Men do not properly discriminate between a personal right and a social act.
25 Personal liberty relates to private conduct. If a man signs the temperance pledge he surrenders his personal liberty or personal privilege to drink; when he votes dry—to prohibit liquor traffic—it has nothing to do with the question of personal liberty.

You have a personal right to eat putrid meat; I have no right to sell it. If
30 your hog dies a natural death, or with the cholera, you have a personal right to grind it up into a sausage and eat it, but you have no right to offer it for public sale. A man has a personal right to corn his dead mule and serve it on his own table. You have as good a right to eat your cat as I have my chicken, or your dog as I have my pig. The Chinese in New York have a dog feast at their New
35 Year's celebration and the police have never interfered with their personal right. But if you opened a meat market and skinned dogs and cats or exposed horse sausage for public sale, the meat inspector would confiscate the entire supply, close up the place as a public nuisance and arrest you for selling what you had a personal right to eat.

40 To abstain is a personal act; to market, traffic and trade is a social act, limited by the social effect of the thing sold and the place where it is kept for sale. This distinction between total abstinence, which relates to personal liberty or personal conduct, and prohibition, which relates to social conduct and the State, is perfectly clear. The one is the act of the individual; the other is the act
45 of the State.

Total abstinence is the voluntary act of one man; it recognizes the right of choice of personal liberty. Prohibition is the act of the community, the State, the majority, which is the State, and is a matter of public policy, to conserve social and civic liberty by denying to an immoral and dangerous traffic the
50 right of public sale.

39. Which of the following does the author use as a synonym for "the majority"?

(A) The right   (D) The State

(B) The God-fearing populus   (E) Men

(C) Society

40. What does the author believe about "personal rights"?

(A) Personal rights must be agreed upon by society.

(B) Personal rights are confined to the privacy of the home.

(C) Personal rights are a fiction—societies have only personal privileges.

(D) Personal rights are forfeit when abused.

(E) Personal rights do not justify all social acts.

41. What means of argument is used in the fifth paragraph?

(A) A series of distinct metaphors

(B) A sustained metaphor

(C) Repetitous legal examples

(D) Satirical pseudo-legal examples

(E) Point by point counter-examples

42. The sentence beginning "You have a personal right" (line 29) is distinct from others in its paragraph in that it serves primarily to

(A) distinguish between personal rights and public acts.

(B) associate liquor with putrid meat.

(C) emphasize the difference between reader and author.

(D) associate the author with the Prohibition movement.

(E) mirandize the reader.

43. The author's tone in the second paragraph can best be described as

(A) annoyed.   (D) impatient.

(B) corrective.   (E) bored.

(C) condescending.

44. Which of the following is described as "immoral" (line 49)?

(A) Right   (D) Traffic

(B) Sale   (E) Liberty

(C) Public

45. What contradiction exists between the first and fifth paragraphs?

(A) The first paragraph uses religious/literary examples, while the fifth paragraph uses legal examples.

(B)   The first paragraph takes liberties with its source to make an example, but the fifth does not.

(C)   The first paragraph assumes the reader is a Christian, while the fifth assumes the reader is a lawyer.

(D)   The first paragraph associates prohibition with eating, while the fifth associates it with sale.

(E)   The first paragraph is about fruit, while the fifth is about meat.

46.   The author uses all of the following to refer to Satan EXCEPT

(A)   Beelzebub.   (D)   the enemy.

(B)   a liar.   (E)   a brewer.

(C)   the devil.

47.   What is the purpose of the sentence beginning "Whether a man drinks" (lines 19-23)?

(A)   to ridicule drinkers for comic effect

(B)   to exaggerate the evils of alcohol and so demean the opposition's credibility

(C)   to demonstrate that even a personal liberty can become a social concern

(D)   to explain the pervasiveness of personal liberties

(E)   to argue that personal liberties are inherently a social burden

48.   According to the passage, the purpose of prohibition is to

(A)   conserve social and civic liberty.

(B)   limit hazardous personal liberties.

(C)   deny public sale to immoral and dangerous traffic.

(D)   enforce the will of God on weak men.

(E)   eliminate the profit from liquor consumption.

49.   In the first paragraph, the author implies that

(A)   Satan is a lawyer.

(B)   Satan was correct.

(C)   the Eden story is historic fact.

(D)   the fruit is analagous to alcohol.

(E)   Eden is abstinence.

50. Which of the following does the passage say is the distinction between total abstinence and prohibition?

    I.   One relates to personal conduct; the other relates to social conduct.

    II.   One is the act of the individual; the other is the act of the State.

    III. One recognizes personal liberty; the other is a matter of public policy.

    (A) I and II only.   (D) All of the above.

    (B) I and III only.   (E) None of the above.

    (C) II and III only.

51. In the context of the passage, what does "dry" mean?

    (A) To be sober

    (B) To have signed a temperance pledge

    (C) To not offer alcohol

    (D) To outlaw the sale of alcohol

    (E) To thirst for alcohol

52. What do the closing lines imply about the speaker?

    (A) His principal concern is the safety of the public.

    (B) He has a strong belief in God.

    (C) He believes laws should uphold morality.

    (D) He wants drinkers to brew their own intoxicants.

    (E) He maintains the majority is always right.

Questions 53 - 60 are based on the following passage. Read the passage carefully before choosing your answers.

First, truly, to all them that, professing learning, inveigh against poetry, may justly be objected that they go very near to ungratefulness, to seek to deface that which, in the noblest nations and languages that are known, hath been the first lightgiver to ignorance, and first nurse, whose milk by little and little
5 enabled them to feed afterwards of toughest knowledges. And will they now play the hedgehog, that, being received into the den, drive out his host? Or rather vipers, that with their birth kill their parents? Let learned Greece, in any of her manifold sciences be able to show me one book before Musaeus, Homer, and Hesiod, all three nothing but poets. Nay, let any history be brought that

can say any writers were there before them, if they were not men of the same
skill, as Orpheus, Linus, and some other are named, who, having been the first
of that country that made pens deliverers of their knowledge to their posterity,
may justly challenge to be called their fathers in learning. For not only in time
they had this priority—although in itself antiquity be venerable—but went
before them as causes, to draw with their charming sweetness the wild untamed wits to an admiration of knowledge. So as Amphion was said to move
stones with his poetry to build Thebes, and Orpheus to be listened to by
beasts,—indeed stony and beastly people. So among the Romans were Livius
Andronicus and Ennius; so in the Italian language the first that made it aspire
to be a treasurehouse of science were the poets Dante, Boccace, and Petrarch;
so in our English were Gower, and Chaucer, after whom, encouraged and
delighted with their excellent foregoing, others have followed to beautify our
mother-tongue, as well in the same kind as the other arts.

53. What is the author's tone in saying "all three (were) nothing but poets" (line 9)?

(A) Negative

(D) Mocking

(B) Condescending

(E) Harping

(C) Satirical

54. According to the passage, the significance of poetry to learning is that

(A) poetry helps break the monotony of more boring subjects.

(B) rhyming aids the memorization required in other subjects.

(C) poetry teaches the student that learning is fun.

(D) poetry builds learning strengths needed for more difficult subjects.

(E) poetry teaches the language, a prerequisite to all learning.

55. The sentence beginning "Or rather vipers" (lines 6-7) serves primarily to

(A) associate the alleged ungratefulness with a most extreme example.

(B) cloud the issue with proverbial references.

(C) imply that others are guilty of the vipers's crime.

(D) allude to the myth that snakes nurse from cows' udders.

(E) link the accused with coldbloodedness.

56. In the context of the passage, "wits" (line 16) means

    (A) jokes.   (D) senses of humor.

    (B) cares.   (E) men.

    (C) minds.

57. What does the passage attribute to Amphion?

    (A) Being the first light-giver to ignorance

    (B) Recording on paper for prosperity

    (C) Beautifying his mother tongue

    (D) Cultivating sophisticated minds

    (E) Building with stone blocks

58. As implied by the passage, which of the following groups of men speak one language among them?

    I.   Dante, Boccace, and Petrarch

    II. Amphion, Thebes, and Orpheus

    III. Homer, Hesiod, and Musaeus

    (A) I only.   (D) I and II only.

    (B) II only.   (E) I and III only.

    (C) III only.

59. What would be the effect of changing "aspire" to "attempt" in line 19?

    (A) "Attempt" conveys the idea that this was a real, tangible task.

    (B) "Attempt" clips the wings off the loftiness of "aspire."

    (C) "Attempt" makes the sentence choppy in contrast to "aspire."

    (D) "Attempt" negates the personification of "language."

    (E) "Attempt" implies impending failure.

60. The passage's primary goal is to associate poetry with

    (A) instruction.   (D) communication.

    (B) language.   (E) education.

    (C) history.

Section 2

TIME: 1 hour and 45 minutes
3 Essay Questions

Question 1 (Suggested time—35 minutes.) This question is one third of the total essay score.

The literary genre of fantasy is characterized by the existence of a fantasy realm in which an alternate mode of existence—an imaginary world—exists in severe disjunction with reality. Characteristics of the alternate world include:

> the quality of the mythical and the imagined (think of unicorns, magical powers, spirits),
> the achievable ideal (dreams and fantasies can be realized),
> distortions of time (time is compressed or lengthened),
> simplification of character,
> expression of repressed desires,
> and alternate values to reality (the world operates by a set of values different from those in reality).

For example, Lewis Caroll's *Alice in Wonderland* is a classic example of literary fantasy: Alice visits an alternate world in which time is distorted, fantastic creatures abound, and the everyday values of reality do not exist.

Such elements that constitute fantasy are also present in the non-literary: campaign speeches, product advertising, cartoon strips, children's toys. Select a topic that can be represented as an alternate world and write a well-organized essay explaining how at least two of the elements of literary fantasy are manifested in that alternate world. Be sure to use concrete details and explanations to back your thesis.

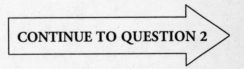

CONTINUE TO QUESTION 2

Question 2 (Suggested time—35 minutes.) This question is one-third of the total essay score.

To market a product successfully, it is necessary to appeal to the targeted consumer group. In addition to consumer needs, desires, personalities, spending habits, etc., advertisers need to tailor all aspects of the language to create an effective, appropriate advertisement.

HEY! Recognize this? [picture of the old Chevron] Sorry, wrong generation.

How about this? [picture of the new Chevron] Nice isn't it? Hard to believe it's from the same generation that spawned bell bottoms, platforms, the Village People, and expressions like "groovy" and "far out." Whoa, that was when our parents were cool.

But hey, we're a a new generation, and now we're wearing Levis and flannel, cowboy boots and metal, and well, bell-bottoms and platforms. Like those classics, the Chevron is back, only it's not a car just for our parents anymore. It's our time now, and with the newly designed Chevron, we can express ourselves with power, speed, and sleek styling that shouts, "Hey, it's me!" Best of all, with the most standard features in its class, it still won't break the bank. So it'll leave you with enough money for all the CDs you need to listen to, concerts you need to attend, cities you need to visit, bridges you need to bungee-jump from…

Write a brief essay explaining why and how this ad is appropriate for the intended audience. Consider such elements as language, tone, syntax, and diction in your explanation.

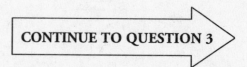

CONTINUE TO QUESTION 3

Question 3 (Suggested time—35 minutes.) This question is one-third of the total essay score.

Examine the following poem by William Wordsworth. Write an essay that explains what view of the world the speaker is presenting to the reader and how elements of language such as syntax, diction, imagery, and tone persuade the reader to share this view.

The world is too much with us; late and soon,
Getting and spending, we lay waste our powers;
Little we see in Nature that is ours;
We have given our hearts away, a sordid boon!
This Sea that bares her bosom to the moon,
The winds that will be howling at all hours,
Are up-gathered now like sleeping flowers,
For this, for everything, we are out of tune;
It moves us not—Great God! I'd rather be
A Pagan suckled in a creed outworn;
So might I, standing on this pleasant lea,
Have glimpses that would make me less forlorn;
Have sight of Proteus rising from the sea;
Or hear old Triton blow his wreathed horn.

EXAM IS FINISHED

AP Examination in English Language & Composition

TEST III

ANSWER KEY

Section 1

1.	(C)	21.	(C)	41.	(C)
2.	(A)	22.	(B)	42.	(B)
3.	(D)	23.	(D)	43.	(B)
4.	(D)	24.	(E)	44.	(D)
5.	(E)	25.	(D)	45.	(D)
6.	(A)	26.	(E)	46.	(B)
7.	(B)	27.	(A)	47.	(C)
8.	(D)	28.	(B)	48.	(A)
9.	(E)	29.	(C)	49.	(D)
10.	(D)	30.	(E)	50.	(D)
11.	(C)	31.	(C)	51.	(D)
12.	(D)	32.	(A)	52.	(C)
13.	(A)	33.	(D)	53.	(C)
14.	(C)	34.	(B)	54.	(D)
15.	(B)	35.	(D)	55.	(A)
16.	(E)	36.	(C)	56.	(C)
17.	(C)	37.	(D)	57.	(E)
18.	(E)	38.	(A)	58.	(E)
19.	(A)	39.	(D)	59.	(B)
20.	(D)	40.	(E)	60.	(E)

Detailed Explanations of Answers

Test III

Section 1

1. **(C)** The rephrased sentence reads: **Landmark discoveries in astronomy eventually forced religious scholars to interpret biblical passages less and less literally.** The ideal for these sentences is that they be clear and concise, and above all else maintain the meaning of the original sentence. The change "to interpret" is the most concise and maintains the meaning. (E) "into interpreting of" is disqualified by "of," which makes the phrase awkward and would distort the rest of the sentence. (A) "to the interpretation of" is possible but too wordy, and (D) "to be interpreting" is less workable and too wordy. (B) "with interpreting" is incorrect because "forced...with" is incongruous.

2. **(A)** The rephrased sentence reads: **Most consumers express concern for the environment in opinion polls, but too few are willing to pay more for the safety constraints suggested by experts.** This sentence is simply two conflicting clauses linked by a conjunction that demonstrates their conflict. "Although" can precede either clause. However, "but" in most cases is placed between the two clauses. The omission of "Although" requires what preceded it to become the beginning of the sentence, rendering (A) "Most consumers express" correct. (B) "Most express" is less clear because it does not identify to whom "most" refers. (C) "but consumers are too willing" is a major and erroneous change to the original sentence. Although it is not actually wrong, (D) "but too few consumers" will sound repetitious after "Most consumers" in the beginning of the sentence, and similarly fails to be concise. The extraneous inclusion of "then" in (E) "But then too few" makes it incorrect.

3. **(D)** The rephrased sentence reads: **The new employee tried to make a good impression with a suggestion for a more economical resource deployment system.** The word "proposing" is a verb and uses the remainder of the sentence as its object, but "suggestion" is a noun and needs the remainder of the sentence to be in an adjective prepositional phrase. (D) "for a more economical" begins that prepositional phrase. (A) "for more economical" is awkward without "a" as in (D). (B) "to deploy a system" is a rearrangement that no longer describes the "system." Any use of "that resources" of (C)

in keeping with the original's meaning will be wordy and awkward. (E) "that is more economical" would work at the end of the sentence, but would be more wordy than (D).

4.   **(D)**   The rephrased sentence reads: **The columnist's implication that the "eye witnesses" behind Trader's conviction were compensated by the state was the real incendiary to the scandal.** This answer, "implication that," is the simplest change, allowing "that...prosecutor" from the original to remain unchanged. (A) "implication of" and (E) "implication concerning" require a noun clause to follow, which would cause extensive changes to the sentence. (B) "implication having been" is an inappropriate and inconsistent verb tense. (C) "implication because he" would at best eventually be wordy and would only possibly ever be clear.

5.   **(E)**   The rephrased sentence reads: **Buying his way into people's confidences, Lawrence is gaining enough backing to make a bid for office.** Beginning the sentence with "Buying…" makes a dependent clause, which needs to be set off with a comma, and followed by the subject and verb. (E) "confidences, Lawrence is" best fulfills these needs. The failing point of (A) "confidences he is" is that "he" would have no antecedent and the sentence's meaning would be less specific. (B) "confidences by which Lawrence is" makes a dependent clause of what must be the independent clause. The "so" of (C) "confidences, so Lawrence is" is a conjuction, but it cannot be used to link the two different kinds of clauses. (D) "confidences is how Lawrence is" attempts to use the dependent clause "Buying…confidences" as a noun clause, which it is not.

6.   **(A)**   The rephrased sentence reads: **The administrator's treatment of female employees demonstrates why so few ever work here longer than a year.** The change makes "demonstrates" the verb of the sentence and requires that "how…treats" become the subject—the noun that demonstrates. Thus, (A) "The administrator's treatment" is the answer because it is a successful conversion to the needed noun and subject. (B) "The fact of the administrator's treatment" is awkwardly workable, but wordy. Both (C) "Due to the treatment" and (E) "On account of the administrator's treatment" place the needed subject in a phrase where it cannot serve the needs of the sentence. (D) "The administrator treating" is workable, but slightly awkward. It is incorrect only because (A) exists.

7.   **(B)**   The rephrased sentence reads: **Portraying its product as a catalyst for male-female interaction implies an end to loneliness is but a purchase away.** In this sentence, we have an independent verb clause and a dependent verb clause. The change makes the independent dependent; so we must make the dependent independent. (B) "implies" puts the formerly dependent verb in the same tense as the original independent verb. (A) "will imply" and (C) "have implied" change the verb tense of the sentence. (D) "then interacts and (E) "will interact" alter the wrong word and fail to address the needs of the sentence.

8.   **(D)**   The rephrased sentence reads: **Despite a very limited budget, the theater company's performances never labor under frugality.** This sentence has two indepen-

dent clauses which express contradictory ideas. The conjunction which links them must point out this contradiction, as "and yet" did in the original. Conjunctions "but" and "although" are alternatives. (C) "Although the theater company operates" successfully accomplishes the conversion from one conjunction to the other and is a good answer, it is not the best answer. (D) "Despite a very limited budget" creates more structural changes; but in doing so, it maintains the meaning of the original sentence and expresses it more concisely. (D) transforms a simple compound sentence into a brief complex sentence. (A) "A very limited budget" never introduces the contradiction between the sentence parts. (B) "Although a very limited budget" needed "on" ("Although on a…") if it were to work. (E) "Whereas the theater company operates" fails to introduce the conflict.

9. **(E)**   The rephrased sentence reads: **Merging onto a busy highway requires that you match the speed of the flowing traffic and pray the other motorists get out of the way.** The word "require" is one of those verbs that may be paired with another, such as "ask to leave," "tell to leave," "permit to leave," etc. It may be followed by the infinitive form of the second verb, or by a sentence clause. The sentence clause takes the direct object from, for instance, "ask him to leave" into the subject of the sentence clause—"ask that he leave"—making the entire sentence clause the direct object. "What is required? that he leave." Notice that "to leave" became "leave" in this transformation. Similarly, (E) "and pray" shows the conversion from "requires you to match…and to pray" to "requires that you match…and pray." Both "match" and "pray" are predicates to the subject "you." (A) "and prays" assumes a third person singular subject. (B) "and praying" is the wrong verb tense. (C) "and should pray" has a change to the conditional, which differs from the original. (D) "and to pray" fails to recognize that "pray" needs the same conversion as "match."

10. **(D)**   The rephrased sentence reads: **In Shakespeare, there is a role which is perhaps the most demanding in King Lear.** The construction "there is" is a declaration of existence, presenting either a noun or a noun clause. The declaration of (A) "one demanding" does not carry the weight of "most demanding" in the original. (C) "role is" is incorrect because the verb has already been provided. Now, one potential rewrite which meets the specifications and the original's meaning is "In Shakespeare there is perhaps no more demanding role than King Lear." However, it contains "more demanding" and "role than," (E) and (B) respectively. Because two options cannot both be correct, they must both be wrong. The answers that the test makers expect is (D) "most demanding in," such as "In Shakespeare, there is a role which is perhaps the most demanding in King Lear." Remember, competing answers that logically require one another must both (or all) be wrong.

11. **(C)**   The author suggests that "injustice is part of the necessary friction" of government, implying that government does not react to the injustices it encounters. This gives the impression of a lack of awareness and concern. The idea that your life should "be a counter-friction to stop the machine" implies that the machine cannot be operated, that it is going about its purpose and can only be sabotaged. For these reasons,

the answer is (C) "single-minded and unfeeling." The passage says nothing favorable about the "machine," eliminating (A) "efficient and reliable" and (E) "labor-saving." The author finds the government as efficient as being lost but making great time. The passage also is not optimistic about the "machine," as notable in the "let your life be a counter-friction" quotation; so (D) "reparable" is incorrect. Nowhere does the author complain literally about machines; so (B) "noisy and polluting" is also incorrect.

12. **(D)** A quick scan of these questions will tell you that these are not "topics to be covered in the essay"; so (A) is incorrect. Also, one will note that these are the legitimate concerns of the author, so (C) "He is satirically posing the questions of those he disagrees with" is incorrect. At no point in the essay does the author antagonize his reading audience; so (E) "He wants to polarize his readers…" is incorrect. The idea of (B), that the author "expects…the reasons," seems possible at first with the beginning questions, but the last question, "Why does it always crucify Christ,…pronounce Washington and Franklin rebels?" obviously is accosting different governments of different centuries. These questions of the author do not function truly as questions—they have no addressee and expect no answers. The author is complaining about the traditional abuses of government, even "good" government. (D) "He is rhetorically stating what the government does and should not" is the correct answer.

13. **(A)** The speaker's primary goal is to address the injustices of the state so they may be undone. He would obviously prefer a simple tax revolt; so (B) "encourage an armed revolution" is incorrect. However, this is a means, not an end; so "reduce the tax burden" (E) is incorrect also. The author never refers to the taxes as weighty or unfair, only misused. He would certainly not "attract persecuted minorities to Massachusetts" (C), because Massachusetts supposedly "imprisons unjustly." The author cannot be said to "promote a political party" (D), because his proposal of a tax revolt would not exchange a single elected official for another person. The author seeks to "evoke the moral responsibility of the reader" (A), as in "Under a government which imprisons any unjustly, the true place for a just man is also a prison."

14. **(C)** The passage suggests that men not pay their taxes, which is "a proposal of peaceful protest" (A). The passage refers to the governments of Christ, Copernicus, and Washington, which are "historical references to other governments" (B). The passage states, "But even suppose blood should flow. Is there not a sort of blood shed when the conscience is wounded?," or "justification for bloodshed" (D). The passage opens with a series of rhetorical questions, which are "unanswered questions" (E). By elimination, the answer is "criticism of specific persons," (C), which never occurs in the passage.

15. **(B)** The passage reads "…in her prisons…It is there that…," so the correct answer is (B) "prison." The same paragraph refers to (A) "Massachusetts," but at best you would have to say "Massachusetts prisons" to capture the same meaning. Neither (C) "legislative building," (D) "church, nor (E) "the grave," occur in the paragraph to be potential antecedents.

16. **(E)**   The lines being paraphrased are "A minority is powerless while it conforms to the majority; it is not even a minority then; but it is irresistible when it clogs by its whole weight." (A) "A minority…so it can disable the majority" is an inaccurate paraphrase because the minority should clog the "machine" of government, not assault the majority. (B) "A minority is an important part of the majority…" is obviously wrong. The minority is an important part of the people, but, by definition, not any part of the majority. (C) "A majority exists…" is incorrect because it transposes "minority" and "majority." (D) "A minority…brings injustice upon itself" is incorrect because lines 34-36 say nothing of the kind. The answer is (E) "A minority that complies to the will of the majority ceases to exist, but a minority that fully commits itself to impeding the unjust action of the majority is unconquerable" because it accurately hits all the points of the original.

17. **(C)**   The author says to the tax-gatherer "if you really wish to do anything, resign your office," which is (C) "quit his job." The author never suggests (A) "steal the state's funds" or (B) "submit counterfeit money." Nor does the author threaten the officer, as (D) "expect gunshots for greetings" and (E) "sleep with one eye open" suggest.

18. **(E)**   First (C) "the governors" can be eliminated because it is plural while "it" and "its" need a singluar antecedent. Line 10 refers to "its citizens," which allows us to eliminate (A) "fault of…," (B) "evil of…," and (D) "deceit of…" because, while governments can have citizens, faults, evils and deceits are not said to have citizens. Now it will be important to note the author's distinction between "the government" and "government." The use of "the" implies the specification of a specific one or example, while its conspicuous absence implies a generalization. If you heard someone say, "The man is prone to violence," you would respond, "Lock him up" or "Get him help"; but if that person had said, "Man is prone to violence," you would respond, "Is it the culture or the species?" The paragraph refers to the different governments of Christ, Copernicus, and Washington as if they were one or as if he were stating a general truth. Therefore, "it's" meaning is best captured by (E), "government."

19. **(A)**   The question asks you to contrast "What I have to do is to see, at any rate, that I do not lend myself to the wrong which I condemn" with "Under a government which imprisons any unjustly, the true place for a just man is also a prison." (B) "…only react to what he sees…" takes "to see" from the original in the too literal sense of vision when the author meant "to see" as in "to make sure." Similarly, "…neither borrower nor lender be…" (C) takes "lend" too literally when the author used "lend myself" to mean "aid." (D) "…it is enough to condemn justice…" is incorrect because, in the original, the author insists that beyond condemning injustice, he must not assist its function. (E) "…advise a man to circumvent the wrongs of his state…" is incorrect because the author nowhere advises avoidance of problems—he always advises protesting to them, whether by strike or opposition. "In lines 19-20, the author is content not to participate in injustice; but in lines 21-22, the existence of an injustice compels the author to give up his freedom in protest." (A) accurately paraphrases the conflict of the original lines.

20. **(D)** The entire sentence referred to in this question is "Cast your whole vote, not a strip of paper merely, but your whole influence." The key word is "influence," which helps to identify (D) "do everything you can to influence lawmaking" as the correct answer. "Vote in every election…" (A) does not convey the "whole influence" of a person, and neither does (B) "vote…across the board" or (E) "vote…your conscience." "Run for office" (C) suggests one's whole influence is given, but nowhere does the passage imply that the author is suggesting everyone run for office.

21. **(C)** While (A) "the author has been unjustly imprisoned" or (B) "the author has a loved one…imprisoned" are conceivable, they are not inferred by lines 22-25. Nowhere is it suggested that (D) "Massachusetts' prisons are overcrowded." When the passage says the state "put out and locked out" some citizens, it is metaphorically referring to imprisonment (note line 23 "in her prisons"), not the banishment suggested by (E) "…banished citizens…" While one may argue that imprisonment is a form of banishment, the correct answer must reflect most precisely what the passage's lines imply. These lines say the principled men in Massachusetts should be in prison; thus, the answer is (C) "the author is either in prison or not in Massachusetts."

22. **(B)** The change from "it" to "they" would not significantly alter the strength of the argument, so (A) "…lose impact" is incorrect. Another problem with (A) is a problem for (C) "…no longer lump all governments…"; while they refer to changes that may or may not be accurate, they are not "changes in tone" as the question requires. "…More accusatory…" (D) and (E) "…more condescending…" claim changes in tone, but these changes do not occur with the stated substitution. The correct answer is (B) "…less condemning and more of a general complaint:" by not lumping the governments into one, as (C) mentioned, the accusation becomes buckshot, covering several targets instead of a single strike at a single entity.

23. **(D)** Because the questions of the opening paragraph are never answered, (A) "question, answer, enact" is incorrect. Because the opening paragraph does not intend to address the government, it cannot be said to prod anyone or anything into action; so (B) "goad, insult, attack" is incorrect. Similarly, (C) "taunt, imply, condemn" is incorrect because the government must be addressed to be taunted. "Argue, reason, propose" (E) is a reasonable answer; but (D) is better and correct because the opening of the passage is best described as criticizing. Also, the passage does more than merely "suggest" and "propose." It follows through to "inspire" action.

24. **(E)** These lines do not necessarily assume (A) "the State is a democracy" because any government gets its power from the tolerance of the people. While (B) "…all…act simultaneously" would be the best means of enacting the author's proposal, it would not be necessary to its success. To say that "the prisons won't be large enough" (C) is to assume the government has little imagination concerning where to put people and how else to punish them. "The women will not bail out the men" (D) ignores the option of prisoners to refuse bail. The assumption behind lines 36-37 is (E) "'all just men' are a

significant number" of which the government will need to take notice. "All just men" is best in quotation marks because it is, as the author defines them, implicitly "those who agree with me."

25. **(D)** The clause begins at line 15 with "for books are…," and so "books" (D) is the correct answer. Books are bred by "authors"; (B), so that is not the correct option. "Souls" (A), "lives" (C), and "children" (E) do not occur in the sentence as plurals and so cannot be the antecedent of "them."

26. **(E)** The passage lacks the personal tone of both "a letter" (A) and "a conversation" (C). The author is reacting to an event "ye have ordained" (line 5) but not in a point by point way like one would react to an argument in the form of "a rebuttal" (D). The religious nature of the discussion makes the passage most like "a sermon" (E). Because a sermon is a form of "a lesson" (B), that answer seems correct but (E) is more detailed and more accurate.

27. **(A)** The passage says in lines 23-25, "Many a man lives a burden to the earth; but a good book…(has) a life beyond life," which affirms both statement I and statement III. Lines 35-36 say, "books are…some of good, some of evil substance," which contradicts statement II. Therefore, the only correct answer is (A) "I and III only."

28. **(B)** The passage says that the significance of God's command was "leaving the choice to each man's discretion" (lines 40-41). This does not support "…each man's task, not the government's, to destroy evil books" (A) because it concerns consumption as in eating or reading, not destruction as in killing or banning. "Read whatever books…" (C) ignores the choice by limiting the choosing to one—everything. (D) conveys an interesting idea that has nothing to do with the passage. (E) "…perils for the mind and soul" has the ring of something with which the author might agree; but he never suggests this. The correct answer "men should be able to choose" (B) is exactly the argument made by the passage.

29. **(C)** The passage says, "he who destroys a good book…kills reason itself, kills the image of God," (lines 22-23) verifying (D) and (A) respectively. Lines 16-18 say books "do preserve as in a vial…that living intellect that bred them," which verifies option (E) "a vial of living intellect." A less direct connection is made in lines 19-20, "(Books) are…may spring up armed men," verifying (B). The word "vault" does not occur anywhere in the passage; so the answer is "a vault" (C).

30. **(E)** The author makes a warning in lines 7-11 that does not suggest (A) "…a ban on all books" or (B) "…a black market." He worries that regulation will "hinder…discovery…in religious and civil wisdom," but to hinder is not the same as to (C) "discourage…" To make something more difficult is not automatically the same as to make it less desirable. The author is not concerned that religion will be a target as (D)

"suppress the word of God" suggests. One of his concerns is that regulation will "(blunt) our abilities in what we know already," as in (E) "inhibit the distribution of knowledge."

31. **(C)**   The author seems to be addressing a legislative body, and is very tactful and diplomatic. He is not (A) "scolding" or (B) "sarcastic." The author does not concede any agreement (E) until the following paragraph. Although he is making an appeal (D), the author should not be characterized as "pleading," which implies self-deprecation. His tone maintains his own personal audience's "love of truth (and)…uprightness of…judgement" (lines 3-4).

32. **(A)**   The author begins the second paragraph by not only acknowledging the dangers of books, "I deny not…" (line 12), but also by agreeing that some books should be "confine(d), imprison(ed)" (line 14). "Acknowledgment to denial" (C) and "acknowledgment to justification" (D) are incorrect because "acknowledgment" is not strong enough to describe the author's concession. "Concern to wariness" (E) is inaccurate because line 12's "it is of concernment to the church" is not the author's concern but the author's acknowledgment of the church's concern. The paragraph proceeds to suggest that by killing books, you also kill good books. The author's position is not distant enough to be "disagreement" (B). The answer is "agreement to warning" (A).

33. **(D)**   The author's true feelings about censorship are expressed in the beginning of the second paragraph, "it is of the greatest concernment in the church and commonwealth to have a vigilant eye how books demean themselves, as well as men; and thereafter to confine…and do sharpest justice on them as malefactors" (lines 12-15). He is not (A) "…against it in every form," nor does he find it (E) "…a necessary evil." He has an approval of censorship that is not limited to religion as (B) "…apply to blasphemous texts" and (C) "…determine by the church" suggest. His belief is most accurately expressed by (D) "it should occur after the books exists, not before the book is first circulated." The ordinance that the author is reacting to forbids the publishing of books that have not been "approved" by the state.

34. **(B)**   The sentence beginning "And yet on the other hand…" does not (A) "flatter…" anyone; nor does it (E) "introduce the first metaphor" or the second or the third. This sentence begins a change, but not to (D) "…an unrelated topic." It begins to show the potential hazards of regulation, not by (C) "contradict(ing) the preceding…" but by explaining the consequences of improper banning. The sentence serves primarily to (B) "introduce the author's departure from agreement."

35. **(D)**   Any group that would ban books is not likely to be influenced by (A) "quote(d) prominent publishers." The topic is too serious to approach it with (C) "…puns and satire." Because the issue is truly a matter of principle rather than science or commerce, (B) "…graphs…" is not advisable. It is inaccurate to characterize the introduction as (E) "…transparently flattering…"; and, as it is, the introduction cannot

harm the argument. The best proposed change to the essay is (D) "use historic examples instead of religious ones," which would release the limitation of appealing to only Christian faiths.

36. **(C)** The passage in lines 24-25 says, "a good book is the precious life-blood of a master-spirit, embalmed and treasured up on purpose to a life beyond life." The attitude conveyed is certainly positive, eliminating (A) "envy," (B) "suspicion," and (E) "hatred," but we must now distinguish between worship and respect. The lines refer to a purpose without specifying or even remotely describing it. Usually one respects a power, an ability or an authority, but these lines do not emphasis these concepts. The lines have images of death and afterlife, emphasizing religion and suggesting a tone of (C) "worship."

37. **(D)** The closing lines address what men get out of reading, eliminating (A) "...reading is not man's only pasttime" and (B) "...more ways to learn than from books." Similarly, the author is not (C) "...emphasizing that readers are more socially active..." (E) implies that all experience, like all reading, can be positive, but the author would rather emphasize that evil reading can be reacted to in a constructive way. (D) "the author points out that reading is not passive, that men read and react according to their natures" is correct because reading does not "happen" to men. Men are in action when they read.

38. **(A)** The passage only briefly uses the metaphors of (B) "dragon's teeth," (D) "mummies," and (E) "reason itself." While the metaphor of (C) "meat" is used throughout the third paragraph, (A) "men" is used in more lines and in more ways, as the offspring of men, as armed men, as the image of God, and the running death of men metaphor of homicide, martyrdom, and massacre.

39. **(D)** In lines 47-48, the passage says, "Prohibition is the act of the community, the State, the majority, which is the State...," verifying (D) "the State." The passage does not use the words of (A) "the right" or (B) "the Godfearing populus." (C) "society" is never used as a synonym for the majority. While the passage tends toward gender bias, the author does not go so far as to equate the majority with (E) "men."

40. **(E)** The author nevers goes so far as to denounce the legitimacy of personal rights. He does not annihilate all of them by saying they (C) "...are a fiction...." He does not depopulate personal rights by saying they (A) "...must be agreed upon..." or that they (D) "...are forfeit when abused." The author does not restrict personal rights (B) "...to the privacy of the home"; he simply argues that (E) "Personal rights do not justify all social acts"—namely, that the right to eat rotting meat does not create the right to sell rotting meat.

41. **(C)** The fifth paragraph uses examples, not metaphors, eliminating (A) "a series..." and (B) "a sustained...." The examples are in earnest, not (D) "satirical...";

but they are not (E) "point by point counter-examples." The examples of the fifth paragraph, while many, only make one point among them; so they cannot be said to be point by point. They are (C) "repetitious legal examples."

42. **(B)** The sentence beginning "You have a personal right…," (line 29) serves primarily to (B) "associate liquor with putrid meat." The paragraph (A) "distinguish(es) between personal rights and public acts" again and again, but never with so extreme an example as putrid meat. The sentence does not (C) "emphasize the difference between reader and author" because the "you" and the "I" are examples, not distinctions of roles. (D) "associate the author…" is incorrect because the author is in no way seeking to distance himself from his audience. (E) "mirandize the reader" is incorrect because, for the same reason just stated, the author does not assume any authority over the reader.

43. **(B)** The author's tone in the second paragraph is neither (A) "annoyed" nor (E) "bored." There is no sense of him being (D) "impatient," rather there is an atmosphere that a moment's explanation will clear the air. The author's reference to "many good men" dispels the idea that he is being (C) "condescending." The overall tone that simple explanation will convince the many good men that there is no assault on personal liberty is best described as (B) "corrective."

44. **(D)** Line 61 describes (D) "traffic" as immoral, "denying to an immoral and dangerous traffic the right of public sale," not (A) "right," (B) "sale," (E) "liberty," or (C) "public" (which is an adjective).

45. **(D)** Certain differences exist between the first and fifth paragraphs, such as (A) "…religious/literary (vs) legal…," (B) "…takes liberties (vs) not," and (E) "…fruit (vs) meat." However, these differences, while true, do not necessarily mean there is a conflict. Because the paragraphs do not undermine each others' points, they do not truly conflict. (D) "the first paragraph associates prohibition with eating, while the fifth associates it with sale" as eating or consumption. The fifth paragraph labors to convey the idea that prohibition does not limit the personal right to eat, while the first paragraph calls God's forbiddance of eating the fruit of the tree of knowledge "prohibition." (C) is incorrect because in using varying examples, the author does not assume anything about the reader.

46. **(B)** The first paragraph alternately refers to Satan as (A) "Beelzebub," (C) "the devil," and (E) "a brewer." The second paragraph refers to those against prohibition as (D) "the enemy," but there is a secondary meaning implying that "the enemy" is Satan and that he is also against prohibition. The answer is (B) "a liar," which occurs in the first paragraph but is Satan's reference to God.

47. **(C)** The purpose of the sentence beginning "Whether a man drinks" (lines 19-23) is (C) "to demonstrate that even a personal liberty can become a social concern." The sentence is not guilty of (B) "exaggerat(ion)," nor of implying the inevitability of (E) "…personal liberties are inherently a social burden." The sentence is almost comical in

its lengthy list, but it does not go so far as (A) "to ridicule drinkers…" The sentence does demonstrate "…the pervasiveness of personal liberties," but its primary purpose is (C).

48. **(A)** The passage never claims that the law should or does (B) "limit hazardous personal liberties." While allowing people to drink, but not allowing the sale of liquor, may seem to intend (E) "eliminate the profit…," the passage never makes that statement. Nor does the passage outwardly claim that prohibition (D) "enforce(s) the will of God on weak men." The passage claims that prohibition (C) "den(ies) public sale to immoral and dangerous traffic," but that is a definition, not its purpose. The purpose of prohibition, as taken from lines 48-49, is to (A) "conserve social and civic liberty."

49. **(D)** In the first paragraph, the author, to a limited degree, characterizes Satan as a lawyer but never truly implies that (A) "Satan is a lawyer." The concessions of later paragraphs may suggest that (B) "Satan was correct," but the first paragraph does not. The author uses the Eden story as a form of truth without necessarily implying that (C) "the Eden story is historic fact." The first paragraph may imply that Eden was abstinence, but it does not imply that paradise can be regained by avoiding alcohol, that (E) "Eden is abstinence." The author definitely implies that (D) "the fruit is analogous to alcohol," that drinking alcohol is another fall, when he refers to the devil as "a brewer" (line 4).

50. **(D)** Lines 42-43 state, "total abstinence…relates to…personal conduct, and prohibition…relates to social conduct," which verifies statement I. Lines 44-45 state, "one is the act of the individual; the other is the act of the State," which verifies statement II. Lines 46-48 state, "abstinence…recognizes…personal liberty… Prohibition…is a matter of public policy," which verifies statement III. The answer is (D) all of the above.

51. **(D)** The passage does not define "dry" as (A) "…sober" or as (E) "to thirst for alcohol." The passage specifically distinguishes between (B) "(having) signed a temperance pledge" and "dry" in the fourth paragraph. Also, the passage never refers to (C) "to not offer alcohol." Lines 26-27 state, "when he votes dry—to prohibit liquor traffic." The answer is (D) "to outlaw the sale of alcohol."

52. **(C)** The author's belief or disbelief in God is not referred to in the closing lines of the passage, eliminating (B) "He has a strong belief in God." Nowhere does the passage suggest that the author (D) "…wants drinkers to brew their own intoxicants." In the closing lines, the author uses the will of the majority to justify prohibition, but does not (E) "…maint(ain that) the majority is always right." The author expresses (A) "…concern…(for) the safety of the public," but this concern is not implied to be primary. Line 49 refers to "an immoral and dangerous traffic," which implies that the immorality of the product is a reason to restrain it from public sale. The correct answer is that the author (C) "…believes laws should uphold morality."

53. **(C)** The passage intends to exalt poetry; so (A) "negative" is not the tone of line 9. Similarly, the line "all three nothing else but poets" is neither (E) "harping" nor (B) "condescending." The passage is not being serious, but its function is more sophisticated than (D) "mocking." The line is making fun of the idea that these men might be referred to as "nothing else but poets." It is (C) "satiri(zing)" both the attitude and the language.

54. **(D)** The passage does not claim that poetry is more interesting than other subjects; so (A) "poetry helps break the monotony…" is incorrect. Poetry is not limited to rhyming and the author never even refers to the convention; so (B) "rhyming aids…" is incorrect. The passage does not use the word "fun" or anything of a similar meaning; so (C) "poetry teaches the student that learning is fun" is incorrect. While it is an interesting argument that (E) "poetry teaches the language…," the passage does not make it. The answer is (D) "poetry builds learning strengths…," as found in lines 4-5 "(poetry's) milk by little and little enabled them to feed afterwards on tougher knowledges."

55. **(A)** The sentence beginning "Or rather the vipers" is not meant to (D) "allude to the myth that snakes nurse from cows' udders." This test does not require outside knowledge of that sort, only reading and comprehension skills. The sentence might be distantly said to (C) "imply that others are guilty…" and (E) "link the accused with coldbloodedness," but the clearer, more direct function of the sentence is to (A) "associate the alleged ungratefulness with a most extreme example." The sentence does not (B) "cloud the issue with proverbial references," but it might be said to cloud the issue with exaggeration.

56. **(C)** The word "wits" in line 16 is not used in the sense of amusement, which eliminates (A) "jokes" and (D) "senses of humor." The sentence is a discussion of education; so (B) "cares" is incorrect; but both (C) and (E) have potential to be the answer. The sentence reads "wild untamed wits," which is obviously not a reference to savage (E) "men," but uneducated (C) "minds."

57. **(E)** The passage refers to poetry as (A) "being the first light-giver to ignorance" in lines 3-4 and as (D) "cultivating sophisticated minds" in lines 15-16. Orpheus and Linus are credited with (B) "recording on paper for prosperity" in lines 11-12. Chaucer, Gower, and others are said to (C) "beautify his mother tongue" in the closing lines of the passage. In lines 16-17, Amphion is attributed with writing poetry so moving that he used it to (E) "(build) with stone blocks."

58. **(E)** Lines 7-9 refer to Homer, Hesiod, and Musaeus as being from Greece, verifying statement III. Dante, Boccace, and Petrarch are said to aspire to alter Italian in lines 19-20, verifying statement I. Amphion, Thebes, and Orpheus are mentioned in the same sentence in lines 16-18, but Thebes is a city, not a man, disqualifying statement II. The correct answer is (E) "I and III only."

59. **(B)**   A change from "aspire" to "attempt" in line 18 would not (C) "…make the sentence choppy…" While the word "attempt" admits the possibility of failure, (E) "'attempt' implies impending failure" exaggerates the significance of that possibility. The word "attempt" does not (D) "…negate the Personification of 'language'" because it continues to attribute action and intent to "language." While (A) "'attempt' conveys the idea that this was a real, tangible task," the more significant change in tone and effect is (B) "'attempt' clips the wings off the loftiness of 'aspire'."

60. **(E)**   In lines 4-5, the author associates poetry with (A) "instruction." In the closing lines, poetry is associated with (B) "language." Lines 9-10 associate poetry with (C) "history." In lines 21-22, poetry is associated with (D) "communication." Because all of these are true and because they have a cumulative effect, (E) "education" is the answer. "Education" represents all forms of learning, and it is the passage's primary goal to associate poetry with all forms of learning.

Student Response to Essay Question 1:

It seems rare that a young girl of any generation since the invention of the Barbie doll has not been exposed to the phenomenon. With the birth and decline of other less-memorable fads, Barbie has maintained a seemingly immortal position in the toy industry. Barbie's world, however, is an artificial storybook world, a fantastic microcosm of American culture in which the classical elements of literary fantasy can be discerned. As a surrogate world, "Barbie-dom" is characterized by the achievable ideal, and values alternate to those present in reality.

To young girls, Barbie represents an achievable ideal. It cannot be denied that Barbie indeed has it all—every possible symbol of material possession that figures into the American dream can be found in the world of Barbie: her own Corvette, a multilevel mansion, swimming pool, candy store, fast food franchise, a wardrobe of immeasurable size, a steady boyfriend, and a bevy of adoring plastic friends from the same mold. In a nutshell, she is an all-American beauty who dwells in a luxurious world in which every aspect of life is picture-perfect, and moreover, ultimately attainable. As a symbol of the American dream of materialism, Barbie demonstrates that a girl can have anything her heart desires (with the added bonus of no parental supervision).

On a similar note, Barbie's world also operates by values alternate to those present in reality. In her world, the work ethic does not exist and life is instead led in a hedonistic pursuit of fun. Time can be frittered away at the poolside or shopping because Barbie does not need to work for her money. Represented in this fantasy is a mode of living by which Barbie attains everything she desires; but we ask ourselves, *how* does she get it all? For we only see the end rewards in the forms of cars, clothing, and fast-food chains, but are kept ignorant of the processes by which they are attained. Anything Barbie could ever need is begotten by way of wish fulfillment rather than hard work; in reality, as is sometimes all-too-painfully obvious, nothing is obtained that easily.

Ultimately, the world of Barbie can be described as unreal, imagined, idealistic, escapist in short, a fantasy. With her materially-dictated, pleasure-driven lifestyle untainted by the work ethic, Barbie offers the young girl a world of fantasy in which alternate values predominate and impossible ideals are achieved. Barbie, in her material wealth, is the manifestation of an American dream begotten in fantasy, a dream ultimately unattainable in the world of reality.

Analysis of Student Response to Essay Question 1:

This essay effectively accomplishes the assigned task: to represent a non-literary topic or text as a fantasy by illustrating how at least two elements of classic literary fantasy are manifested in an alternate world. By selecting an appropriate topic and by using concrete examples and detailed explanations, the writer demonstrates an understanding of the essay question and the elements of literary fantasy. In this case, the writer chooses to represent the world of the Barbie doll and illustrates, with concrete details, how the fantastic elements of the achievable ideal and values, alternate to those in reality, characterize "Barbie-dom" as an alternative world.

As defined by the essay question, an imaginary world in literary fantasy represents the "achievable ideal" in that dreams and fantasies are fulfilled. In other words, what we dream about or wish for in our everyday fantasies can be realized in the alternative worlds represented in fantasy. Here, the writer depicts how the American dream of ideal materialism and luxury is realized in Barbie's world: her car, wardrobe, and home represent the material possessions of this dream, which, in Barbie's alternate mode of existence, are indubitably attainable. By way of these examples, Barbie, as a girl who "can have anything her heart desires," is shown to be empowered with wish fulfillment. We can recognize wish fulfillment as a means to achieve the ultimate dream.

The imaginary world in literary fantasy operates by a set of values surrogate to those in everyday life. Conventional laws, rules, morals may be altered, reversed, or may even be nonexistent. The writer demonstrates how the work ethic does not exist in Barbie's world. Barbie is able to attain material possessions without the hard work that is normally necessary; since Barbie does not need to work for her money, she can spend her life in a "hedonistic pursuit of fun."

The essay itself is well-ordered, with the thesis clearly stated in the first paragraph and support of the thesis organized in the body. The two chosen elements of literary fantasy are each well-represented and accorded ample analysis in their respective portions of the body. The concluding paragraph reiterates the thesis and summarizes the points made in the essay in a clear and effective manner: "With her materially-dictated, pleasure-driven lifestyle, untainted by the work ethic, Barbie offers the young girl a world of fantasy in which alternate values predominate and impossible ideals are achieved."

Student Response to Essay Question 2:

When trying to reach a specific audience in advertising, one approach is to establish a rapport with the members of that audience through appropriate tone and language. In this case, I chose to adopt a casual, conversational tone to address my intended audience: potential car buyers in their early to mid-twenties. Such a tone is not always conducive to proper grammar or sentence structure and, moreover, would not be suitable for all advertising situations (i.e., marketing investment products to serious investors). Here, however, an easygoing, friendly tone evokes an atmosphere of familiarity, akin to speaking with friends in a twenty-something peer group. The tone puts the reader more at ease and less resistant to a sales message. My ultimate goal is to present the product in a manner that is more like a friend recommending a car, as opposed to a hard-sell sales pitch.

Opening the ad with an emphatic "Hey!" serves to capture the reader's attention much in the manner of calling to a friend (Hey, Joe!). Following with a direct question to the reader (Recognize this?) further emphasizes the tone of familiarity and insinuates a sense of reader involvement.

Informal language and syntax are appropriate companions to the casual tone of the ad. Using such words and phrases as "Hey," "cool," and "living it up" mimics the conventions of informal conversation and everyday slang and bridges the communication gap. The same effect is evoked with the sentence beginning, "But hey, we're a new generation, and it's the age of, well...."

To further identify with the audience, the use of the first person nominative case (we) and the possessive case (our) situates myself as a member of the peer group. I make references to the things "we" want and how this is "our" time. By mentioning current popular trends, such as flannel, platforms, and bellbottoms, I am treading on common ground with the twenty-something peer group. This, along with the affable tone, serves to render less apparent my role as an advertiser trying to sell the product to the consumer and, instead, makes it seem more like a friend recommending the car.

Adopting a casual, familiar tone, using informal language, and identifying with the audience are ways to set a rapport with the audience that facilitates the advertising message. My ultimate goal is to reach the twenty-something consumer by speaking in the language and tone characteristic of this group and by referring to common desires and interests. The desired effect is a more intimate sense of familiarity between myself (the advertiser) and the potential buyer. This approach allows me to present the product to the audience in a manner that is engaging, comfortable, and less obtrusive than a hard-sell sales pitch.

Analysis of Student Response to Essay Question 2:

While advertising and marketing know-how are not required to answer the essay question, an appropriate response should demonstrate a cognizant understanding of the elements of language. As both the advertisement and essay illustrate, the literary elements of tone, diction, language, and syntax can be adapted in advertising to reach a particular audience. Furthermore, the writer furnishes a comprehensive response by explaining both how and why the advertisement is appropriate for its intended audience.

The goal of the advertisement, as stated by the writer, is to present the product in the manner of a friend's recommendation to the targeted audience of twenty-something consumers. To clarify this, the writer explains the choice of a casual tone to establish a rapport with the audience. By capturing the reader's attention with "Hey!" and addressing the reader of the ad with a direct question, the writer establishes an "easygoing, friendly tone," which evokes an air of familiarity and "puts the reader more at ease and less resistant to a sales message." Here, the writer demonstrates both how the casual tone is established and why such a tone is appropriate.

The writer further explains how the use of informal language and syntax ("hey" and "cool" and "it's the age of, well,") complements the casual tone and mimics the slang and conversational style of the twenty-something consumer group in order to "bridge the communication gap." Use of the first person nominative case "we" and the possessive case "our" serves to situate the writer as a member of the audience's peer group. Such an effect is strengthened by reference to popular trends, such as bellbottoms and platform shoes. By such methods, the writer explains, a rapport is established with the audience, which facilitates delivery of the advertising message in the manner of a friend recommending a product to another friend.

Student Response to Essay Question 3:

When considering the structure of society and the movement of human lives within, the following question comes to mind: how far are we from becoming mere automatons in a world structure that places emphasis on "getting and spending" to survive? This is what William Wordsworth warns about in his poem. He laments how people of society have ceased to listen to and appreciate the music of Nature; we have neglected the beauty of our natural surroundings. To William Wordsworth, Nature exists for us to appreciate aesthetically; it is not a mere storehouse of resources to capitalize upon. The beauty of Nature is a gift and we have sacrificed our ability to view and appreciate this gift in exchange for the more material aspects of life.

The poet relays this message as a voice of the conscience of society—a society in which he includes himself initially by the use of the pronoun "we." The use of "we" also serves to include the reader as a member of that society. He observes that we are so restrained by living within society's standards that we are in danger of losing contact with the human side of our nature. We will become mere mechanical entities existing only to function within the confines of the artificial world we have created for ourselves. The phrase, "late and soon,/Getting and spending," invokes a listless, plodding rhythm, evocative of the dull quality of a day-in, day-out existence.

To arouse the reader's sympathy, the poet chooses to personify various aspects of Nature, which elevates Nature to the status of possessing a soul, much like the soul residing within mortals. In this light, an entity with a soul must be treated reverently and respectfully, much as a human soul is treated with respect and reverence. To emphasize the metaphorical image of a personified Nature, Wordsworth capitalizes "Nature" and its aspects (i.e., "The Sea") in the poem. This serves to stress the conception of Nature as an entity to be respected and revered.

Certain phrases and metaphors reinforce the poet's view. In the line, "The world is too much with us," the word "world" is not used in the sense of an earthly connotation; rather, "world" becomes an enveloping term to include all of society, emphasizing our over-involvement in the strictures of society and worldly values. Another detail to note is the phrase "—Great God!" with particular attention to the use of the dashes, which serve to enhance emphatically the shortest line in the poem. Wordsworth is not uttering a blasphemy; rather, the line demands our attention in order to emphasize the extent to which the poet is moved by the condition of our world.

Through these images and phrases, the poet communicates his warning to the reader: the danger of losing touch with our human nature through the loss of our ability to appreciate Nature. Wordsworth tries to elicit the reader's empathy and remove the blinders of everyday existence. While the tone is generally pessimistic, the poet closes the poem with an ancient symbol of hope—an image of the old gods of nature.

Analysis of Student Response to Essay Question 3:

This essay, in an effective and well-ordered manner, begins by answering the question, "What view of the world does the poet present to the reader?" with an insightful interpretation of the poem and a definition of the poet's message. The writer then continues to illustrate not only how the message is relayed, but how the poet, through the manipulation of various literary elements, persuades the reader to accept his view. In addition to providing interpretive remarks, the writer examines specific words, phrases, and images in the poem to illustrate the effects of diction, rhythm, personification, and syntax.

Wordsworth's message is interpreted by the writer as an admonishment to the reader that "we have neglected the beauty of our natural surroundings" and as a warning of "the danger of losing touch with our human nature through the loss of our ability to appreciate Nature." The writer highlights the use of the pronoun "we" as an element of language that establishes the poet as the "voice of the conscience of society," a society in which both the poet and reader are implicated. The element of rhythm is addressed by the writer's allusion to the plodding cadence of the line, "late and soon,/Getting and spending," which evokes the "dull quality" of the mechanical, daily existence of which the poet warns. The personification of Nature, according to the writer, works to arouse the reader's sympathy for an entity (Nature) possessing a soul. The capitalization of Nature and its various aspects further stresses this image. As confirmation of the poet's view, the writer points out the phrase "—Great God!" and explains how the syntactic use of dashes (—) highlights the shortest line in the poem and "emphasizes the extent to which the poet is moved by the condition of our world."

AP

English Language & Composition

Answer Sheets

AP English Language & Composition Test 1

Section I

1. Ⓐ Ⓑ Ⓒ Ⓓ Ⓔ	21. Ⓐ Ⓑ Ⓒ Ⓓ Ⓔ	41. Ⓐ Ⓑ Ⓒ Ⓓ Ⓔ
2. Ⓐ Ⓑ Ⓒ Ⓓ Ⓔ	22. Ⓐ Ⓑ Ⓒ Ⓓ Ⓔ	42. Ⓐ Ⓑ Ⓒ Ⓓ Ⓔ
3. Ⓐ Ⓑ Ⓒ Ⓓ Ⓔ	23. Ⓐ Ⓑ Ⓒ Ⓓ Ⓔ	43. Ⓐ Ⓑ Ⓒ Ⓓ Ⓔ
4. Ⓐ Ⓑ Ⓒ Ⓓ Ⓔ	24. Ⓐ Ⓑ Ⓒ Ⓓ Ⓔ	44. Ⓐ Ⓑ Ⓒ Ⓓ Ⓔ
5. Ⓐ Ⓑ Ⓒ Ⓓ Ⓔ	25. Ⓐ Ⓑ Ⓒ Ⓓ Ⓔ	45. Ⓐ Ⓑ Ⓒ Ⓓ Ⓔ
6. Ⓐ Ⓑ Ⓒ Ⓓ Ⓔ	26. Ⓐ Ⓑ Ⓒ Ⓓ Ⓔ	46. Ⓐ Ⓑ Ⓒ Ⓓ Ⓔ
7. Ⓐ Ⓑ Ⓒ Ⓓ Ⓔ	27. Ⓐ Ⓑ Ⓒ Ⓓ Ⓔ	47. Ⓐ Ⓑ Ⓒ Ⓓ Ⓔ
8. Ⓐ Ⓑ Ⓒ Ⓓ Ⓔ	28. Ⓐ Ⓑ Ⓒ Ⓓ Ⓔ	48. Ⓐ Ⓑ Ⓒ Ⓓ Ⓔ
9. Ⓐ Ⓑ Ⓒ Ⓓ Ⓔ	29. Ⓐ Ⓑ Ⓒ Ⓓ Ⓔ	49. Ⓐ Ⓑ Ⓒ Ⓓ Ⓔ
10. Ⓐ Ⓑ Ⓒ Ⓓ Ⓔ	30. Ⓐ Ⓑ Ⓒ Ⓓ Ⓔ	50. Ⓐ Ⓑ Ⓒ Ⓓ Ⓔ
11. Ⓐ Ⓑ Ⓒ Ⓓ Ⓔ	31. Ⓐ Ⓑ Ⓒ Ⓓ Ⓔ	51. Ⓐ Ⓑ Ⓒ Ⓓ Ⓔ
12. Ⓐ Ⓑ Ⓒ Ⓓ Ⓔ	32. Ⓐ Ⓑ Ⓒ Ⓓ Ⓔ	52. Ⓐ Ⓑ Ⓒ Ⓓ Ⓔ
13. Ⓐ Ⓑ Ⓒ Ⓓ Ⓔ	33. Ⓐ Ⓑ Ⓒ Ⓓ Ⓔ	53. Ⓐ Ⓑ Ⓒ Ⓓ Ⓔ
14. Ⓐ Ⓑ Ⓒ Ⓓ Ⓔ	34. Ⓐ Ⓑ Ⓒ Ⓓ Ⓔ	54. Ⓐ Ⓑ Ⓒ Ⓓ Ⓔ
15. Ⓐ Ⓑ Ⓒ Ⓓ Ⓔ	35. Ⓐ Ⓑ Ⓒ Ⓓ Ⓔ	55. Ⓐ Ⓑ Ⓒ Ⓓ Ⓔ
16. Ⓐ Ⓑ Ⓒ Ⓓ Ⓔ	36. Ⓐ Ⓑ Ⓒ Ⓓ Ⓔ	56. Ⓐ Ⓑ Ⓒ Ⓓ Ⓔ
17. Ⓐ Ⓑ Ⓒ Ⓓ Ⓔ	37. Ⓐ Ⓑ Ⓒ Ⓓ Ⓔ	57. Ⓐ Ⓑ Ⓒ Ⓓ Ⓔ
18. Ⓐ Ⓑ Ⓒ Ⓓ Ⓔ	38. Ⓐ Ⓑ Ⓒ Ⓓ Ⓔ	58. Ⓐ Ⓑ Ⓒ Ⓓ Ⓔ
19. Ⓐ Ⓑ Ⓒ Ⓓ Ⓔ	39. Ⓐ Ⓑ Ⓒ Ⓓ Ⓔ	59. Ⓐ Ⓑ Ⓒ Ⓓ Ⓔ
20. Ⓐ Ⓑ Ⓒ Ⓓ Ⓔ	40. Ⓐ Ⓑ Ⓒ Ⓓ Ⓔ	60. Ⓐ Ⓑ Ⓒ Ⓓ Ⓔ

Section II

Use the following pages on which to write your essays. During the official exam, you will be given 12 lined pages for your essays. Since we are providing fewer pages, be sure to use your own standard ruled paper on which to complete additional pages, if needed.

_____

_____

_____

_____

_____

_____

_____

_____

_____

_____

_____

_____

_____

_____

_____

AP English Language & Composition Test 2

Section I

1. Ⓐ Ⓑ Ⓒ Ⓓ Ⓔ
2. Ⓐ Ⓑ Ⓒ Ⓓ Ⓔ
3. Ⓐ Ⓑ Ⓒ Ⓓ Ⓔ
4. Ⓐ Ⓑ Ⓒ Ⓓ Ⓔ
5. Ⓐ Ⓑ Ⓒ Ⓓ Ⓔ
6. Ⓐ Ⓑ Ⓒ Ⓓ Ⓔ
7. Ⓐ Ⓑ Ⓒ Ⓓ Ⓔ
8. Ⓐ Ⓑ Ⓒ Ⓓ Ⓔ
9. Ⓐ Ⓑ Ⓒ Ⓓ Ⓔ
10. Ⓐ Ⓑ Ⓒ Ⓓ Ⓔ
11. Ⓐ Ⓑ Ⓒ Ⓓ Ⓔ
12. Ⓐ Ⓑ Ⓒ Ⓓ Ⓔ
13. Ⓐ Ⓑ Ⓒ Ⓓ Ⓔ
14. Ⓐ Ⓑ Ⓒ Ⓓ Ⓔ
15. Ⓐ Ⓑ Ⓒ Ⓓ Ⓔ
16. Ⓐ Ⓑ Ⓒ Ⓓ Ⓔ
17. Ⓐ Ⓑ Ⓒ Ⓓ Ⓔ
18. Ⓐ Ⓑ Ⓒ Ⓓ Ⓔ
19. Ⓐ Ⓑ Ⓒ Ⓓ Ⓔ
20. Ⓐ Ⓑ Ⓒ Ⓓ Ⓔ

21. Ⓐ Ⓑ Ⓒ Ⓓ Ⓔ
22. Ⓐ Ⓑ Ⓒ Ⓓ Ⓔ
23. Ⓐ Ⓑ Ⓒ Ⓓ Ⓔ
24. Ⓐ Ⓑ Ⓒ Ⓓ Ⓔ
25. Ⓐ Ⓑ Ⓒ Ⓓ Ⓔ
26. Ⓐ Ⓑ Ⓒ Ⓓ Ⓔ
27. Ⓐ Ⓑ Ⓒ Ⓓ Ⓔ
28. Ⓐ Ⓑ Ⓒ Ⓓ Ⓔ
29. Ⓐ Ⓑ Ⓒ Ⓓ Ⓔ
30. Ⓐ Ⓑ Ⓒ Ⓓ Ⓔ
31. Ⓐ Ⓑ Ⓒ Ⓓ Ⓔ
32. Ⓐ Ⓑ Ⓒ Ⓓ Ⓔ
33. Ⓐ Ⓑ Ⓒ Ⓓ Ⓔ
34. Ⓐ Ⓑ Ⓒ Ⓓ Ⓔ
35. Ⓐ Ⓑ Ⓒ Ⓓ Ⓔ
36. Ⓐ Ⓑ Ⓒ Ⓓ Ⓔ
37. Ⓐ Ⓑ Ⓒ Ⓓ Ⓔ
38. Ⓐ Ⓑ Ⓒ Ⓓ Ⓔ
39. Ⓐ Ⓑ Ⓒ Ⓓ Ⓔ
40. Ⓐ Ⓑ Ⓒ Ⓓ Ⓔ

41. Ⓐ Ⓑ Ⓒ Ⓓ Ⓔ
42. Ⓐ Ⓑ Ⓒ Ⓓ Ⓔ
43. Ⓐ Ⓑ Ⓒ Ⓓ Ⓔ
44. Ⓐ Ⓑ Ⓒ Ⓓ Ⓔ
45. Ⓐ Ⓑ Ⓒ Ⓓ Ⓔ
46. Ⓐ Ⓑ Ⓒ Ⓓ Ⓔ
47. Ⓐ Ⓑ Ⓒ Ⓓ Ⓔ
48. Ⓐ Ⓑ Ⓒ Ⓓ Ⓔ
49. Ⓐ Ⓑ Ⓒ Ⓓ Ⓔ
50. Ⓐ Ⓑ Ⓒ Ⓓ Ⓔ
51. Ⓐ Ⓑ Ⓒ Ⓓ Ⓔ
52. Ⓐ Ⓑ Ⓒ Ⓓ Ⓔ
53. Ⓐ Ⓑ Ⓒ Ⓓ Ⓔ
54. Ⓐ Ⓑ Ⓒ Ⓓ Ⓔ
55. Ⓐ Ⓑ Ⓒ Ⓓ Ⓔ
56. Ⓐ Ⓑ Ⓒ Ⓓ Ⓔ
57. Ⓐ Ⓑ Ⓒ Ⓓ Ⓔ
58. Ⓐ Ⓑ Ⓒ Ⓓ Ⓔ
59. Ⓐ Ⓑ Ⓒ Ⓓ Ⓔ
60. Ⓐ Ⓑ Ⓒ Ⓓ Ⓔ

Section II

Use the following pages on which to write your essays. During the official exam, you will be given 12 lined pages for your essays. Since we are providing fewer pages, be sure to use your own standard ruled paper on which to complete additional pages, if needed.

_____

_____

_____

_____

_____

_____

_____

_____

_____

_____

_____

_____

_____

_____

_____

_____

_____

AP English Language & Composition Test 3

Section I

1. Ⓐ Ⓑ Ⓒ Ⓓ Ⓔ	21. Ⓐ Ⓑ Ⓒ Ⓓ Ⓔ	41. Ⓐ Ⓑ Ⓒ Ⓓ Ⓔ
2. Ⓐ Ⓑ Ⓒ Ⓓ Ⓔ	22. Ⓐ Ⓑ Ⓒ Ⓓ Ⓔ	42. Ⓐ Ⓑ Ⓒ Ⓓ Ⓔ
3. Ⓐ Ⓑ Ⓒ Ⓓ Ⓔ	23. Ⓐ Ⓑ Ⓒ Ⓓ Ⓔ	43. Ⓐ Ⓑ Ⓒ Ⓓ Ⓔ
4. Ⓐ Ⓑ Ⓒ Ⓓ Ⓔ	24. Ⓐ Ⓑ Ⓒ Ⓓ Ⓔ	44. Ⓐ Ⓑ Ⓒ Ⓓ Ⓔ
5. Ⓐ Ⓑ Ⓒ Ⓓ Ⓔ	25. Ⓐ Ⓑ Ⓒ Ⓓ Ⓔ	45. Ⓐ Ⓑ Ⓒ Ⓓ Ⓔ
6. Ⓐ Ⓑ Ⓒ Ⓓ Ⓔ	26. Ⓐ Ⓑ Ⓒ Ⓓ Ⓔ	46. Ⓐ Ⓑ Ⓒ Ⓓ Ⓔ
7. Ⓐ Ⓑ Ⓒ Ⓓ Ⓔ	27. Ⓐ Ⓑ Ⓒ Ⓓ Ⓔ	47. Ⓐ Ⓑ Ⓒ Ⓓ Ⓔ
8. Ⓐ Ⓑ Ⓒ Ⓓ Ⓔ	28. Ⓐ Ⓑ Ⓒ Ⓓ Ⓔ	48. Ⓐ Ⓑ Ⓒ Ⓓ Ⓔ
9. Ⓐ Ⓑ Ⓒ Ⓓ Ⓔ	29. Ⓐ Ⓑ Ⓒ Ⓓ Ⓔ	49. Ⓐ Ⓑ Ⓒ Ⓓ Ⓔ
10. Ⓐ Ⓑ Ⓒ Ⓓ Ⓔ	30. Ⓐ Ⓑ Ⓒ Ⓓ Ⓔ	50. Ⓐ Ⓑ Ⓒ Ⓓ Ⓔ
11. Ⓐ Ⓑ Ⓒ Ⓓ Ⓔ	31. Ⓐ Ⓑ Ⓒ Ⓓ Ⓔ	51. Ⓐ Ⓑ Ⓒ Ⓓ Ⓔ
12. Ⓐ Ⓑ Ⓒ Ⓓ Ⓔ	32. Ⓐ Ⓑ Ⓒ Ⓓ Ⓔ	52. Ⓐ Ⓑ Ⓒ Ⓓ Ⓔ
13. Ⓐ Ⓑ Ⓒ Ⓓ Ⓔ	33. Ⓐ Ⓑ Ⓒ Ⓓ Ⓔ	53. Ⓐ Ⓑ Ⓒ Ⓓ Ⓔ
14. Ⓐ Ⓑ Ⓒ Ⓓ Ⓔ	34. Ⓐ Ⓑ Ⓒ Ⓓ Ⓔ	54. Ⓐ Ⓑ Ⓒ Ⓓ Ⓔ
15. Ⓐ Ⓑ Ⓒ Ⓓ Ⓔ	35. Ⓐ Ⓑ Ⓒ Ⓓ Ⓔ	55. Ⓐ Ⓑ Ⓒ Ⓓ Ⓔ
16. Ⓐ Ⓑ Ⓒ Ⓓ Ⓔ	36. Ⓐ Ⓑ Ⓒ Ⓓ Ⓔ	56. Ⓐ Ⓑ Ⓒ Ⓓ Ⓔ
17. Ⓐ Ⓑ Ⓒ Ⓓ Ⓔ	37. Ⓐ Ⓑ Ⓒ Ⓓ Ⓔ	57. Ⓐ Ⓑ Ⓒ Ⓓ Ⓔ
18. Ⓐ Ⓑ Ⓒ Ⓓ Ⓔ	38. Ⓐ Ⓑ Ⓒ Ⓓ Ⓔ	58. Ⓐ Ⓑ Ⓒ Ⓓ Ⓔ
19. Ⓐ Ⓑ Ⓒ Ⓓ Ⓔ	39. Ⓐ Ⓑ Ⓒ Ⓓ Ⓔ	59. Ⓐ Ⓑ Ⓒ Ⓓ Ⓔ
20. Ⓐ Ⓑ Ⓒ Ⓓ Ⓔ	40. Ⓐ Ⓑ Ⓒ Ⓓ Ⓔ	60. Ⓐ Ⓑ Ⓒ Ⓓ Ⓔ

Section II

Use the following pages on which to write your essays. During the official exam, you will be given 12 lined pages for your essays. Since we are providing fewer pages, be sure to use your own standard ruled paper on which to complete additional pages, if needed.

_____

_____

_____

_____

_____

_____

_____

_____

_____

_____

_____

_____

_____

_____

_____

_____

_____

AP English Language & Composition Test __

Section I

1. Ⓐ Ⓑ Ⓒ Ⓓ Ⓔ	21. Ⓐ Ⓑ Ⓒ Ⓓ Ⓔ	41. Ⓐ Ⓑ Ⓒ Ⓓ Ⓔ
2. Ⓐ Ⓑ Ⓒ Ⓓ Ⓔ	22. Ⓐ Ⓑ Ⓒ Ⓓ Ⓔ	42. Ⓐ Ⓑ Ⓒ Ⓓ Ⓔ
3. Ⓐ Ⓑ Ⓒ Ⓓ Ⓔ	23. Ⓐ Ⓑ Ⓒ Ⓓ Ⓔ	43. Ⓐ Ⓑ Ⓒ Ⓓ Ⓔ
4. Ⓐ Ⓑ Ⓒ Ⓓ Ⓔ	24. Ⓐ Ⓑ Ⓒ Ⓓ Ⓔ	44. Ⓐ Ⓑ Ⓒ Ⓓ Ⓔ
5. Ⓐ Ⓑ Ⓒ Ⓓ Ⓔ	25. Ⓐ Ⓑ Ⓒ Ⓓ Ⓔ	45. Ⓐ Ⓑ Ⓒ Ⓓ Ⓔ
6. Ⓐ Ⓑ Ⓒ Ⓓ Ⓔ	26. Ⓐ Ⓑ Ⓒ Ⓓ Ⓔ	46. Ⓐ Ⓑ Ⓒ Ⓓ Ⓔ
7. Ⓐ Ⓑ Ⓒ Ⓓ Ⓔ	27. Ⓐ Ⓑ Ⓒ Ⓓ Ⓔ	47. Ⓐ Ⓑ Ⓒ Ⓓ Ⓔ
8. Ⓐ Ⓑ Ⓒ Ⓓ Ⓔ	28. Ⓐ Ⓑ Ⓒ Ⓓ Ⓔ	48. Ⓐ Ⓑ Ⓒ Ⓓ Ⓔ
9. Ⓐ Ⓑ Ⓒ Ⓓ Ⓔ	29. Ⓐ Ⓑ Ⓒ Ⓓ Ⓔ	49. Ⓐ Ⓑ Ⓒ Ⓓ Ⓔ
10. Ⓐ Ⓑ Ⓒ Ⓓ Ⓔ	30. Ⓐ Ⓑ Ⓒ Ⓓ Ⓔ	50. Ⓐ Ⓑ Ⓒ Ⓓ Ⓔ
11. Ⓐ Ⓑ Ⓒ Ⓓ Ⓔ	31. Ⓐ Ⓑ Ⓒ Ⓓ Ⓔ	51. Ⓐ Ⓑ Ⓒ Ⓓ Ⓔ
12. Ⓐ Ⓑ Ⓒ Ⓓ Ⓔ	32. Ⓐ Ⓑ Ⓒ Ⓓ Ⓔ	52. Ⓐ Ⓑ Ⓒ Ⓓ Ⓔ
13. Ⓐ Ⓑ Ⓒ Ⓓ Ⓔ	33. Ⓐ Ⓑ Ⓒ Ⓓ Ⓔ	53. Ⓐ Ⓑ Ⓒ Ⓓ Ⓔ
14. Ⓐ Ⓑ Ⓒ Ⓓ Ⓔ	34. Ⓐ Ⓑ Ⓒ Ⓓ Ⓔ	54. Ⓐ Ⓑ Ⓒ Ⓓ Ⓔ
15. Ⓐ Ⓑ Ⓒ Ⓓ Ⓔ	35. Ⓐ Ⓑ Ⓒ Ⓓ Ⓔ	55. Ⓐ Ⓑ Ⓒ Ⓓ Ⓔ
16. Ⓐ Ⓑ Ⓒ Ⓓ Ⓔ	36. Ⓐ Ⓑ Ⓒ Ⓓ Ⓔ	56. Ⓐ Ⓑ Ⓒ Ⓓ Ⓔ
17. Ⓐ Ⓑ Ⓒ Ⓓ Ⓔ	37. Ⓐ Ⓑ Ⓒ Ⓓ Ⓔ	57. Ⓐ Ⓑ Ⓒ Ⓓ Ⓔ
18. Ⓐ Ⓑ Ⓒ Ⓓ Ⓔ	38. Ⓐ Ⓑ Ⓒ Ⓓ Ⓔ	58. Ⓐ Ⓑ Ⓒ Ⓓ Ⓔ
19. Ⓐ Ⓑ Ⓒ Ⓓ Ⓔ	39. Ⓐ Ⓑ Ⓒ Ⓓ Ⓔ	59. Ⓐ Ⓑ Ⓒ Ⓓ Ⓔ
20. Ⓐ Ⓑ Ⓒ Ⓓ Ⓔ	40. Ⓐ Ⓑ Ⓒ Ⓓ Ⓔ	60. Ⓐ Ⓑ Ⓒ Ⓓ Ⓔ

Section II

Use the following pages on which to write your essays. During the official exam, you will be given 12 lined pages for your essays. Since we are providing fewer pages, be sure to use your own standard ruled paper on which to complete additional pages, if needed.